Knock

Blakeney Overfalls

the return of the tide

the return
of the tide...

on the Saltmarsh Coast of North Norfolk

edited by Ian Scott and Richard Worsley

Foreword by Lord Butler

This book is a sequel to 'The Turn of the Tide' published 2005

Copyright text © 2010 Ian Scott, Richard Worsley and the Contributors
Copyright endpaper map © 2010 Godfrey Sayers
Copyright drawings © 2010 Nicholas Barnham

Designed by Graham Hiles, Station Farmhouse, Barney

First published 2010 by JJG Publishing
Sparrow Hall
Hindringham
Fakenham
Norfolk NR21 0DP

ISBN 978-1-899163-90-8

Printed in China through Colorcraft Ltd, Hong Kong.

Contents

Foreword

by Lord Butler of Brockwell

When I was a junior civil servant, a story was told about Sir Matthew Stevenson, Permanent Secretary of the Ministry of Housing and Local Government. Someone, objecting to a change Sir Matthew was proposing, said, "If you do what you are suggesting, life will never be the same again." "That's true," said Sir Matthew, "but, you know, we have to accept that life does change. That's what distinguishes it from death."

This book is about change – change in a part of North Norfolk which many value because they think that it has changed so little. Yet those who think so are wrong. Whether the perspective we take is millions of years, or thousands or hundreds or even tens, change has happened all the time. That's life.

Of course, not all change is for the better. I've reached a stage of my life when almost all the physical change I notice in myself is for the worse. Nor is all change inevitable or a consequence of nature or the human condition. Ever when changes are brought about by nature, we human beings may be able to offset them, though our efforts are often puny in the face of the forces of nature and may be beset by ignorance about what the actual consequences will be. Other changes are certainly brought about by human action, and that may be for the better or the worse.

When we see change taking place in something we love, our disposition is to think that change is for the worse. If we regard something as nearly perfect, change in it seems like loss, even if it is ultimately replaced by something else good or even better. In that sense we are all conservative in relation to the things we love.

As the chapters in this book bring out, much change is taking place in North Norfolk – environmental, social, economic, aesthetic. The contributors to the book are experts in all those fields and have interesting things to say about them. Some see the danger of change for the worse, others see opportunities for improvement. In two respects, they all agree. One is that they share a love – even a passion – for this coast. The second is that they all believe that the actions and decisions made today matter, that they will make a difference for better or worse.

It must also be true that not all change will be equally good or bad for everybody. Some will gain or lose more than others. The aim must be to do the greatest good for the greatest number, and the largest part of that greatest number will be our children, their children and those who follow them.

One of the changes which is needed is in the way in which decisions are made.

A common theme running through the book is that too many decisions are made in London or by a remote quango, and that the best decisions are likely to be made if those who live on, and care for, this coast have a big say in them. This book provides a local voice. If its themes are taken up and echoed by others, it stands a greater chance of influencing even what is decided in Westminster and Whitehall, to the benefit of all who love this unique coastline. For that reason, I believe that those who conceived the book and those who have contributed to it have performed a valuable service. I wish the book well.

Robin Butler

Preface

by the Editors

In December 2000 a group of friends, acquaintances and (then) strangers began to talk about a book of contrasting perspectives on the future of the Saltmarsh Coast of North Norfolk. The *Turn of the Tide* was published in June 2005. In 2008, knowing it had helped some people appreciate the area's vulnerability, persuaded others it was more vulnerable than they had thought and echoed in some other vulnerable places, we asked its publisher, Jeremy Greenwood, if he was ready for a sequel. He was. This is the result.

The idea for another book was driven by four perceptions: that the coastal area defined by lowland Britain's last wilderness was even more vulnerable than it had been eight years earlier; that new threats and opportunities had emerged; that, as a result, its future was increasingly uncertain; and that what its authors might say about it would resonate in other places facing comparable challenges.

The Turn of the Tide was put together by choosing twenty interesting authors – some locally born, some incomers, some professional writers, most not – before deciding what they would write about. They sought to raise awareness about the issues they thought were important to the future of the coast between Holme and Salthouse, to provoke debate about those issues in the population at large and to stimulate dialogue between those who had always lived there and those who had recently arrived. For *The Return of the Tide* we chose the topics before seeking twenty authors willing and able to write about them. As diverse as their predecessors, they have contrasting views, opinions and priorities but little in common save longstanding affection for and attachment to a place whose magical qualities – despite many economic, social, political, cultural and physical changes in the last fifty years – remain remarkably intact.

We made no attempt to cover the waterfront that might be covered in a comprehensive text and chose the issues in light of what we saw as their urgency, significance and tractability. Many readers will wonder why we left some things out. Others will wonder why we put some things in. All, we hope, will be stimulated by what they read, disagree with parts of it and understand why the authors disagree with each other. But regardless of whether readers like our choice of issues we think they will be duly impressed by the fact that the authors' knowledge of the Saltmarsh Coast has been acquired over a collective period of more than 800 years: like them or not, these are expert opinions.

The authors have approached their chapters from personal but not, for the most part, autobiographical perspectives. They have written without colluding, have not amended their stories in light of what others have written and bear no responsibility for this preface or the first chapter although their views are reflected in the final chapter of conclusions. Their backgrounds, interests, political opinions, attitudes and values are often transparent as they walk the line between objectivity and sub-jectivity, raise questions and suggest answers. We hope readers less familiar with the area than they are will share their enthusiasm for the wonders of a small piece of England and want to know it better. We hope those who know it intimately will share their hopes and concerns about its future, their conviction that if its magic were to evaporate it could not be retrieved and their certainty that complacency about this vulnerable place is decidedly out of place.

Several chapters in this book address aspects of our past, present and future relationships with the North Sea: how it has shaped and reshaped our 25 mile long coastline; how the area economy has always depended on it; how our saltmarshes are nourished and replenished by the deposition of sea-borne solids; how new marshes are forming at Holkham Gap and Wells where it seems only yesterday there were sandy beaches; how our dunes are configured and reconfigured by wave action; how our relationships with the sea have changed and will continue to change the way we live and the things we do; and what the sea might mean for us in the not distant future. Some of those changes are measured in centuries, some in years, some – like the intertidal landscape – in hours.

Most chapters, attempting in one way or another to bound the plausible future, focus on onshore issues: demographic trends; the outlook for young people; access to affordable housing for local families; the built environment; the future for wildlife; the outlook for locally sourced food and drink; what we do in our spare time; whether the things that inspire artists, poets and writers to paint, draw and write about this place could lose their charm; whether painters, photographers and film makers will continue to see the things that have made this coast a mecca for image-makers; whether relationships between incomers and local people might change; what might happen to relationships between national, regional and local government.

The book is organized in three sections. The first explores issues arising from cur-rent and plausible changes in our natural and built environments: Richard Hardman considers alternative physical futures in the context of changes over geological time; Tim O'Riordan and Sophie Nicholson-Cole appraise issues related to shoreline man-agement; Richard Girling assesses the area's past, present and future relationship with the sea; Ron Harold evaluates issues confronting the area's habitats for plants, birds and animals and Nicholas Hills looks at the future of our built environment.

In the second section which focusses on aspects of how we live on the Saltmarsh Coast, Glynis Anthony considers the future for the area's children and young peo-ple; Cyril Southerland discusses issues of access to affordable housing for local people with low incomes; Sally Festing evaluates how we use our spare time in an extraordinary playground; and Galton Blakiston looks at the future of locally sourced food and drink.

The third section asks how we view our world and ourselves. Godfrey Sayers describes the thoughts and feelings of local people about those who have come from elsewhere to live here; Raymond Monbiot writes about the human environment from the perspective of a fairly recent arrival; Kevin Crossley-Holland, Nicholas Barnham and Lady Fraser consider the sources of inspiration for creative artists from the perspectives of poet, painter and patron; Jim Ring appraises the way creative artists have interpreted the Saltmarsh Coast in words, music and images; and Henry Bellingham and Norman Lamb (in interviews) talk about current and future political issues as seen from here and Westminster.

We suggested earlier that the authors of this book had little in common but affection for a magical place and shared concerns about its vulnerability. That is not quite true because they also share a spirit of generosity that persuaded the professional writers among them (who are normally properly paid for their work) and those who earn their livings in other ways (to take time they could have used more profitably) to share their concerns and passions about the future of the Saltmarsh Coast. Not just because they care but also because they believe in the possibility that what they say here could make that future different. A tall ambition? Certainly. An unrealistic one? We shall see.

As co-editors, we are very grateful to all of them. Grateful also to Lord Butler for writing the Foreword. To Jeremy Greenwood who, having taken a chance on *The Turn of the Tide,* has taken a chance on its successor because he cares too. To Graham Hiles who designed this book. To Nick Barnham who wrote a sub-chapter, painted the cover illustration and drew the images that appear thoughout the text. To Godfrey Sayers who wrote a chapter and drew the endpaper maps depicting the coast as we know it and the coast we might know in the future. And to our readers. Not because by buying this book they will greatly increase our collective net worth but because they are curious to read what we have to say. We would be even more grateful if, having read it they felt inclined to do something about the issues we discuss.

We have no idea if there will be a sequel to this sequel. But if, in three or five years time, another group of authors agree it's time for another book about the future of the Saltmarsh Coast we hope some at least of the issues discussed in this one will have receded, that some of the threats will have diminished, that some of the opportunities will have been grasped and that the essence of this place will remain. We also hope that what we have to say about its future will strike responsive chords in other vulnerable places and may even prompt concerted preservative action. This is after all, a common cause. The world has a finite number of irreplaceable places and if we fail to preserve them – or do not even try – they will become memories and our successors will hold us accountable for their loss.

Ian Scott and Richard Worsley
July, 2009

Ian Scott

A retired Director of the World Bank, Ian Scott fell in love with North Norfolk in 1961 having previously fallen in love with his Wells-born wife at University College London. Married in Wells in 1964, they spent most of the next thirty years working and living in North and South America, Africa and the Caribbean but ensured their four children had Norfolk roots by spending summers in their converted barn at Binham; their grandchildren are now growing Norfolk roots of their own.

Since retiring from the World Bank Ian has divided his time between North Norfolk and the Chesapeake Bay and his efforts between advising public, private and voluntary organizations on strategic issues; academic positions at the London Business School and Oxford University (where he is Executive Director of the Emerging Markets Symposium); long distance driving (a circuit of South America and London – Sydney); wooden boat restoration; and writing. He edited *The Turn of the Tide* and his other publications include *Urban and Spatial Development in Mexico*, *A Month of Summers*, *Mudlark's Ghosts*, *What on Earth is a CKO* (with Michael Earl), numerous articles and more than 250 newspaper columns.

Introduction:
An Even More Vulnerable Place

Ian Scott

The Soft Edge

The top edge of Norfolk is bookended by the red-and-white chalk cliffs of Hunstanton and the white chalk cliffs of Kelling. Far from homogenous but all of a piece it is one of the most distinctive coastal areas in Europe. The saltmarshes between Holme and Burnham Overy Staithe and between Wells and Morston look much as they have looked for more than a thousand years. The reclaimed marshes at Cley, Blakeney, Holkham and Overy, protected by shingle banks, sea walls and mixed woodland have looked much as they do now since they were captured from the North Sea between 1639 and 1859. In the mind's eye of most visitors this is a tranquil, sunlit place. Sailing in Blakeney Harbour or Norton Creek (that separates Scolt Head Island from the British Isles) on fine summer evenings it is hard to remember the winter nights in 1953 and 1978 when the North Sea hurled itself against the soft edge of Norfolk, smashed sea defences, reversed centuries of patient reclamation, destroyed property and took human and animal life. It is easier to remember the night of November 9, 2007 when, if high water had coincided with the storm surge, the sea wall at Blakeney would have been overtopped and Blakeney Freshes would have been flooded.

When I came to Wells fifty years ago agriculture was still a major employer, Branthill Farm fielded a cricket team, the inland villages had schools and enough children to fill them, most had shops, some had post offices and all had one or more pubs, some with what my father-in-law used to call 'spit and sawdust' floors (although few served food). The year was still punctuated by traditional festivals. My wife's grandfather talked about rods (though not as I recall, poles or perches). University vacations were filled with back-aching field work except at Christmas when I carried a post bag. There were few holiday cottages and even fewer week-enders but then there was no M11, there was no dual carriageway in the county and London seemed a long way off although you could get there and back from Wells by train the same day.

Some local people – by which I mean people who have always lived here and whose ancestors lived here before them – complain about the changes that have rolled across the Saltmarsh Coast since the 1960s. But I think they overlook the facts that the world is never still, the sea is never still, the marshes are never still, the soil is never still – and never have been. Those who would pickle the present should perhaps ponder the fact that when Hamlet tells Rosencrantz and Guildenstern, "There is nothing either good or bad, but thinking makes it so," he's not indulging in ethical relativism but stating the unvarnished truth that what we choose to see depends on where we choose to sit.

I sympathize with those who would like to stop the world not because they want to get off but because they yearn for a simpler time. Those my age and older have lived through (some might say survived) much simpler times. But there are always several sides to a story.

The side some choose to remember is what they lost as many villages were dispossessed of working farms, schools, shops, post offices, pubs and cricket teams; the fact they knew the names of all their neighbours (and those of their children and grandchildren); the certainty everyone would look out for everyone else; and that nobody would die alone. They mourn the loss of communities that no longer exist that few people in our urban world even know existed.

A second side, familiar to everyone who has lived in a small community is the downside of intimacy, the probability your neighbours will know more about your business than you know yourself and the possibility they will know before you do what you will eat tonight.

A third side is that while everyone in the still tight-knit communities of North Norfolk in the 1960s was better fed than they had been in the 1930s, every child went to school and everyone had access to healthcare, by no means everyone had television, few had cars and even fewer took foreign holidays. Now most people have all those things; what troubles some is whether they are really better off. Human nature being human nature the vast majority will say why can't we have it both ways? Why not community *and* prosperity? Why did we have to lose human values to gain material ones? I'm not sure they did although I have seen the same process unfold in other parts of the world and I'm almost but not quite convinced the trade-offs are part of the process and that most people in most places have lost something to gain something. Yet I know there are exceptions and that the spirit of some village communities remains strong.

The fourth side is that the price of *relative* prosperity – the Saltmarsh Coast is less well off than the country as a whole and has significant levels of deprivation – is measured in demographic, social and cultural change. Villages have been repopulated by weekenders and holiday makers. Houses and cottages have been remodelled. The range of goods on offer in local shops has widened. Churches once used only on Sundays are now venues for midweek summer concerts. And whereas in the 1960s you had to drive out of the area to find a good restaurant you are now spoiled for choice and had best book early – even in February. But as we shall see later in this chapter, not everyone has been swept up in a wave of prosperity and there are marked contrasts between 'fashionable' and 'less fashionable' villages and even stronger contrasts within them.

But suppose, when employment in agriculture, mills, granaries and fishing fell off in the 1960s and '70s the tourism and recreation industries had *not* grown; suppose weekenders and holiday home owners had *not* fallen in love with the Saltmarsh Coast; suppose they had *not* bought second homes and retirement homes; suppose demand for what economists call superior goods had *not* blossomed; suppose nobody had sought fine food, good wine and delicatessens? What then would have happened to the housing market, to pubs and shops? Would our villages now resemble once thriving villages in Northern Tuscany where handfuls of elderly residents live among empty houses? Would all the pubs have closed? Would the range of goods be even smaller than it was 50 years ago? Probably not. But the economy would be weaker, young people would have little choice other than to move away, fewer schools would be open, and parish churches would be even emptier.

Although there is abundant evidence that economic development and cultural change go hand in hand, I regret what we have largely lost because it was valuable. I regret the crass and patronizing behaviour and insensitivity of some of those who have come to live here and fail to understand why local people are upset when they say that if they want higher incomes they should work harder. I regret the fact that although the new economy has benefitted people who build, restore, repair and maintain houses and has created new jobs in the tourism and restoration sector, most of those jobs do not provide sufficient income to get families on the housing ladder – thereby widening the gap between relatively wealthy incomers and relatively poor local people. I regret the fact that 'born heres' and 'come heres' sometimes relate to each other like ships in the night without navigation lights. And I regret the fact that some local people refuse to accept that if the incomers had not come they would be even worse off.

Then and Now

In the four and a half years it took to convert the *The Turn of the Tide* from a rough idea to a published volume the horizon remained more or less unchanged. The threats evolved and opportunities loomed larger or smaller but lists of both remained more or less stable the lack of movement reflecting the reality of what most people who live here and nearly all visitors think of as a slow paced place. But there were notable differences between that process and the process that unfolded over the sixteen months it took to take this book from concept to print. One was that the issues changed so fast we wondered at times how to keep up with them, always concluding that since we were not writing a newspaper we would not and should not try. The other was that the mood of the area changed and questions we might have asked ourselves in 2005 had different answers in 2009.

In 2005, asked if the Saltmarsh Coast was part of the world or a place apart we might have said it was still, in many ways, a place apart; that although it was closer to London than it had been in 1960 or even 1990 there was still a perceptible contrast in the rhythm of life; that we intuitively understood the 'slow' movement[1] because we had unwittingly helped invent it; that we continued to value people, as we had always done, for their intrinsic worth rather than their extrinsic status; that although stresses and strains had crept in to the social fabric of the area as 'old' and 'new' people met, merged and sometimes clashed, the traditional culture was still alive and reasonably well; that there was a perceptible contrast between the Saltmarsh Coast and much of Southern England which, viewed (perhaps complacently) from here, seemed homogenized and pasteurized by decades of shaking and stirring; and that this area was both a special case (and thus a place apart) but also a case in point – in the sense it was a microcosm of the larger world and the issues it faced were essentially similar to those that affected other vulnerable places in Britain, Europe and beyond.

By 2009 the rhythm had accelerated. There was a sense that people – at least some people – were in a greater hurry to go places and do things; the area seemed more part of the world: the recession arrived with little lag (and welcome deviations as some British tourists decided to stay home rather than go to Europe); local conversations turned to global warming and offshore and onshore windfarms; people seemed more concerned about local and national political issues, more upset about the 'democratic deficit', more inclined to participate in local politics and more aware of the 'butterfly effect'[2] although my favourite measure of global connectedness was the question "Have you been to Kerala recently" overheard at a local sailing club.

The transition – if there is one – from a place apart to a part of the world may have profound implications. Some people believe the rare essence of the Saltmarsh Coast that gave the area its hard-to-define character was partly the product of a distinctive human, natural and built environment that matured over centuries and partly a function of relative separation from the rest of the world. Looking ahead they fear that the more *this* world is integrated with *the* world the more that essence will be diluted. Yet despite these changes it seemed to me as I set out to write this introductory chapter that the imperative of this book was essentially the

---

[1] The 'Slow Movement' began in Italy in the late 1990s with the 'Slow Food' organization and developed into a subculture in other fields including cities, travel and design.

[2] The phrase refers to the notion that a butterfly's wings might create tiny atmospheric changes that could ultimately alter the path of, delay, accelerate or prevent events in a given location. The flapping wings represent a small-scale change that triggers a chain of events with large-scale outcomes.

4

same as the imperative of the *The Turn of the Tide*. Now as then I see no alternative than for local people to come to terms with economic, cultural and social realities. Now as then I see no alternative than for those new to the area to stuff their criticism, wait their turn, restrain themselves from telling local people how to run things and understand that although they may believe they are smarter, more worldly and wiser, they must realize that without the people whose ancestors fashioned the human landscape of the Saltmarsh Coast it would be a different place. And now more than then I see an urgent need for mutual engagement, mutual empathy and mutual respect because, as the area is confronted by the possibility of transformational change, they will surely need each other.

Sizing Things Up

Although the Saltmarsh Coast is all of a piece – to the extent even first-time visitors know when they reach it and sense when they leave it – it is not monolithic. Roughly coterminous with six electoral wards (four in North Norfolk, two in King's Lynn and West Norfolk) its distinctiveness is offset by palpable contrasts. Wells is not Warham, Blakeney is not Binham, Burnham Market is not Brancaster. Yet the contrasts do not mask the fact that the six wards are in many ways more different from England as a whole, the East of England and, in some ways, the rest of Norfolk than from each other.

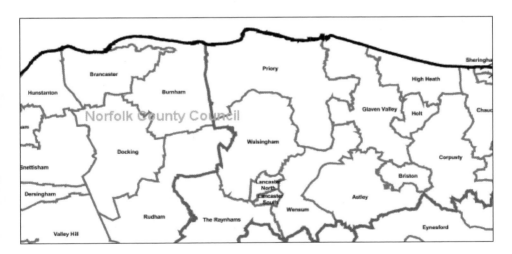

Chart 1: The Electoral Wards of the Saltmarsh Coast

The wards are shown in Chart 1. From west to east the Brancaster Ward includes part of Holme, Thornham, Titchwell, Brancaster, Brancaster Staithe and Burnham Deepdale; the Burnham Ward includes the Burnhams (except Deepdale) and North

5

Creake; the Priory Ward includes Holkham, Wells, Warham, Stiffkey, Cockthorpe, Langham, Binham and Hindringham; the Walsingham Ward includes Great and Little Walsingham, Great Snoring, Houghton, the Barshams, Sculthorpe and Wighton; the Glaven Valley Ward includes Morston, Blakeney, Wiveton, Glandford and some villages to the south that are not part of what most people define as the Saltmarsh Coast; and the High Heath Ward includes Cley, Salthouse plus a few places (Weybourne, Kelling, Upper Sheringham) that also lie outside the Saltmarsh Coast. The geographic match is imperfect but serviceable. All data on which the following charts are based are taken from the Norfolk Insight website maintained by the Norfolk County Council[3].

The dominant demographic feature of the Saltmarsh Coast is that the people who live here are older – in some wards much older – than in the three larger areas of which it forms part (Norfolk, the East of England and England). As Chart 2 shows, the contrast is most pronounced in High Heath where the proportion of over 60s is more than twice the average for both the East of England and the country as a whole. There are correspondingly large proportions of retirees in all wards and low proportions of under fifteens, most notably in Brancaster.

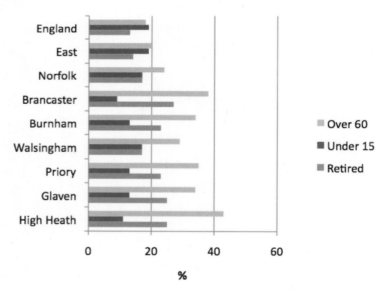

Chart 2 Demographics 2007

The strongly skewed age distribution has numerous implications: the relatively small working age population means those who work[4] cannot support those who

---

[3] norfolkinsight.org.uk Most of the data underlying these charts are for 2006, 2007 or 2008. Some are estimates for 2009 and a few are from the 2001 Census. These differences inevitably cause distortions but do not affect overall patterns of consistency and contrast.

[4] That is to say those who report themselves as in paid work all or most of the time

don't; the small school age population and low rural population density means an inexorable trend towards village school closures and consolidations and longer journeys to school even for young children; and a broad correlation between old age and chronic ill health means demand for healthcare and social services is higher than in many other areas.

There is a popular misconception in the area and the nation (reinforced by certain Sunday newspapers) that the Saltmarsh Coast is an enclave of well-off retirees and weekenders. Recent trends in residential property prices, the much photographed and written about presence of high income consumers in local harbours, shops and restaurants, the high density of expensive late model cars in some villages and the visual contrast between incomer wealth and the more modest circumstances of the indigenous population confirm the existence of new money. But the facts do not support the myth. Reality is approximated in Chart 3 where four things stand out:

- The proportion of families with yearly incomes over £50,000 is lower in every ward than in Norfolk, the East of England and England as a whole; in some wards (Priory, Walsingham and Brancaster) it is much lower.

- The high proportion of households (except in High Heath and Glaven) with yearly incomes of less than £20,000 is higher than in Norfolk, the East of England and the country at large.

- There is a strong contrast between the best off wards (High Heath, Glaven) and the worst off (Priory, Walsingham, Brancaster). Whereas in Norfolk, the East of England and England as a whole, more families have incomes above £50,000 than below £20,000, the opposite is true in every ward of the Saltmarsh Coast.

- The relationship between household incomes under £20,000 and over £50,000 is better in High Heath and Glaven than elsewhere and worst in Priory which suggests the best off wards may have relatively better income distribution than others.

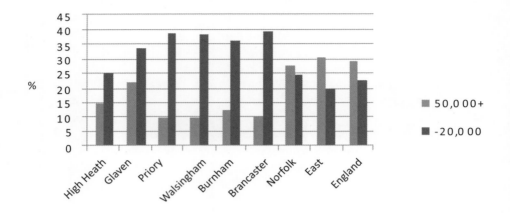

Chart 3 Household incomes 2009 (£000s)

Some of the consequences of the fact that household incomes are generally modest are revealed in Charts 4-6.

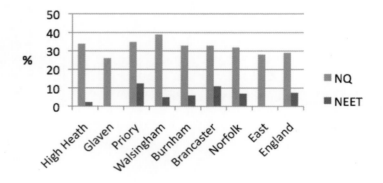

Chart 4 Social Deprivation

Chart 4 shows adults who had no qualifications (NQ) in 2001 and the percentages of 16-18 year olds not in education, employment or training (NEET) in 2006. Priory and Brancaster have the least favourable scores on both indicators and both are worse off than the comparators[5].

There is a similar pattern in Chart 5 which shows the percentages of families self-described as financially 'hard pressed' (2008), those that receive income ('Y') support (2007) and those in social Grade 'E' (2001) which includes individuals who receive benefits, work in the lowest paid jobs and/or are unemployed. The internal contrasts between High Heath and Glaven on the one hand and Priory and

[5] There are no NEET data for the East of England

Brancaster on the other stand out as does the fact that most wards have relatively more people in grade 'E' than the comparator areas.

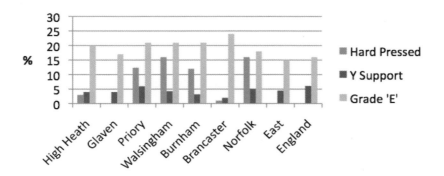

Chart 5 Economic deprivation

The most obvious implication is that despite outward shows of plenty and touches of luxury the area is less prosperous than it looks. It also suggests there are parallel, separate and unequal social systems. One includes people who have lived and worked there a long time, are not well off and are concentrated in Priory, Walsingham and to some extent Brancaster, although some of the scores for the Burnham Ward are lower than most people would expect given the popular image of Burnham Market. The other system includes people who have bought weekend and holiday homes in the area or have retired there, are on the whole, better off and are concentrated in High Heath, Glaven and Burnham. This will not surprise anybody who has observed and contrasted weekenders and local people on summer Saturdays on the quays at Morston, Wells and Burnham Overy Staithe and noticed differences in clothes, voices, vehicles and conversations.

Chart 6 describes relative affluence in terms of people classified as 'Affluent Greys' (those over age 60 who are financially well off) and people who are 'Comfortably Off' (households with relatively modest but adequate means). The contrast between the better off wards (High Heath, Glaven, Burnham and in this case Brancaster) and the poorer wards (Priory and Walsingham) is again clear.

Taken together, these data reveal significant contrasts in economic and social conditions between the wards that make up the Saltmarsh Coast and between the Saltmarsh Coast as a whole and England as a whole; less significant contrasts between the Saltmarsh Coast and the East of England as a whole; and some contrasts between the Saltmarsh Coast and the rest of Norfolk. In almost every instance the comparisons are unfavourable to the Saltmarsh Coast.

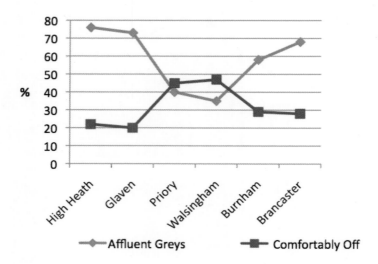

Chart 6 Affluence and comfort 2007

Although there are no ward level data on the area economy and no economic data specific to the area (aggregated District level data for North Norfolk and King's Lynn and West Norfolk are meaningless for this purpose) we know with some certainty that the area economy depends on recreation and tourism, that agriculture and fishing have been eclipsed by construction and maintenance, that the retail sector is weak except in Wells and Burnham Market, that home-based employment has gained some ground in recent years as Broadband has become available throughout the area (and the Internet has enabled footloose businesses to operate as well there as anywhere else); that the growth of car ownership has put the Saltmarsh Coast within commuting distance of Norwich and King's Lynn; and that increasing numbers of people who live there travel fifty miles (or more) to and from work. We also know the area's dependence on tourism means it is potentially vulnerable to national trends although the recession that got under way as this book was being written may benefit local tourism if consumers substitute British for foreign holidays.

Sorting Things Out

In the early 17th century William Camden commented that Norfolk *"is at present and has always been reputed the most fruitful nursery of lawyers and even among the common people you shall meet many who ....if they have no just quarrel, are able to raise out of it the very quirks and niceties of the law[6]"*. Thomas Fuller later

---

[6] William Camden, 'Brittania', 1607

told the world that *"these same people will enter an action for their neighbour's horse but looking over their hedge[7]"*. And Wyndham Ketton Cremer writing about Norfolk in the Civil War observed that *"The litigiousness of Norfolk people was proverbial and was emphasized by contemporary writers to the point of boredom[8]"*. Few of us now think of Norfolk as exceptionally litigious or unduly confrontational; the daily bread of Saltmarsh Coast lawyers comes from deaths, taxes and property transactions rather than slander, libel and assault. Yet anyone who has penetrated the surface of some North Norfolk communities knows that when neighbours fall out seemingly small issues can become big issues and lifetime associations can rupture.

I don't know if that is more true of North Norfolk than the rest of the county, or more true of the county than the rest of the country. Friends who live in rural areas from Cornwall to Cumbria tell me village life is village life and that some of their otherwise reasonable neighbours are occasionally deranged by what outsiders see as trivial issues. To the extent it happens it may simply suggest that people in small communities are more apt to take sides than people who live in urban anonymity because issues are joined against the background of lifetime relationships and long memories. In a recent conversation about a mutual acquaintance with someone I know well he said, "I don't trust him." "Why?" "Because he promised to play in an away match, didn't turn up and left us one short." "So when was that?" "I should think that was 1972."

But just as there are economic and social contrasts between the six wards of the Saltmarsh Coast there are contrasts in the extent to which their villages are perceived as relatively cohesive or divisive. In a series of candid conversations with people who have lived in the area a long time[9] (and in most cases in more than one village) I found remarkable consistency in their perceptions of the extent to which village communities were more or less cohesive. I also found rough consensus that whereas some village communities seem to thrive on conflict others appear to settle their differences through amicable conversation; that some seem to avoid confrontation while others lurch from conflict to conflict; and that different communities have distinctive ways – ranging from decorous to down and dirty – of settling disputes.

Those who think every issue on the Saltmarsh Coast revolves around conflicts between long term residents and recent arrivals might expect social cohesion to be a function of population changes since the 1960s. They might, for example – assuming 'new' populations do not harbour 'old' tensions – expect villages in the High Heath and Glaven wards (including Salthouse, Cley, Blakeney, Morston and

---

[7] Thomas Fuller, 'The History of Worthies of England', 1662
[8] Wyndham Ketton Cremer, 'Norfolk in the Civil War', 1969
[9] Not a truly scientific sample but a representative array of eighty people with intimate knowledge of area communities

Wiveton) to be relatively cohesive by virtue of high concentrations of second homes[10] (Chart 7) and the fact that many well off retirees have settled there[11]. But most observers agreed that some of those villages are far from cohesive[12] and that there was comparable incoherence between demography and cohesion in the villages of the central (Priory, Walsingham) and western (Burnham, Brancaster) wards.

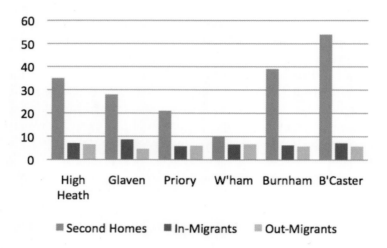

Chart 7 Second homes and migration (2003)

If the mix of 'old' and 'new' populations fails to explain the contrasts, can they be attributed to distinctive values, attitudes and behaviours among those who have moved to the area from elsewhere? There was support for the proposition that some villages (e.g. Stiffkey, Wiveton, Wighton, Warham, Binham, Langham, Burnham Thorpe and Burnham Norton) where early incomers (starting in the late 1960s) sought peaceful co-existence, kept their opinions under wraps until they had been there a while and did not seek to supplant local leaders (e.g. on parish councils) are now among the most cohesive whereas many people see other villages (e.g. Burnham Market, Cley and Blakeney) as places where early incomers set local teeth on edge by competing with local leaders (and each other) and created enduring tensions.

There was also a shared perception that the extent to which this happened was partly a function of the extent to which it was allowed to happen. Some people distinguish between villages that in the 1970s had ineffective or apathetic local lead-

---

[10] Second home ownership being a surrogate for relative prosperity

[11] An influx of retirees does not necessarily indicate relative prosperity but in light of high property values in these villages it probably does

[12] See Godfrey Sayers comments on contrasts between Blakeney and Wiveton in his chapter in this book

ership and those (e.g. Morston and Brancaster Staithe) where established local leaders made it clear they planned to retain their roles. In Wells, which for several years had a co-opted council because too few candidates were willing to stand for election, resurgent interest led to a 2007 contest in which almost all of the successful candidates were locally born and bred and those who were not had been there a long time.

The most important force for cohesion may be village size. Wells (estimated 2008 population 2600) is not strictly a village having once been the smallest Urban District in England[13] and the fact it is often viewed as divisive may simply mean it is and has long since been (having once been much larger)[14] too big to be cohesive. There is ample evidence from around the world that settlement size tends to be inversely correlated with a shared sense of belonging. Size has certainly been a critical parameter in efforts (e.g. at Poundbury[15]) to synthesize the social virtues of organic communities. It remains to be seen however if social cohesion can be manufactured and if there is a threshold (the original village at Poundbury has 2500 inhabitants) above which cohesion becomes elusive or impossible. Many people on the Saltmarsh Coast perceive the largest villages (Wells, Burnham Market, Blakeney, Cley, Hindringham) as relatively less cohesive than others although the fact they also perceive some smaller ones as divisive or moribund suggests small is not necessarily beautiful and that cohesion is not a simple function of size.

External and internal perceptions of village communities are rarely identical. While some outsiders perceive Wells as fractious, those who live there – who know it is sometimes portrayed as being at odds with itself and that over the years successive projects have been roiled in acrimonious debate[16] – feel they belong to a strong and healthy community. Conversely, while casual observers see Burnham Overy Staithe as idyllic some insiders see it as something else. And some people who live in Burnham Market and Blakeney – both of which are perceived as divisive by many outsiders – are puzzled by the disparity between the way they see their communities and the way they know they are seen by others. The obvious explanation is that larger settlements contain sub-communities that confer a strong sense of belonging on their members but lack what planners might call 'whole settlement cohesion'.

Tilting at Windmills

Social cohesion matters because it affects the capacity of village communities to identify issues of common interest, confront real or imagined threats and seize

---

[13] Until reverting to parish status in the Local Government Act of 1964

[14] Wells had a population of more than 3000 in the mid 19th century

[15] The 'new' village like development in Dorset that seeks to replicate the virtues of small communities

[16] Examples include the Wells Harbour Project and the Fish Handling Facility

potential opportunities. In recent years, as villages on the Saltmarsh Coast have been tested in different ways, some have split over what outsiders have seen as trivial differences, others have made common cause. Those who know them will recall the issues. But as this book was being written – in Brancaster Staithe, the Burnhams, Wells, Wiveton, Morston, Hindringham, Congham, Norwich and London – a new phenomenon emerged that delighted those who saw it as a source of jobs, public revenues and private incomes and horrified those who saw it as the most serious threat to the area since Viking longships loomed through offshore mists in 866 AD.

The British Government approved the first windfarm project for North Norfolk in April 2002, has since approved more and is considering others. Under current plans and proposals[17] the Docking Shoal Windfarm would place up to 177 turbines 14 kilometres off Wells and 19 kilometres off Skegness, the Race Bank Windfarm would place up to 206 turbines 27 kilometres northwest of Blakeney Point, the Dudgeon Shoal Windfarm would place up to 168 turbines 32 kilometres off Cromer and the Sheringham Shoal Windfarm would place 88 turbines 17 kilometres off Sheringham. There are also plans to locate windfarm support facilities in Wells Harbour (initially for the Sheringham Shoal Windfarm) and in and around the town.

Until 2008 when wind turbines in the Wash first became visible from Brancaster, Scolt Head Island, and the coastal Burnhams few local residents gave them much thought. But in 2009, as information about the new projects – all but one of which would be more visible from the Saltmarsh Coast than those in the Wash – began to seep in to public consciousness it provoked sharply different reactions.

Those who lined up in support included many people who live on and care deeply about the Saltmarsh Coast and its future. They believe windfarms promise viable alternatives to nuclear power and an opportunity to reduce Britain's looming energy deficit and improve its environmental health. Whether they believe increased concentrations of anthropogenic greenhouse gases have caused most of the increase in global average temperatures since the mid-20th century or put them down to other causes, they see an imperative to exploit every form of renewable energy. And they insist that since the inshore waters of the North Sea are well suited to windfarm development and offer relatively low construction and transmission costs it is meet right and proper to build them there.

Some of those who support the proposed developments acknowledge there are valid questions about windfarm efficiency but argue that alternative technologies, including wave and tidal energy, are not yet commercially proven, that meanwhile, we should use every available source of green energy and that the proposed windfarms plus those in operation,[18] under construction or approved would generate more than enough power to service every home in Norfolk and are essential parts

---

[17] Published data from government and other sources shows inconsistent figures for windfarm locations, turbine size, numbers of turbines and anticipated capacity

[18] Lynn, Scroby, Inner Dowsing

of the Government's commitment to generate 20% of the nation's electric energy output from renewable sources by 2020.

Another part of the local community believes windfarm construction and maintenance offers the prospect of diversification for an onshore economy dominated by the recreation and tourism industries; the potential for new jobs, particularly for young local people who have found it hard to find work that pays them enough to allow them to live where they were born and raised; the possibility of higher incomes that would allow those same young people to get a foot on the housing ladder; the power of expanding markets for locally produced goods and services; and the concomitant growth and diversification of local businesses. What, they ask, are the disadvantages of creating a new economic sector, a new lease on life for area businesses and the chance to build a more stable economic base?

But not everyone thinks windfarms are a blessing. Some question the long run economic and financial returns on windfarm investment, argue that none of the proposed schemes would be viable without government subsidies and price controls, say that windfarms are an expensive fig leaf to cover the Government's embarassed need to present a green face to the world and argue that current plans for windfarm development are a panic reaction to make up for actions to confront a looming energy deficit that should have been taken years ago.

Others are concerned that the unique land and seascapes of the Saltmarsh Coast will be irretrievably spoiled by windfarms; that its visual amenity value will be ruined by the erection of highly visible metal towers within a few miles of the shoreline; that windfarms will threaten migratory and resident bird populations on the nationally and internationally important reserves that stretch like a string of pearls from Holme to Salthouse; and that increased boat traffic generated by windfarm support activities will damage the saltmarsh around Wells.

Others worry there may be fewer direct employment opportunities than meet the eye because the new jobs will require locally unavailable skills and windfarm developers have poor records of keeping promises to train local people to fill them; that while secondary jobs may be created, both the size of the potential multiplier effect[19] and the nature of indirectly generated jobs are uncertain; that the fact windfarm developers do not plan fixed investments in land-based activities demonstrates a lack of long term commitment to the area; that tourism and recreation will suffer from the visual intrusion of windfarms along the shoreline and changes in the visual attractions of the beach and foreshore at Wells where semi-continuous dredging will conflict with recreational activities; and that there will be a negative impact on local fisheries because some of the towers would be built on fishing grounds, because there are no known plans to compensate fishermen, and because claims by windfarm developers that turbines in other locations have created favourable habitats for fish and shellfish are irrelevant because boats will not be allowed to fish near them.

Yet others object on what might be called political grounds; some because they feel the project has not been adequately publicized by press and media; and some because they think there was inadequate public consultation about the environmental, economic and social implications before decisions were made[20]. Others

---

[19] Where an initial increase in demand for goods and services in the Wells area economy would lead to an increase in the supply of goods and services in aggregate output that is a multiple of the initial change.

[20] The development companies (Centrica, Statoil and others) dispute that claim

think organizations that might have been expected to protest have failed to do so with sufficient vigour[21]. They acknowledge that the King's Lynn and West Norfolk Borough Council and the Norfolk County Council have raised objections to aspects of some of the proposed developments (although they doubt the objections will make any difference) and fret because the North Norfolk District Council has not done likewise. And in Wells, part of the community is distressed by the prospect that the town could revert to the industrial port it was until the early 1990s (to the detriment of the tourism and fishing port it has since become) and that by promoting developments that would affect the harbour (for which they have jurisdiction) and the town (for which they do not) the Wells Harbour Commissioners have exceeded their mandate[22] and will be unable to control future events.

The extent to which Saltmarsh Coast communities successfully address issues arising from windfarm development will depend on the extent to which they believe their collective interests are directly or indirectly affected; their capacity to achieve internal consensus; their sense of whether they believe their voices would influence outcomes; and, above all, by whether they are relatively cohesive or divisive.

The impact of windfarm development will necessarily be greater in coastal than inland villages and greater where windfarms are close inshore than where they are further out. None of the planned and proposed developments would have anything like the visual impact they have had at Scroby[23] but under normal atmospheric conditions they would (at varying distances) be readily visible from the marshes, beaches and foreshores. And although they could not be seen from inland locations they would affect those who enjoy access to the coast but do not actually live on it.

Beyond possible outcomes in individual villages the prospects for whole coast collaboration are not good: partly because the implications vary from one part of the coast to another (notably because their negative impact will affect the coast as a whole whereas the benefits will be concentrated in Wells); partly because the record of cooperation between North Norfolk communities is poor; and partly because there are no cooperative mechanisms. The most likely outcome is that they will decide it is a waste of time to tilt against government mandated windmills.

---

[21] The RSPB on behalf of birds that will be killed by turbine blades as they approach the end of migratory journeys across the North Sea; the Norfolk Coast Partnership because it has been mute about the impact of windfarms on the visual appreciation of the Area of Outstanding Natural Beauty it exists to protect; Natural England which they believe should have engaged government on the grounds that windfarms will intrude on a site of Special Scientific Interest and a Special Area of Conservation; and the Environment Agency and other organizations for not having acted to protect one of England's most important Heritage Coasts.

[22] The Commissioners were created by Royal Statute in 1663 and have been governed, like other Trust Ports by successive Revision Orders. The Commissioners' mandate is to care for and operate the port and harbour of Wells.

[23] The windfarm at Scroby Sands near Great Yarmouth is less than five kilometers offshore

17

Collective attitudes could change if the initial schemes led to much larger developments (windfarm economics suggest high densities are most profitable) and some of those who now support them revised their opinions. If, meanwhile, they choose to protest they would do well to avoid special pleading, recognize they are dealing with local manifestations of national and international issues and anchor their arguments in the proposition that *all* power infrastructure should be sited where it does least damage to natural and cultural heritage[24]. The counter arguments: that the North Norfolk Coast offers shallow inshore water, short transmission lines and good access to the National Grid and onshore supply and maintenance facilities; and that exempting it and other eligible sites would raise windfarm operating costs, reduce returns on investment and hit business and residential consumers with higher electricity prices, are valid. Successful opposition to large scale windfarm development in North Norfolk and comparable areas would hinge on demonstrating that the social cost of destroying national and international heritage would exceed the financial and economic costs of exemptions.

Because Britain has waited far too long to exploit renewable energy sources the government must now exploit every available option *including windpower*. But because windpower is inherently expensive, inflexible and inefficient and has a far higher net carbon cost than is generally understood, it is essentially a stop-gap solution. And because wind power is neither a viable nor sustainable long term option windfarm policy should evolve to protect National Parks, Areas of Outstanding Natural Beauty and Heritage Coasts – including the Saltmarsh Coast of North Norfolk. Not in the interests of those who live in or near them but because they are priceless and irreplaceable assets. It would be a great shame if the long term value of those assets were irretrievably compromised by the pursuit of chimerical short term opportunities.

More specifically, the Sheringham Shoal and Dudgeon Shoal Windfarms on the Saltmarsh Coast will not overwhelm the Saltmarsh Coast and will be built no matter what. The proposed Race Bank and Docking Shoal Windfarms are another matter. They should not be built. First because they would impede access to and activity on the area's main fishing ground and threaten the survival of local fisheries (already threatened by depleted stocks)[25]. Second because they would be highly visible from every part of the Saltmarsh Coast, threaten its status as a wildlife preserve, severely compromise the visual environment that defines its character and undermine its comparative advantages for recreation and tourism which are and – unless spoiled in a well intentioned but frantic search for short term solutions – will continue to anchor its economic future.

Windfarms are not dark satanic mills. But if the copse-like footprint of the Sheringham Shoal Windfarm were allowed to grow into an industrial forest the essence of the Saltmarsh Coast would be destroyed as surely as the once magnificent landscapes of West Yorkshire were destroyed by industrial development two centuries ago. It need not and should not happen.

---

[24] I recently returned to Rye, Sussex for the first time in more than 50 years. The town remains a jewel but the once pristine seaward view of Romney Marsh from Ypres Castle has been blighted by a nuclear power plant, transmission towers, power lines .. and a windfarm.

[25] The future of the North Norfolk fisheries has recently been promoted by the construction of a new fish handling facility on Wells Quay.

Our Environment

How we see the physical, natural
and built world around us

Richard Hardman

Richard Hardman was born on some of the oldest rocks in the British Isles – the pre-Cambrian of Anglesey – in 1936. His grandfather, a former clergyman and keen amateur natural historian who had retired there, had a marvellous collection of butterflies but a small knowledge of geology. Richard decided to read geology at Oxford to be able to add to his grandfather's knowledge. Unfortunately, his grandfather died before that became possible but he left Richard with a great love of landscape and everything on it.

Richard first came to North Norfolk in the early 1980s and was entranced by the skyscapes and a land which melted away into the sea. His career as a geologist had taken him to many lands to study rocks and the processes by which they were formed, vital knowledge for those who seek to find oil and gas. He says that North Norfolk has many of the ingredients that give an understanding of beach process-es and sand accumulation and that many oil fields have been found in reservoirs created out of similar sands.

Richard has worked more than 45 years in oil and gas exploration and has enjoyed every minute. It was personally rewarding and in the 28 years he was involved in North Sea exploration he found several fields and was awarded the Petroleum Group's Silver Medal, the Geological Society's William Smith Medal and was made CBE in 1998. He is a former President of the Geological Society and member of the Natural Environment Research Council and throughout his com-mercial career has maintained a keen interest in the academic side of the science.

Shifting Sands:
North Norfolk Unzipped

Richard Hardman

For a long time North Norfolk has had me under its spell. Ever since, as an undergraduate at Oxford, I stumbled upon an anthology of short stories by Irish authors in which Lord Dunsany described the marshes of East Anglia in terms of beauty, mystery and fear. This description of an area which is neither land nor sea captured my imagination from that day until now. Beauty with an edge is how I see it, as one never knows when the incoming tide could lead to disaster. When, later in my adult life, I visited the Gulf Coast of America in the company of Jim Coleman, a well known expert on beaches and river systems, I understood the underlying realities. North Norfolk is comparatively rare in Britain being an aggradational coastline – an area where new land is being added. More of this later, but before we look at the coast in detail we need to consider the geological background and in particular geological time.

Time and the Importance of History

"With the Lord one day is like a thousand years, and a thousand years are like one day"

the Second Letter of Peter, 3:8

Man is an egotistical being and finds it difficult to comprehend any period of time that much exceeds his own life span. His egocentric perspective decided that he was so important that the whole of the solar system revolved around the earth and anyone who had the temerity to disagree was persecuted. Then Archbishop Ussher interpreted the Bible to determine creation happened 4003 years, 2 months, 11 days and 6 hours before the birth of Christ and, moreover, insisted the whole of Britain believe this. Today there are still those who would like to persecute anyone who disagrees but if we are going to understand the North Norfolk Coast we have to jettison biblical interpretations and turn to science.

It is interesting to note that geological science owes its origin more to the free-thinkers of Scotland than the establishments of Oxford and Cambridge which were unable to cope with radical ideas lacking the blessing of the Anglican Church. John

Fuller reports that in England as late as the 1865 meeting of the British Association for the Advancement of Science a motion supported by 716 signatories was put up which said, *"It is impossible for the Word of God as written in the book of nature and God's word as written in Holy Scripture to contradict one another."* This left out the question of who had determined the age of the earth and whether they were a reliable interpreter of either bible or nature. Scotland was fortunate in that the guiding light behind the Church of Scotland, Calvin, suggested that if you wanted to understand the creator you had better study his creations. Scientific enquiry was thus actively encouraged in Scotland. Today it can be established beyond reasonable doubt that the world is about 4.5 billion years old with the oldest rocks being just under 4 billion years. Nevertheless the creationists are making a come-back as they attempt to deny the advances science has so painstakingly made. Does Calvin turn in his grave? I think so.

To understand the geological framework of East Anglia we need to have a feeling for geological time. There are two guiding geological principles which were set out by a Scottish Geologist, Charles Lyell, in 1830-33. These are, *"The present is the key to the past"*, and the rule of superposition, *"If a rock layer or bed overlies another bed it must be younger (unless there has been an overturning)"*. What these mean are: firstly, if we study the geological record we should be able to find rocks which were laid down by similar processes to those exhibited by the present coast of North Norfolk; and secondly, although it is demonstrably true about superposition, the age difference between two layers, one underneath and one on top, could be five minutes, five years or five million years or more. In Norfolk we are aware of juxtaposed rocks where the age difference is 100 million years! Time is important and vital to our understanding of the earth.

Geological Framework

Driving over the undulating low reliefs of North Norfolk, it is hard to imagine the geological turmoil of the past. 400 million years ago the Caledonian plate tectonic collision created a mountain chain stretching from Scandinavia through Britain to what is now North America. As millions of years passed, the mountains were worn down by the heat of the sun, the cold of the night, rain water and rivers until a large flat area was created. Named the Anglo-Brabant Massif by geologists, it underpins East Anglia and London itself. A recent study concludes that the present coast line in Norfolk coincides with the edge of this old massif which today lies at a depth of between 500 and 1000 metres below the surface.

During the passage of the 100 million years which it took for the mountains to be eroded, a gently north-east sloping upland area was developed. It was a time when all the plates coalesced and the earth's land surface was one huge super-continent where hot desert conditions prevailed. Winds blew sands around this flattened landscape and a thin veneer of reddened desert sediment was laid down filling in irregularities and covering the old land surface. These deposits known to geologists as of Permian and Triassic age (200 -300 million years) are commercially important in the North Sea. To the northeast of Norfolk much of our inheritance of natural gas has been found reservoired in sandstones of these ages. Two of the companies involved in North Sea exploration even drilled several wells in North Norfolk hoping that gas would have migrated from deep under the North Sea to be trapped in the shallower Permian sandstones of Norfolk. They were mistaken but perhaps for the good of the countryside this was no bad thing.

The failure to find gas was caused by the lack of an effective seal to cap the sands and trap the gas. The uplands of North Norfolk had to wait over 20 million years before any rocks were laid down over the older sands. Then, in a landscape dominated by dinosaurs who roamed in the swamps and shallow seas, clays and sands were laid down over the older desert sediments. In the shallow seas shelly organisms flourished but, perhaps under the influence of increased global warming, icecaps melted and sea levels continued to rise. About 100 million years ago, in the sea over North Norfolk calcareous algae called coccolithophorids bloomed in huge quantities. On death the calcareous skeletons of these organisms rained down to collect on the sea bed and form the rock we now know as chalk, familiar to us from the white cliffs of Dover. The sea bed at that time was not very congenial for life in general. There was not much to live on but burrowing shrimps, and sea urchins seemed to live quite happily as did siliceous sponges. On death, the sponges disintegrated and provided silica to infill the shrimp burrows and become the flints well-known and perhaps detested by Norfolk farmers, but a source of employment if you were a flint-knapper.

About 65 million years ago, a comet or large meteorite struck the globe near the present Yucatan peninsula. The dust thrown up circled the globe, blotting out the sun and leading to at least ten years without a proper summer. This led to severe global cooling and the extinction of the dinosaurs. Sea levels fell as ice caps grew and in places which had formerly been shallow seas such as Norfolk, the Chalk which stretched from the United Kingdom in the west to as far east as Kazakhstan was exposed. Chalk slowly dissolves in rain water and as a result it was gradually eroded to leave a thin capping of soil embedded with obdurate, unweathering flints covering chalk which in turn was supported by the older rocks of the Anglo-Brabant platform. Geologists divide rocks into solid and drift with the solid being consolidated and generally old and the drift being unconsolidated and young. For those interested only in solid geology, this was the end of the story but in many ways the greatest geological interest in North Norfolk was yet to come, brought about by the ice ages and the coming of glaciers.

Yesterday, Today and Tomorrow

Yesterday

Young rocks, less than 1.8 million years old, are known to geologists as the Quaternary. Despite within the sediments themselves rock fragments giving evidence of from whence they have been derived, truly diagnostic age criteria are often absent. It is difficult to be specific about which glacier exactly laid them down and at what time. This makes them a splendid battleground for academics.

My views are based on the Bulletin of the Geological Society of Norfolk, 1984, backed up by Field Guide Number 1 compiled for the 13th International Sedimentological Conference in 1990 by I.N. McCave of Cambridge and P.S.Balson of the British Geological Survey.

The Quaternary was the time of Ice Ages and the first glacier reached Norfolk perhaps 250,000 to 300,000 years ago. The glacial front of what we know as the "Anglian stage" glacier pushed ice over the rim of the old Chalk platform which arrested further forward motion of the ice. A terminal moraine, the rock fragments pushed forward by the ice or derived from fragments caught up in the ice, was the result. The largest and most impressive accumulation of ice marginal sediments on the east coast of England thus occurs in North Norfolk. It is generally referred to as the Cromer Ridge. Where the ridge reaches the sea in the Trimingham – Overstrand coastal strip it comprises sands, gravels and muds more than 75 metres thick, deposited over earlier Chalk deposits. These unconsolidated sediments, often referred to as "crags", are significant sediment providers to the North Sea. The people who have built houses upon them clearly forgot about the biblical parable about building one's house on sand as despite rock dumping and wooden barriers the sea continues to eat away at the soft sediments, causing destruction of property and much grief to the householders. We will consider the significance of the products of erosion below. Meanwhile the householders continue their battle for more cliff protection or compensation from the local council for their misfortune.

Later glacial activity also left markers upon the North Norfolk landscape but with much less impact. There are glacial sediments younger than Anglian but experts are uncertain whether it was one or two additional glaciers which terminated in North Norfolk; Wolstonian 128,000 years, and Devensian perhaps 18,000 years ago. At Sidestrand one of the later glaciers, probably the Devensian ripped up a huge chalk raft from the sea bed and rammed it into the Anglian Crag sediments. The power of moving ice is amazing and well illustrated by this example. The Chalk in the cliff at Sidestrand is the youngest chalk found onshore in Britain. Such chalk is well known to us from the Norwegian and Danish sectors of the North Sea where it contains billions of barrels of oil and associated gas. The last glaciers left several other marks of their presence. Near Holt there is a well developed esker or kame, a sinuous gravel bank formed by a stream flowing within the ice-walled tunnel of a glacier, which has been exploited for building material. The Waveney Valley has thick glacially derived sands and gravels and much of North Norfolk is covered in glacial till. The Somerton borehole penetrated 86 feet of glacial till before drilling 94 feet of Norwich Crag, showing that glacial till is no mere veneer. The aerial extent of the till is shown by the little book *Classic Landforms of the North Norfolk Coast* and covers almost the whole of North Norfolk.

Although glaciers have long been absent from the landscape because they dumped so much unconsolidated sediment in North Norfolk, they continue to play an important part providing distinctive landforms to the scenery and a source of sands and gravels to the building industry. Glacial material is also the major source of new sediment to the North Sea around Norfolk although modern rivers can also be important.

Sea level has risen continuously from the time the last glacier started to melt. 12,000 years ago the sea level in the area was 90m below where it is today. 7800 years ago it was a mere 20m lower, and sea level continues to rise. It is reckoned that Norfolk is sinking at the rate of perhaps 1 metre every thousand years, but of course as sea level continues to rise it is hard to know whether this a relative or absolute measurement. We need to bear this in mind when we start to consider the conditions of North Norfolk today.

Today

The company with which I explored for oil and gas came to study the North Norfolk barrier island coast in 1988. Essential features of such coasts are a string of ribbon like sand dunes parallel to the shore (the barriers), with lagoons on the landward side and high tide and low tide beaches on the seaward side. The high tide and low tide beaches are developed because in the tidal cycle most time is spent by waves at the high tide and low tide marks which develop these well recognised features. Normally geologists who wish to study barrier coasts go to the Carolinas on the Eastern Seaboard of the United States where they are particularly well developed. Barrier coasts reflect two important geological principles, *"The present is the key to the past"* and Walther's Law of 1894 which stated, *"The rock types that occur conformably next to one another in a vertical sequence will be the same as those found laterally in adjacent depositional environments."* If Walther's law applies what this means is, if near Wells-next-the-Sea we stand on the marshes or reclaimed fields, there should exist beneath our feet the same sequence of rocks as we can see going out to sea – viz: marsh, dune sands of a barrier island complex, high tide beach, low tide beach and beach slope sands with muddy sands at the greatest depth. As time goes by the land should continue to migrate seawards always in exactly the same sequence. The requirements for this are;

- Space for the sediments to accumulate ;

- An adequate supply of sand and mud;

- A tidal range sufficient to allow low tide and high tide beaches to form;

- Winds which occasionally blow onshore strongly enough to form dunes and barrier islands

- Lagoons developed behind the barrier islands where mud accumulates bound in place by sediment trapping plants

We were interested because sands of these types form excellent reservoirs for oil and gas and we needed to understand how they are developed. We have seen that the Norfolk Coast is sinking to provide plenty of accommodation space for the accumulation of sediment. So we had every expectation that in boreholes in the area we would find a duplication of the sequence our eyes could see on the surface. It did not prove to be the case. The subsurface sequence was more complex and we learned that simplicity at surface does not always imply simplicity subsurface. To understand why we need to look at the detailed picture of the past and consider the part human beings have played in altering the natural state.

The present North Norfolk barrier coast is a very young coast. It was not until the glaciers had totally disappeared that anything like the barrier coastline we know today could start to form, the shore line lying far off to the north. At Cley, a basal peat bed beneath the barrier coast sequence is dated by the radiocarbon method as 6610 years before present. At Brancaster, Funnell and Pearson report a basal peat of 6460bce (before common era, previously reported as BC before Christ) and a later one of 1520bce. These peats represent plant material, predominantly reeds (*Phragmites communis*), developed in lagoons trapped behind older barrier islands which existed when sea level was lower. This is probably the main reason why Walther's Law is not demonstrated by the present North Norfolk subsurface. The older barrier coastline has been overwhelmed by the rapidly rising sea level. There was just not enough sediment being delivered to keep up with subsidence.

The other reason is the interference with natural processes by human beings.

Our voyage of understanding starts at the cliffs of Overstrand and Sidestrand. The cliffs in this area are about 50 metres high and they are composed of very soft sediments of the Norfolk Crag dumped by the Anglian Glacier. Every attempt has been made to lessen erosion and to give comfort to those living atop the cliffs but, despite rock dumping and a wooden barricade, cliff retreat continues at about 1.8 to 2 metres per year. This yields an estimated 750,000 cubic metres per year of sediment of which 400,000 is sand. (In order to visualise the enormousness of this consider a dump truck is of about 25 cubic metres capacity. 16,000 dump trucks would be needed to move just one year's supply of sand.)

My brother-in-law who was a fisherman for 40 years observed, using the sophisticated electronic instruments with which his boat was fitted, that when the wind blows onshore, sediment is removed from the beach but when it blows offshore it is brought back to the beach. To understand this we have to think about near shore water comprising two layers, a surface layer and an under layer. In calm conditions the two layers are one and move controlled by the tidal pulse. With an offshore wind the surface water is held back from coming to the beach but water below the surface responds to the tidal pulse and brings sand in. With an onshore wind the reverse is true and the surface water is strongly impelled shoreward by the wind and balanced by the under-tow carrying sediment out. The prevailing wind in North Norfolk is from the south-west. The tidal range is from 5 to 6 metres in springs and 2 to 3 metres in neaps which gives plenty of energy for sand movement. Generally when the wind is in the prevailing direction sediment will be brought back to the Overstrand and Sidestrand areas but with onshore winds it will be taken out to sea. Eventually sediment will be partitioned between sediment going south and that going west with the driving mechanism in both cases being the prevailing south-westerly wind. Figures produced by various authorities suggest that the split is 2:1 in favour of the southerly direction but from year to year, depending on the exact average wind direction the split can differ with perhaps as much as 350,000 cubic metres out of 400,000 going west along the North Norfolk coast. Note we are only considering sand and fine gravel. Mud needs quiet waters to settle and once settled is much more difficult to move than sand. Mud generally accumulates behind barrier islands where it falls out onto the sea-bed and is then fixed by plant growth.

The North Norfolk Coast has a plentiful supply of sand and mud, but only so long as the cliffs of Sheringham, Cromer, Overstrand and Sidestrand keep eroding. The sediments from these cliffs drift from east to west along the coast under the influence of the prevailing south-westerly wind. Should the sediment supply diminish a combination of rising sea level and sinking land would mean that the North Norfolk coastline we know today would retreat back to the Chalk Platform. Wells-next-the Sea for instance would once again prove to be an excellent port but the recreational facilities of the barrier coast enjoyed by so many would no longer exist. A good example of what can happen is provided by travelling westwards along the coast to Titchwell.

At Titchwell on the mid-tide beach a forest bed of tree trunks and stumps embedded in peat is exposed. Radiocarbon dating suggests for these eroding sediments an age of 2790 to 3470 BP (before present). It is suggested that this area is being starved of sediment which is thus left open to active erosion as the land sinks.

There are two possible reasons for the sediment starvation: The aforementioned efforts of local Councils to reduce cliff erosion at Sidestrand with a consequent diminution in the overall volume of westerly drifting sediments: Channel dredging particularly at Wells-next-the-Sea which is breaking the pattern of sediment flow. The case of Wells is fascinating. If you look at detail of the Wells area on Google Earth you can see that there is a huge build up of sand on the east side of the dredged channel. The tidal stream velocity in the channel acts as a barrier and prevents the natural westerly drift of sandy sediment. Look at the northern limit of the channel where you can see a spur of sand attempting to bridge across the channel mouth and continue its westerly migration. Sand has piled up on the east of the channel forming a dramatic ebb tidal delta which continues to build out northwards. For one or both reasons Titchwell is no longer obtaining its natural sedimentary share and erosion occurs.

The barrier coast is being interfered with in other ways:

- Barrier islands which were naturally stabilised by marram grass (*Ammophilia arenaria*) and sand twitch(*Agropyron junceiforme*) were planted with Scots Pine in the last century, to give much greater protection against wave and wind reworking.

- Marshes have been reclaimed by building high sea walls. The resulting rich agricultural land is now being used profitably for both arable and pastoral farming.

- East of Blakeney gravel has been bull-dozed into a bank to protect the coast near Cley from inundation by storm surges and high tides. It is understood this may not continue but I await with interest the response after the first serious inundation of a very beautiful part of Norfolk.

The barrier island coast of today which started out as a work of nature owes much of its present existence to human activity. It is only when exceptional events occur that nature is able to reassert itself. Walls are breached, islands are flattened and floods occur and everyone is surprised. Given enough of these unexpected events Walther's law would undoubtedly start to apply.

Tomorrow

During geological time significant changes in climate have always occurred. As a result of tectonic plates moving around the globe, carrying the continents like limp passengers, parts of our continent have seen desert conditions, have been at tropical latitudes with well developed swamps, and have frequently been submerged under temperate seas. In addition to climate change as a result of plate tectonic movements there is also climate change as a result of global cooling and warming. We have been exceptionally lucky to have had a stable climate for about 12,000 years. There is no guarantee that stability will continue forever. Indeed we should not expect it to do so. Today, we enjoy a temperate climate with a prevailing south-westerly wind which brings the rain vital for agriculture and life in general. We are worried about global warming and sea level rise but we in Britain should be much more worried about global cooling. It was not warming that finished off the dinosaurs but a dramatic 10 year burst of intense cooling. Cool equals no food. After the dinosaurs had eaten each other what was left? Not a pretty thought if you are a mammal unused to extreme physical hardship. Whereas global warming may prove an expensive inconvenience cooling would be disastrous for North West Europe with its teeming millions. A land with the same climate as the Canadian tundra could not possibly support today's population. A warmer climate does however spell danger to the North Norfolk Coast with the implication of a rising sea level.

As the world burns fossil fuels to derive energy, greenhouse gases such as carbon dioxide are released and are increasing in the atmosphere. The number of parts per million carbon dioxide in the atmosphere has increased from 280 in the 18th century to more than 360 at present and continues to increase. It has been observed from Greenland ice cores that in the Quaternary, increased carbon dioxide in the atmosphere and interglacial climate warming show a one-for-one correlation. More carbon dioxide equates with warmer conditions. To date we estimate that the increased carbon dioxide has resulted in an increased global temperature by perhaps 0.6°C. It is believed increases will continue and we should perhaps expect 2°C even if efforts to reduce greenhouse gas emissions are successful. Increasing global temperatures result have two main impacts. Firstly, evaporation rates are higher leading to the expectation of greater levels of rainfall, and secondly, the climate system – with rising global temperatures we should expect more storms. Storms driven by offshore winds in Norfolk, the prevailing south-west direction, will have only minor impact but more frequent storms driven by northerly winds particularly if coinciding with high tides will be devastating for the coastline. Add the predicted increased level of storms to a sinking coastline, and add to the mix sediment supply restrictions both by preventing erosion of cliffs and by dredging and you have a devastating scenario. The real question is what do we want? What do we want our elected representatives to sanction? Do we want to protect the status quo at what looks like greatly increasing cost or do we wish nature to reassert its influence? How do we decide between saving the homes of people who live on top of glacial cliffs and the need to maintain the sediment flow to the barrier island complex of North Norfolk? At a time when world food shortages are likely to occur do we really want to see the reclaimed marshes once again flooded? We could take a geological view and simply shrug our shoulders and say fatalistically, let nature reign and see what happens! As Edmund Wilson said, "Nature triumphs but men and women may be inconvenienced."

I suppose the future lies half way between these extremes. The North Norfolk Coast is a magical place and we can steer a course at a reasonable cost to protect it and maintain a living future. I have the following suggestions. We should:

- Stop protecting the glacial cliffs at Sidestrand and Overstrand with rock dumping and wooden barricades. Instead we should use the money saved to compensate the cliff top dwellers for the eventual loss of their homes.

- We should encourage the development of a wind farm in the Sidestrand/Overstrand area with dense spacing just offshore and use the revenue from this to help the local council cope with road replacement and general repair of infrastructure. The wind farm will have two major benefits besides generating "green" electricity. In an onshore wind, i.e. the wind which leads to an attack on the cliff base, the foundation of the wind turbine towers will break up the waves and lessen cliff erosion. Also, the windmills themselves will absorb wind energy and reduce wave strength, both contributing to more benign conditions at cliff base. Despite the anticipated increase in stormy weather, the wind farm should help prevent the rate of erosion being any greater than it is today – if it does what is predicted.

- Stop all dredging forthwith allowing sediment to be dispersed naturally. It is expected that eventually the channel out of Wells Harbour would be diverted in a westerly direction but still remain passable by the fishing boats and ships that use it today. It is understood that plans are afoot to dredge a deep water harbour to the south-east of the lifeboat house for vessels engaged in servicing wind farms. In my view this would be misguided. Study of tidal channels shows that there are two deltas associated with such channels, ebb tide and flood tide deltas. We have seen the huge ebb tide delta to the east of the shipping channel. Where is the flood tide body? At present it is south-east of the lifeboat house squashed by the wall built to keep the sea out of reclaimed land housing the caravan park. It is understood this is exactly where dredging is intended to provide deep water for the harbouring of vessels servicing offshore wind farms. All I can say is the best of luck. Sisyphus had a greater chance of getting the stone to the top of the hill than the dredgers of keeping this area sand free.

Conclusions

North Norfolk is a place of great allure and its future needs to be considered in the round. The barrier island coastline is fragile and the gentleness of the inland scenery with its unique heritage of glacial features could too easily be destroyed. In this brief description of some of the inherent features I hope you have reached the realisation there are few easy options. Conservation costs money but nature has a power that only a great deal of money continuously applied can even hope to keep in check. The money that will inevitably be spent should be used sensibly, defending the defensible. Schemes which need large amounts of money continuously expended should be avoided.

In the case of cliff erosion we must bow to the inevitable. There is no point in trying to prevent erosion especially since this would also cause problems further along the coast to the west. However a suggestion has been made to reduce erosional impact at minimum cost. Not everyone likes wind turbines but if they can be used to protect the coast, generate green electricity, and income for the local taxpayers it strikes me that this would not be a bad option. Of course there will be objections. Bird lovers are not fond of them and from the landscape aspect they are not everyone's cup of tea but they have a majesty all of their own. Perhaps the way to overcome objections is to let local people own them either through the Council or by setting up a cooperative. A radical solution perhaps but if there was profit involved for those most affected then objections would probably be muted.

Stopping dredging should be an easy option as it actually saves money. However consultation with those seemingly affected would be a good idea. The people who plan a deepwater anchorage near the lifeboat house should also be consulted and an attempt made to understand their plans. If they are as I have outlined perhaps they can be persuaded that there is a better solution.

I would hope that in 50 years time someone appraising this area will write that North Norfolk is still a wonderful example of nature and people living in balance; that beauty would still have an edge; and that all the mystery had not been driven out of this most magical of landscapes.

Professor Tim O'Riordan

Professor Tim O'Riordan is Emeritus Professor of Environmental Sciences at the University of East Anglia. He is a Deputy Lieutenant of the County of Norfolk, and a Fellow of the British Academy. He holds an MA in Geography from the University of Edinburgh, an MS in Water Resources Engineering from Cornell University, and a PhD in Geography from the University of Cambridge.

He has edited a number of key books on institutional aspects of global environmental change, policy and practice, led two international research projects on the transition to sustainability in the European Union (1995-2002) and edited two editions of the text book, *Environmental Science for Environmental Management*.

Professor O'Riordan is a member of the UK Sustainable Development Commission and of the East of England Sustainable Development Round Table. His research deals with the themes associated with better governance for sustainability. He is also active in the evolution of sustainability science partnerships. His direct work relates to designing future coastlines in East Anglia so that they are ready for sea level rise and the creation of sound economies and societies for a sustainable future.

He is a core member of the Prince of Wales' seminar on Business and the Environment, has many contacts with the business world, is an assessor for the Prince of Wales Accounting for Sustainability project and sits on the Corporate Responsibility Body for Asda PLC and on the Growth and Climate Change Panel for Anglian Water Group. Professor O'Riordan is also Executive Editor of *Environment Magazine*. His other research interests cover interdisciplinary approaches to pursuing the transition to sustainability, risk perception and communication, business and social virtue.

Tim O'Riordan plays classical double bass in a Norwich orchestra he has managed for over 25 years.

Dr Sophie Nicholson-Cole

Dr Sophie Nicholson-Cole joined Atkins' Climate Change and Environmental Futures team in October 2008 from her previous position as a Senior Research Associate in the Tyndall Centre for Climate Change Research's Sustainable Coasts and Adaptation Programmes. Sophie is recognised widely for her expertise in the social dimensions of climate change (both mitigation and adaptation). She has a particularly sound understanding of the challenges relating to the policy and practice of adaptation in the UK and abroad (including social justice, human rights, adaptive governance, perceptions of vulnerability and how these issues interact with the design and delivery of adaptation to climate change). She also has a solid grounding in the practice of stakeholder engagement (including public participation) – a critical component in decision-making processes concerned with uncertain and often contentious environmental issues which interact with social and economic systems.

Sophie's PhD training, teaching experience and research involvement with a range of public sector projects at different scales have enabled her to acquire strong skills associated with the planning, management and practice of social science research, engagement with external stakeholders, presentation of climate change research to different audiences, organisation and facilitation of workshops and other events. Her most recent academic post, which involved an investigation of the governance challenges facing adaptation to coastal change, gave her the opportunity to work extensively with coastal management and related stakeholders in different sectors at national to local levels. Her earlier work concerned public perceptions and the communication of climate change and involved working with members of the public and national government.

Turning the Tide in North Norfolk

A Case Study of Adaptation to Coastal Change

Tim O'Riordan and Sophie Nicholson-Cole

This chapter substantially reproduces material included in Coastal governance in transition: A case study of adaptation to coastal change in North Norfolk, UK, *by Sophie Nicholson-Cole, Tim O'Riordan, Jessica Milligan-Bryson and Andrew Watkinson, which has been accepted for publication in the Journal of Environmental Planing and Management.*

Preface

The coastline is a combination of affection for what is there and unease over what it might become. In many ways, the coast is the test case for adapting to climate change. Coasts are on the front line. What this chapter will reveal is that we cannot know with any confidence just how coasts will be affected by sea level rise, flooding and erosion. What we do know is that such damage will inevitable occur over the rest of this century, and that all attempts to control these outcomes will affect the vulnerability of the coast even more. So the challenge is how to design a robust and resilient coastline that allows for flourishing economies and communities to adapt with vigour and purpose, how to plan future settlement and infrastructure so that the consequences of such decisions are not at risk in the future, and how to work with businesses and residents and visitors to ensure that a fair and just outcome is reached with appropriate funding and management arrangements to enable the transition to be joyful and effective. This is not an easy task as this chapter reveals.

Introduction

The geologically soft coastlines of Eastern England are dynamic and diverse in both their geomorphology and ecology, with a complex legacy of hard-engineered coastal defence (Brennan, 2007; Bridges, 1998). In north Norfolk, the coastline encompasses rapidly eroding glacial cliffs, with shingle banks and sand dunes protecting a low-lying interior. Much of this is at or below sea level, including the internationally famous wetland habitat and member of the UK national park family, the Norfolk Broads.

The risks of coastal flooding and erosion in the region are increasing as a result of climate change (Hulme et al., 2002; IPCC, 2007) and natural coast level adjustments following the melting of the glaciers after the last ice age (Shennan, 1989). Sea level rise, which could be of the order of one metre or more by the end of the century (IPCC, 2007), and the prospect of more extreme storm events, present real challenges for long-term coastal management. New projections for sea-level rise (McKie, 2009) suggest that coastal inundation may be greater and more immediate than previously estimated. Yet it is on conservative projections of the current science, that current coastal adaptation and investment is being assessed.

The consequences of well-intentioned efforts to protect the coast using engineered coastal defence works (e.g. sea walls, groynes and revetments, off-shore reefs which have enabled development to take place in previously risky locations) add to the problem. Hard-engineered defence works have interrupted the natural process of long-shore drift, encouraging the removal of protective sediment from unprotected coastal zones, and hence increasing their future vulnerability to coastal erosion and flooding (French, 2004; Leafe et al., 1998). This context means that it is particularly difficult to make decisions about planning sustainably for new housing and other types of regeneration and development in coastal areas.

This chapter examines the mix of policies and organisations and funding arrangements which address coastal change in England. It also reviews the difficulties of matching the genuine uncertainty as to what the coast may look like in 50 or more years' time with the needs to maintain local confidence in community wellbeing and economic prosperity. It concludes that there is a need to redesign the future coastline in accord with the best available science, genuine and well delivered community participation and consent, and a wide array of innovative funding arrangements to bring confidence to the coastline.

Policy and Governance on a Changing Coastline in England

Since 2005 there has been significant change to the national strategic approach to flood and coastal erosion risk management policy in England. This is reflected in the government's policy, entitled *Making Space for Water* (MSW). This new policy arena signals a move away from investing in expensive "hard" engineered defence toward designing a more naturally functioning and adaptable coastline (Defra, 2005b). Amongst other things, it promotes a more risk-based and holistic approach, favouring more long-term probabilistic assessments, and embeds flood and coastal erosion risk management across a range of government policies, including planning, urban and rural development, agriculture, transport and nature conservation. It also involves new, restraining, forms of cost-benefit analysis, where the economies of possibly affected coastal economies are reduced to crude assessments of property values rather than their functioning social and commercial networks (Milligan et al., 2006; Risk and Policy Analysts, 2008).

Making Space for Water also signalled the passing of strategic responsibility for the management of the coast to the Environment Agency in April 2008. Despite all this, there is still no coherent, co-ordinated or integrated approach to managing the coast, and the coastal governance arrangements are somewhat disjointed and fragmented. There is complex web of elected and statutory agencies, non-governmental organisations and interest groups, with different organisational cultures, plans, strategies and responsibilities where the coast is concerned (CoastNet, 2007). A serious coastal flood event would uncover this institutional gap and could lead to calls for much more co-ordination and integration. Hopefully this should not arrive on the back of damage and distress.

Figure 1 charts the three main central government players in England for coastal management. The Department for Environment, Food and Rural Affairs (Defra) is responsible for both policy and the coastal management agencies – the Environment Agency (EA) and Natural England. The Department for Communities and Local Government (CLG) is responsible for planning, community cohesion and regeneration, and all relevant local authority activities. While the Treasury controls overall government spending, including broadly how much funding is provided for Defra and the Environment Agency, it is Defra and the EA that maintain overall control of the level of spending pertaining to the delivery of flood and coastal erosion. Defra allocates resources to the EA, which in turn funds flood and coastal erosion protection works based on strategic policy through a system of shoreline management plans, and a priority scoring system for timing protection schemes. It is the responsibility of coastal local authorities to support EA financed works with erosion protection investments of their own. In general these two bodies work together, but as we report here, such arrangements are rare and often messy. Regional government provides additional economic stimulus, though not fully linked to possible realigned coastal configurations. As a result, there is a lack of co-ordination and organised management. Understandably, where there is inaction through lack of funds or because of a disjointed local policy regime, which advocates no intervention or retreat, local people can and have been known to take matters into their own hands, for example, coastal communities or individual property owners may provide privately sourced funds for the construction of temporary defence works. In amongst this complex governance structure there is a gap – a clear lack of overall leadership and vision.

Shoreline management plans (SMPs) cover the 6000km of coast in England and Wales, and provide a large-scale assessment of the risks associated with current and potential "best guess" future coastal processes. They form an important element of the strategy for flood and coastal erosion, and present a long term policy and management framework to reduce these risks. The recent shoreline management plan for the north Norfolk coast (sub-cell 3b) proposes some highly contentious recommendations including suggestions for no active intervention and managed realignment along parts of the frontage where previously the line was held (Anglian Coastal Authorities Group, 2006). Policy preferences for shoreline retreat and realignment mean no future guarantees of protection, or even mainte- nance of existing defence works. At a time when many existing defence structures require maintenance or replacement, and where no compensation or other meas- ures exist to support the transition to what could be a major change on the coast in some places, many coastal communities of varying size in Norfolk (and other English counties, for example, Yorkshire, Lincolnshire, Suffolk, Essex and Kent) are now facing a situation of considerable unease and anxiety about their future.

Figure 1. Current tensions between the key institutions presently involved in governing England's coast

Case-study Research in North Norfolk

The research on which part of this chapter is based was commissioned and carried out along the coastline of north Norfolk in 2005-6 (Milligan et al., 2006). Its aim was to investigate the implications of the draft second generation Shoreline

Management Plan for sub-cell 3b on north Norfolk coastal communities. The purpose was to explore the complex issues relating to changing property values, adjustments to social well-being and how a cross section of communities understood and viewed the draft SMP. The study took a participatory approach and involved working with established community forums, parish councils, local businesses and local recreational and residents associations. Following discussions with the North Norfolk District Council (NNDC) and some key community contacts, a series of workshops were held in 2005, in four communities in north Norfolk. These enabled the research team to meet a wide range of local people as well as members and officers of the NNDC, and to gain a sense of the ways in which the shoreline management planning process and its draft proposals were perceived by and affecting the communities of North Norfolk. .

Whilst there was a high level of awareness about the SMP itself, the primary response was one of feeling let down, of being treated unfairly, and of not being properly consulted. All of this resulted in a combination of resigned helplessness and deep resentment. There was a clear feeling that the SMP process did not fully take into account the deeper social and economic consequences of uncertainty, blight and reduced business confidence brought about by the policy change.

"Most of us realise that we have no legal entitlement to sea defences, but the game has been changed with little or no prior warning allowing us to make plans for the future."

The findings showed that businesses and residents are already suffering from the threat and uncertainty brought about by the SMP, illustrated by dwindling confidence (e.g. reluctance to improve/maintain property, invest in business improvement, blight on property prices and more widely, etc.). Businesses create investment and jobs, and service both visitors and residents; there is no guarantee of a viable future social economy on this coastline if businesses are not offered reasonable guarantees of their economic future. It appears that those who are economically disadvantaged are especially exposed to uncertainties in the local economy and to falling business confidence. This theme is reflected in other research carried out in North Norfolk (Ash et al., 2008; Risk and Policy Analysts, 2008).

"Not having been able to afford to invest in anything into the business for the past few uncertain years, equipment breaks down, the property looks run down and one is afraid to borrow funds to update accommodation to today's high standards because of the prospect of impending total loss. No one who has worked and paid taxes over a long time deserves to face the sort of bleak retirement that I now anticipate."

Around half of participants agreed that coastal change is inevitable and a natural process. A strong majority of both residents and businesses agree however, that even if the coastline cannot be held, compensation or other adaptation solutions must be agreed – particularly where coastal change is happening in the light of policy change (the line having been previously held, and their livelihoods having been established in this regard). The study strongly indicated that leaving matters as they are is not an option, politically, or in terms of establishing sustainable future coastlines. The current management and financing arrangements are not appropriate to support the adaptation process that is required.

"When our sea wall goes because it can't be maintained it will be a disaster. The adaptation toolkit could be the saving or the breaking. It is now that we need to be doing things about long-term decisions. If they are seriously going to let it go, this village needs to move, and people will need homes to go to. The council can't do that without some financing. It's all about putting the nitty-gritty in place to enable this to happen." Community representative, 29th November, 2007.

"There is little movement on the adaptation front. While £30 million has been allocated over three years for adaptation, there is no indication about how the fund will be spent and no answers are being given. It is critical that the money is used for case-work in real communities to guide future spending." NNDC, 29th November, 2007.

Recent research into the costs of coastal change and adaptation commissioned by the NNDC (Ash et al., 2008; Risk and Policy Analysts Limited, 2008) explored the

costs of no active intervention as a policy (monetised and non-monetised impacts and losses), costs of facilitating roll-back and different options for funding packages. This goes further than the narrow economic appraisal of damages based on number of properties affected compared with the costs of providing coastal protection works carried out as part of the SMP. The study also raises issues of distributive justice concerned with who bears the costs of no active intervention policies over 100 years.

> "The total costs of no active intervention have been estimated at almost £100 million (discounted), although this excludes significant community impacts that cannot be valued in monetary terms. On-going repair and replacement of key assets and infrastructure is estimated to cost around £2.6 million over the next 20 years, while roll-back is estimated to cost £39 million and funding for adaptation between £20,000 (for streamlined planning permission only) and £240 million (for purchasing properties from their existing owners at the not at risk market value)." (Risk and Policy Analysts Limited, 2008, p.ix)
>
> "Trust has been eroded here. People who have experienced the SMP 3b process have no belief in Government to handle the situation properly...This has been a pioneering effort by North Norfolk District Council. This has never been done anywhere before. And it seems there has never been the closeness of association between authority and its people in addressing these problems. It has been a huge success and we should recognise that NNDC have stretched the bubble."

Community representative, 29th November, 2007

Moving Forward

This chapter has examined, in the context of a case study, why governance for a future sustainable coastline is so dysfunctional at present, and why it is failing to create the conditions for adjustment to a changing coastline. It contributes to the evolving policy arena in coastal management in England and further a-field by clarifying some of the underlying challenges facing adaptation to coastal change. Current coastal governance arrangements are ill-equipped to tackle the totality of coastal change because of un-coordinated approaches and a deep seated reluctance to invest in adaptation initiatives.

However, the situation is not entirely bleak. The changes witnessed in the research reported in this paper are characterised by a creative and increasingly adaptive approach to managing coastal change, and a shifting mood of growing confidence and cooperation between the local authorities, other coastal management stakeholders, and coastal communities. The North Norfolk District Council

(NNDC) continues to work with Defra, the Environment Agency, local communities and other coastal management stakeholders to establish adaptive and creative ways of enabling residents and businesses to adjust to a changing coastline. They have embarked upon seeking options and expectations which accept a degree of erosion and flooding, so long as an appropriate mix of defence and adaptation support is in place.

Planned adaptation to inevitable coastal change is absolutely critical. Adaptation needs to be managed in the short-term, in order to prepare for change that will occur 25, 50 or 100 years into the future. This requires enabling policy, funding, tools and mechanisms for delivering long-term adaptation, which incorporates options for those people at most risk in the next 20 years. Foremost, policy making and delivery across sectors needs to be much more integrated and inclusive with clear and common objectives. This will demand a partnership model of governance combining public, private and civil society into new co-ordinating arrangements, which will help to address the tension between national strategic frameworks, and local flexibility for delivery. It will also help in the development of new and positive approaches to looking at options for the future of our coast within a framework that proactively seizes the opportunities arising through change.

As part of further policy movement, the flood management team in Defra issued an important consultation paper (Defra, 2009) with a view to re-examining the policy on adaptation. Many of the ideas being floated in this discussion document reflect the points outlined in this chapter. There is a proposal for up to £28 million being made available for adaptation over the period 2008 – 2011, with £8 million being specifically allocated to help coastal communities devise and carry out pilot schemes in coastal adaptation. In addition, a new fund of £5 million will be allocated to help households build in flood proofing measures to deal with flood risk. On top of this is a proposal to enable a selection of coastal authorities to bid for "pathfinder status" to test out ways of positively and proactively designing coasts for ecological and economic transition so that the outcome is more resilient in the face of climate change. The discussion document suggests that new forms of financing may be made available from local, regional and national sources to help deal with these adjustments.

This consultation signals a fresh approach to coastal change in the UK. It recognises that we may have actively to design sustainable future coastlines aimed at accommodation to climate change and sea level rise, and providing new forms of coastal ecologies and economies that provide for prosperity and peace of mind. This will not be at all easy as coastal residents are naturally wary of promised and proposals that usually fail to stay the course.

For financing this fresh approach, here are some suggestions:

1   Ensure that the shoreline management plan is a statutory process embedded in coastal action plans coupled with creative adaptation schemes. The SMP should evolve into a sustainable coastal action plan, and the creation of the new coastal partnerships.

2   All coastlines should be mapped on the basis of future flood and erosion risk, based on the best modelling available and put in it the context of scenario driven sea level rise projections.

3   Each "risk vulnerable" coastal area should be assessed on the following lines:

    a   The scope for coastal erosion for funding coastlines elsewhere (sacrificial cliffs)

    b   The scope of future flood risk when property should be progressively moved away, and no new planning permission granted.

    c   Zones of projected risk (50 – 100 years hence) designated for progressive removal of property and a prohibition against any new development unless clearly informed as to probable risk and requiring appropriate flood proofing.

    d   Zones for relocation and coastal redesign, for new socio-economic ecological investment for genuinely sustainable redesign.

On the basis of this arrangement, financing could be found as follows:

- *Sacrificial cliffs*: Funded by the flood defence budget, and boosted by carbon levy revenue, to buy out any property at fair market prices.

- *Vulnerable zones*: find a process to buy or lease back for a combination of carbon levy trust funds and planning betterment monies, where any development offered in a zone protected by coastal defence pays a public interest levy for a coastal management trust fund.

- *For new sustainable coastal opportunities*, use of a combination of rural development money, local authority economic development money, EU regional/social adjustment money (notably of adaptation to climate change) and EU environmental biodiversity assessment funds (on the back of LIFE funds and the overall biodiversity enhancement cash). This last tranche should also make maximum use of any new environmental schemes.

To conclude, a combination of interactive science, imaginative modelling, creative visioning, profound and prolonged community engagement, and innovative use of levies and sustainable development cash, coupled to a process of cooperative coastal governance and community coastal adaptation trust funds, could do the trick.

To leave the present governing and financing arrangements as they are will never lead to substantial coastal adaptation. All this would lead to is an unsatisfactory atmosphere of betrayal, distrust, vigilante coastal protective measures, and single-minded community resentment that plagues the endangered coastlines of today.

Acknowledgements

This research was carried out as part of a project funded by the Tyndall Centre for Climate Change Research and North Norfolk District Council. Additional research projects carried out in partnership with the Environment Agency, Defra, English Nature (now Natural England) and Great Yarmouth Borough Council contributed to the reflections presented in this paper. Any errors and the views expressed in this paper are the sole responsibility of the authors.

References

Anglian Coastal Authorities Group 2006. *Kelling to Lowestoft Ness Shoreline Management Plan*. First Review. Final Report, November 2006.

Ash, J., Fenn, T., Daly, E., Frew, P., Young, R., et al. 2008. *North Norfolk Coastal Management Plan – Assessing the Potential and Costs of Adaptation to Coastal Change*. Flood and Coastal Managment Conference 2008, Manchester, UK, Defra and the Environment Agency.

Brennan, R. 2007. The North Norfolk Coastline: A Complex Legacy. *Coastal Management* 35, 587-599.

CoastNet 2007. *Scoping study regarding current coastal activity and the national ICZM programme, and implications for East of England*. Essex: Prepared by CoastNet for the Sustainable Development Round Table – East.

Defra 2005. *Making Space for Water: Taking forward a new Government strategy for flood and coastal erosion risk management in England. First Government response to the autumn 2004 Making space for water consultation exercise*. London: Department for Environment, Food and Rural Affairs.

Defra 2009. *A strategy for promoting an integrated approach to the management of coastal areas in England*. Department for Environment, Food and Rural Affairs, London.

French, P. W. 2004. The changing nature of, and approaches to, UK coastal management at the start of the twenty-first century. *Geographical Journal*, 170: 116-125.

Hulme, M., Jenkins, G. J., Lu, X., Turnpenny, J. R., Mitchell, T. D., et al. 2002. *Climate Change Scenarios for the United Kingdom: The UKCIP02 Scientific Report*. Norwich, UK: Tyndall Centre for Climate Research, School of Environmental Sciences, University of East Anglia.

IPCC 2007. Summary for Policymakers. *In* S. Solomon, D. Qin, M. Manning et al., eds. *Climate Change 2007: The Physical Science Basis. Contribution of Working Group I to the Fourth Assessment Report of the Intergovernmental Panel on Climate Change*, Cambridge, UK and New York, USA.: Cambridge University Press.

Leafe, R., Pethick, J. and Townend, I. 1998. Realizing the benefits of shoreline management. *The Geographical Journal*, 164: 282-290.

McKie, M. 2009. Scientists to issue stark warning over dramatic seal level figures. *The Observer*, 8th March 2009.

Milligan, J., O'Riordan, T., Watkinson, A., Amundsen, H. and Parkinson, S. 2006. *Implications of the draft Shoreline Management Plan 3b on North Norfolk Coastal Communities. Final report to North Norfolk District Council*. Norwich: Tyndall Centre for Climate Change Research.

Milligan, J., O'Riordan, T., Nicholson-Cole, S. A. and Watkinson, A. R. 2009. Nature conservation for sustainable shorelines: lessons from seeking to involve the public. *Land Use Policy*, 26: 203-213.

Nicholson-Cole, S. A. and O'Riordan, T. 2009. Adaptive governance for a changing coastline: science, policy and the public in search of a sustainable future. *In*: N. W. Adger, I. Lorenzoni and K. O'Brien, eds. *Adapting to climate change: thresholds, values,*

Risk and Policy Analysts Ltd. 2008. *North Norfolk Coastal Management Plan Evidence Gathering Study 01 Final Report*. Loddon, Norfolk: RPA Limited, for North Norfolk District Council.

Shennan, I. 1989. Holocene crustal movements and sea-level changes in Great Britain. *Journal of Quaternary Science*, 4: 77-89.

Table 1 Key findings from residents questionnaires

Residential	Key findings
Awareness of the draft SMP (Shoreline Movement Plan)	84% heard of draft SMP. 71% knew what it was about. 24% had no idea what the draft SMP proposed. 37% aware via local newspapers, 8% via public meetings.
Opinions about the SMP process and outcome	Greatest influence on opinion is newspapers (29%). Formal SMP process accounted for 4%, local authority website accounted for 5%, friends (7%), this study (5%). Others: other media, action groups, village meetings, etc.
	57% felt angered by unfairness and lack of fair treatment in the outcomes of the draft SMP. 22% had joined an action group to fight the SMP.
	"It condemns an entire community based upon imprecise science and inaccurate economics...The government count only the cost of defence and see this as a cost saving exercise. The lives and well being of thousands are not valued at all."
Involvement in the SMP process	0% of respondents noted that they were involved in SMP public consultation process run by the local authority, NNDC.
	"I should have been consulted, I was chairman of the Parish council of the village that is most affected. The golf club was consulted but not the parish council."
	"No consultation with locals took place. The draft was leaked to the press hence the uproar."
Perceptions of impacts of SMP on property prices	20% did not want to talk about the draft SMP for fear that further publicity may further lower their house prices. 56% didn't know if there was any change in property value, 12% felt that there was no decrease, 28% felt there was some with most information about this coming from neighbours (30%), estate agents and solicitors (27%) and action groups (32%).
	"I have lost three potential buyers for my property, with the draft SMP being given as the reason in each case."
Awareness of local coastal change and its causes	46% felt they knew a little about the history of coastal change, with 27% knowing nothing (21% knowing a lot, and 6% no answer). 51% agreed that coastal change is historical and inevitable in the area. 70% agreed that offshore dredging is causing the loss of beach material (2% disagreed, others ambivalent/don't know).

Residential	Key findings
Views on the management coastal change, including compensation	74% agreed that the coastline should be held irrespective of costs. 69% disagreed that as they have no legal right to coastal protection they cannot assume compensation. 69% agreed that the coastline should be held until a compensation solution is agreed. Agreement was evenly split in response to a statement that those who benefit from improved coastal defences should help pay for those whose property will not be guaranteed protection. 74% felt there should be a scheme to insure against coastal flooding and erosion.

"What about my human rights? Compensation must be given especially to those who purchased properties before the shoreline management plans existed."

"The government first attracted investment in coastal communities by originally providing coastal protection. If it now intends to remove that protection by letting it fail, it should compensate those who lose their homes; those whose property values are adversely affected and those who suffer a degrading village lifestyle." |
| How uncertainty about the coast has affected personal confidence, family and community relations, job and health prospects | The effects of uncertainty were most marked in terms of personal confidence (66% overall perceiving some degree of effect). Marked effects on community (31%), health (28%), close family (22% overall), and jobs (5%) were also noted.

"The sea will not reach this property in 25 years, but the psychological effect is most significant. The loss of amenities, i.e. access to the beach, loss of the lifeboat, and cliff top café, decrease in vitality and confidence of the village. We are also concerned about the decreased value of our house."

"By the time our property is threatened, much of my village may by that time be lost already. Amenity areas such as the beach will be affected. Wealth generated by the holiday industry for the village will quickly decrease."

"I am an old age pensioner. I cannot take out equity from my home to help me in my old age because the plan has changed the rules with regard to the coastline. So my lifetime's achievements have been totally devalued." |

Residential	Key findings
Demographics, residential history and location in relation to the coastline	Greatest proportion of residents in 55-64 (30%) and 65-74 (24%) age groups.
	Residential history dominantly 1-5yrs (23%), 5-10yrs (27%) and 10-20yrs (27%). 94% ownership of dwellings. Distance from coast , less than quarter of a mile (31%); approx 0.25 mile (45%); approx 0.5 mile (13%). In-migration from outside East Anglia (40%) and Norfolk (19%). 89% agreed that they would like to stay in the area for the rest of their lives. Main income groups <£10k (23%), £10-20k (34%), £20-40k (17%).

Table 2 Key findings from business questionnaires

Business	Key findings
Nature of business, duration in location, reasons for running business in location	Types: tourist accommodation (hotels, B&B's, caravan, chalet and holiday parks); beach facilities (shops, cafés); community and visitor facilities (post office, greengrocers, MOT centre, petrol station, retail, pub/restaurant). Coastal location for reasons of tradition, potential and beach access. 90% agreed that they would like to stay in the area for the rest of their lives, with 10% disagreeing.
Awareness of draft SMP and opinions about its effect on business	90% aware of draft SMP.
	"Changing attitudes to investments and customers. Some customers are very uneasy about returning, having seen the erosion at Happisburgh. Some are just interested. The SMP has had little effect on business. However, the blight of the area has probably lowered property values."
Estimates of how business activities influence the local economy (spending by visitors, local spending by staff; purchases of local produce, links to other local businesses)	"This village works as a community, using local shops and businesses in support of each other. The loss of any one business has an adverse effect, directly or indirectly on the other businesses."
	"There are many links through tourism, trade, associations, business and village life. Probably in the region of 120 major links and a further 50 minor links."

Business	Key findings
Perceptions of possible future effects on business if draft SMP implemented (on plans for renovation, extension, employment, turnover, local business confidence)	While 45% noted no or unknown effects, others commented: "It came as a shock at first and has put any plan for the future on hold 'till we know what the outcome for our village is going to be." "Have undertaken only the most necessary renovation for the past 4 years since the failure of the proposed protection scheme in 2000." Respondents most notably reported an impact on business confidence (40% citing falling investment in area, decline in / negative impact on local business confidence) and turnover (40% noted reduction or more difficult to maintain; 20% no effect). "There is now absolutely no confidence in the village and indeed a sense of depression in all the coastal areas." "Most people we have spoken to have lost confidence in the future of the area. There is a general feeling of having worked hard all our lives and now being let down."
Awareness of local coastal change and its causes	Responses were evenly split between agreement and disagreement about the causes of coastal change in the area being historical and inevitable. 85% agreed that offshore dredging is causing the loss of beach material (others ambivalent/don't know).
Views on the management of coastal change, including compensation	60% agreed that the coastline should be held irrespective of cost (25% ambivalent, 15% disagreeing). 70% disagreed that the coastline should be defended if costs outweighed benefits. 80% disagreed that as they have no legal right to coastal protection they cannot assume compensation (10% agreed, others neither). 80% agreed that the coastline should be held until compensation solutions are agreed. 55% agreed that those who benefit from improved coastal defences should help pay for those not guaranteed protection (20% disagreed, others ambivalent). Given compensation, the majority would choose to stay in the area (60%) with 30% choosing to move away. 75% felt there should be a scheme to insure against coastal flooding and erosion. "A strategy of the future is necessary which incorporates compensation for losses of property in the future." "As central government is not prepared to spend money to aid coastal areas, perhaps a levy on council tax in all counties bordering the sea could be a way of funding the management of our coastline."

Richard Girling

Richard Girling is a senior feature writer for *The Sunday Times Magazine*, of which he was formerly managing editor. In 2002 he was named Specialist Writer of the Year in the UK Press Awards, and in 2008 was Journalist of the Year at the Press Gazette Environmental Press Awards. In their citation, the judges said: "He argues complex issues with clarity, an unassailable knowledge of his subject, intelligence, and humour, offering all sides of the debate without preaching." He is the author of six books, including *Sea Change* (2007) and, most recently, *Greed*. He lives in North Norfolk.

Sea Change

Richard Girling

My earliest memory of the sea is not of the sea itself but of a photograph. It was taken two years after the end of the second world war on the beach at Skegness, by my mother with the ubiquitous Box Brownie. I am 18 months old, dressed in a knitted romper suit and taking peculiar interest in a black leather bag. Inside it, apparently, is a packet of Smith's crisps.

My newest memory of the sea is from yesterday. I am on a marsh near my home in Norfolk, gazing upon the same North Sea that lured my parents all those years ago to Skegness. The place is beyond beauty. It is *sublime*. The tide is high, changing a landscape of creeks and sand bars into a rippling sheet of silver. Geese, ducks and gulls pepper the surface. Wading birds graze the softened mud. A pair of seals raise their heads above water that has surged across a footpath.

Nowhere in the UK is more than 72 miles from the sea. Every aspect of our lives – our climate, diet, trade, politics, art, suspicion of foreigners, even the blood in our veins – is affected by it. As a people, we are not so much *by* the sea as *of* it. Transmuted through the deep-fat fryer, it taints the air in every city and town. Along Wells harbour-front, tendrils of scent work like pheromones on people who didn't even realise they were hungry. Powerless to resist, they perch on the wall and feed like gulls. Somehow it is in their nature.

The sea is our favourite day out, our pride and national identifier. We can't know when the first Norfolkman launched himself on a log. By sometime between 1890 and 1700BC however, Bronze Age Britons were advanced in the art of building proper, internally braced planked boats with caulked seams and keels. We lagged behind the Egyptians, who had the technology at least 700 years earlier, but few nations on earth have left a more powerful wake. Julius Caesar arrived to find an energetic maritime nation ploughing a well-furrowed sea and with a well-established tradition of shipbuilding.

The eastern shoreline is dynamic and ever-changing. Cliffs are nibbled away, sand swept by the tide to raise new beaches further south. Whole towns and villages lie beneath the waves, and more will follow. And yet, in the wild places, there is a feeling of unchangingness. A Bronze Age man, a Neanderthal, any half-sapient hominid from the entire span of human evolution, could return to a place like this and fail to notice the passing millennia. It is an illusion, but one worth hanging on to.

Like every other place in the world that gives me pleasure, from central London to sub-equatorial Africa, North Norfolk is best seen on foot. A good walk is like a well-thumbed book – something you can travel again from end to end, or dip into for lingering enjoyment of a favourite page. Knowing the shape, tone and structure of the whole, you can bury yourself ever more intimately in the detail. The analogy is imperfect only in the sense that, once in a while, you turn a familiar page and find that the script has been rewritten. The change may be subtle – an unfamiliar quality of light; new combinations of seasonal colour. Or it may be so dramatic – after flooding, a gale or deep snow – that you lose your bearings and are transformed in an instant from confident habitué to bewildered stranger. Such was my experience yesterday.

As long-distance routes go, the Norfolk Coast Path is short – a little under 50 miles. Strictly speaking it starts at Hunstanton, but I've always skipped the first couple of miles and begun at Holme, where it meets the Peddars Way. Once, to oblige a magazine, I walked the 44 miles to Cromer in two hot summer days and made my feet bleed. Three days would be more comfortable; four perfect for those who want to inquire properly into what this unique landscape has to offer. As I plod into my seventh decade, I am pleased to be overtaken by the Gore-Texed map-and-compass regiment who march as if to battle. It's not the miles that count, or the cardio-vascular work-out. It's the *seeing*. Psychological wellbeing comes surprisingly high in the health industry's endorsement for this most primitive form of transport. Men who walk more than two miles a day apparently face half the risk of dementia as those who walk less than a quarter of a mile. Walkers are also less likely to be depressed and can expect to enjoy what psychologists (who perhaps should get out more) like to call "better cognitive function", by which they mean thinking, remembering and learning.

It's not a new idea. In a somewhat overwrought essay published in 1913, the historian G.M. Trevelyan declared that he had two doctors – "my left leg and my right" – which he would summon to carry him off for the day whenever "that combination of mind and body which I call my soul" was "choked up with bad thoughts or useless worries". He went on: "I have often known the righteous forsaken and his seed begging their bread, but I never knew a man go for an honest day's walk... and not have his reward in the repossession of his own soul."

Walkers also notice things, though the things you notice are not always the best medicine for depression. In town and country alike, you bang your nose against the piecemeal idiocies of post-war planning and transport policies; the debasement of architecture; the corrosive imprint of the Common Agricultural Policy; the Disneyfication of heritage; the contempt for history; designer pubs. In comparison with much of the rest of lowland Britain, North Norfolk gets off lightly. It is precisely because of its beauty, out of sheer love, that we resist the kinds of encroachment that would wreck its uniqueness. But people distort the green case when they

muddle it with Luddism, technophobia or stalled imagination. Great minds gave us steam power, electricity and the petrol engine, and great minds will create energy for the future. Carbon-neutral biofuel from algae? Why not? A low-carbon economy that stimulates growth in the developing world as well as the developed?

Why should we think it impossible, or, worse, see no reason to care? Conservation is not about blocking progress.

But nimbyism is fine. It's not resistance to progress that makes people reject ugly or misplaced building. It is because they want to protect their right to be involved in their communities and not to be bullied by commercial insurgents who don't have to live within sight of their own creations. They *do* want affordable homes for teachers, nurses and firemen (and for their own children, too), but not as a spin-off from unaffordable executive sprawl. They don't want to be swallowed by development "corridors"; they don't want their high streets blighted by out-of-town retail parks; they don't want their lives splintered by new runways or roads; they don't want rubbish tips, incinerators, prisons or power stations; they don't want ugliness. They can't always get what they want, or avoid what they don't, but good arguments should give way only to better.

The convention is to walk the coast path from west to east, with the prevailing westerlies at your back and the evening sun behind you. Always (though I've never done it) I feel tempted to do the reverse, for Holme itself would make a tumultuous finale. The seaward side is classic saltmarsh, sage-coloured with creeks draining to chocolate at low tide, yielding to sand in the east. It was here in 1999 that 55 buried posts circled around an upturned oak made their first recorded appearance for 4000 years and entered the textbooks as "Seahenge". Don't waste time searching for it. Despite a sit-in by Druids, English Heritage long ago took away the timbers for conservation. The path here follows a bank dominated by sea buckthorn, a spiky olive-coloured shrub which in autumn bears orange berries popular with fieldfares. They also provide a medicinal oil which its advertisers say is "an amazingly effective natural remedy for all health problems related to damaged mucous membranes of the gastrointestinal tract".

Throughout the walk you will be reminded that this is a landscape in flux. Dunes creep. New channels cut the sandflats and slow, glassy tides spread thin smears of mud to build slick upon slick into new marsh. Here grows the samphire which, given a few moments in boiling water and a knob of butter, makes the god-given partner to fish; and the immense blue meadows of sea lavender that electrify the landscape in summer. Across the dunes between Holme and Thornham, around Gore Point, is one of the few places along the route where the word "beach" answers to its classic description: clean, unmarked sand with a booming sea.

Not all beaches are so lucky. Even in North Norfolk there is garbage, tidelines delineated not just by wrack and driftwood but by cans and plastic bottles. In most other parts of the coastline, closer to shipping lanes and urban populations, it is very much worse. Readers of *the Sunday Times* in the late 1970s did much to make such disfigurement illegal. Hundreds of them joined in a beach litter survey which, by recording and de-coding serial numbers on plastic bottles, showed what everyone had always suspected but never proved – that Britain's rim of rubbish was the gift of the merchant marine, garbage dumped from ships. Armed with their data, the Department of the Environment (as it then was), had all the evidence it needed to ratify Annex V of the International Convention for the Prevention of Pollution from Ships, known as MARPOL, outlawing the dumping of rubbish at sea, which came into force in December 1988.

Twenty years later we might expect to and find pristine beaches unscarred by anything worse than seashells or worm-casts. Well we *might*, but we would be disappointed. Every September since 1993, the Marine Conservation Society has run a "Beachwatch" survey, and it is still waiting for good news to report. The contribution of the shipping industry may have declined (though the precise amount is open to question), but the UK's scum-line now is thicker, more persistent and more dangerous than ever.

In 2008 the survey clocked a total of 2,195 pieces of garbage for every kilometre of coast – that's one for every human stride, more than double what it was in 1994 and 7% more than 2007. You would expect plastic bags to be a nuisance, and so they are, but at 46.5 per kilometre they could reach no higher than 14th in the shoreline litter league. More persistent offenders included dog ends (60 per km), plastic drinks bottles (71), pieces of glass (76.8), cotton-bud sticks (100.5) and polystyrene (142). The absolute chart-toppers, as always, were plastic fragments. Pieces ranging from less than a centimetre to half a metre in length totted up to an astonishing 487.3 per km – very nearly one every two metres.

The offensiveness of all this is not just aesthetic. Glass, drinks cans and the all-too-accurately labelled "surgical sharps" are obvious risks to human feet. Plastics are promiscuous killers of wildlife. More than 170 marine species are known to mistake litter for food, resulting in starvation, poisoning and fatal stomach blockages, and at least 144 species including turtles, whales, dolphins, seals, sea lions, seabirds and fish, have been found entangled in debris. Leatherback turtles, for example, feed on jellyfish, which closely resemble plastic bags. No surprise: 34% of leatherbacks washing up dead have plastic in the gut.

Six years ago the US National Academy of Science calculated that 6.4m tonnes of litter entered the oceans every year – a total that is hardly likely to have reduced in the meantime. Closer to home, we're told that 20,000 tonnes of waste goes into the North Sea every year. Seventy per cent of this sinks to the bottom, 15% stays in the water and 15% hits the beaches. What this means in terms of pollution is largely, though not wholly, visible to us all. Plastics never disappear – they simply break down into smaller and smaller fragments. Analysis of 45 seemingly clean sand samples taken from the Northumbrian coast showed that every one of them contained microscopic plastic fibres at densities of up to 10,000 per litre of sand. More have been discovered in plankton samples dating back to the 1960s. Already there may be no such thing as a clean beach.

There may also be no such thing as clean water. After visitors and the fishing industry, the third most prolific source of rubbish on the beach is what the jargon calls SRD – Sewage Related Debris. Two phenomena contribute to this – the public's unshakeable belief that solid objects somehow dematerialise if they are flushed down a lavatory, and the inadequacy of drainage systems built in the age of the carriage horse. In comparison with other parts of the country, North Norfolk once again is blessed with good luck. Water around the coast is routinely sampled and tested by the Environment Agency for sewage-borne bacteria such as *Escherichia coli*. In recent years the waters of North Norfolk have been regularly classified as "excellent" or, at the very worst, "good". On the face of it, this seems to conform with national trends.

The Environment Agency states correctly that water at British beaches is cleaner than it was ten years ago. Bathing water is tested against two benchmarks laid down by the EU – a "mandatory" standard and a higher "guideline" standard, defined by the number of bacteria. In 2008, 97% of the 495 designated bathing waters in England and Wales met the mandatory, and 72% the guideline standard, an improvement of a third since 1998. Most of North Norfolk's beaches reached guideline standard – only Hunstanton Beach was stuck on mandatory – and Cromer, Sheringham and Hunstanton Main Beach all achieved the MRC's more stringent "recommended" grade. But passing the test does not mean the water is clean, only that concentrations of faecal matter are low in comparison with others.

It has been argued – for example by the World Health Organisation in 1998 – that illnesses can be caused at bacterial concentrations far lower than the manda-

tory limit. What is boils down to is that swimmers at almost half of Britain's 776 coastal bathing beaches – the 333 that failed the guideline test last year – have on average a one in seven chance of catching a sewage-related disease. Even at the MCS's "recommended" standard the risk hovers at around 4% per swim. There are also doubts about the accuracy of the Environment Agency's sampling system. Incredibly, on the very day in August 2008 that Sunderland City Council found the promenade and tideline at its South Whitburn beach awash with "sewerage debris and dirty run-off water" in quantities "too much to estimate", EA logged the water quality as "excellent".

The fact is that the only safe amount of sewage to swim in is none at all. Another fact is that since the best-ever year of 2006, the graph has taken a downward turn. Water quality is no longer improving. It is getting worse. Last year 78 bathing beaches failed to reach even the minimum mandatory standard – the highest total of the century so far. Ominously, EA and Defra put this down to overactive combined sewer outfalls (CSOs), which divert untreated sewage into rivers, estuaries and the sea when public sewerage and drainage systems are overloaded, and worsening "diffuse pollution" – ie dirty storm water from streets and fields. It is ominous because both these malfunctions are associated with heavy rainfall, and heavier rainfall is a feature of climate change, which is progressive. Already, many of the outflows are spilling even in dry weather. All it takes is an influx of holiday-makers putting pressure on the lavatories. This is a blatant contravention of EC policy, which is that CSOs are to be used only for emergency flood relief after "unusually heavy rainfall", not as regular conduits for sewage. This is why the EC has instigated four test cases against the UK, citing outflows at Torbay, London,

Kilbarchan in Renfrewshire and Sunderland's notorious Whitburn South which it says are discharging constantly.

On the beach at Thornham we may with good cause feel privileged, but we should not be tricked into complacency. Parochialism is its own worst enemy. Our concern for the oceans must extend beyond what we can see (otherwise what we see will assuredly change for the worse). It is not enough even to think nationally. Water is like time. Every drop links to every other drop, and what happens in one place may have terrible impacts somewhere else in future. Only 24% of the UK's sewage is still discharged raw, but in the Mediterranean it's 53% (so don't look too closely at what the fish are nibbling in the bay). Even this doesn't make it a particular black spot internationally. The figure for Latin America and the Caribbean is 86%, slightly better than Eastern Asia (89%) but worse than the South East Pacific and West and Central Africa (83% and 80% respectively).

The consequence is not just swimmers with their heads down the lavatory. Pollutants including agricultural as well as human wastes are causing algal blooms and creating oxygen-deficient "dead zones" – marine graveyards in which nothing can live. This is exacerbated by climate change, which is causing shifts in winds and ocean currents. The UN Environment Programme (UNEP) reports that the number of dead zones worldwide has doubled in every decade since the 1960s. In 2006 there were 200, and they are not small. Off the coast of Oregon, oxygen was sucked out of 3000 sq km (1150 sq miles), suffocating everything that lived. No fish swam. The seabed was littered with carcasses, and the shore with dead seabirds. Migrating salmon starved, and the whole episode lasted 17 weeks. Similar zones have appeared in Scandinavia, the Gulf of Mexico, and off the coasts of South America, Ghana, China, Japan, Australia, New Zealand, Portugal and yes, even the UK, though nothing yet on the scale of Oregon.

According to Greenpeace, soupy "plumes" of agro-chemically-enriched river-water have created areas of de-oxygenation in the southern North Sea, Liverpool Bay and the Clyde estuary, and worse has befallen our neighbours. In 2000 the EC Commission for the Protection of the Marine Environment of the North East Atlantic (OSPAR) reported widespread problems "in particular estuaries and fjords, the Wadden Sea, the German Bight, the Kattegat and the eastern Skaggerak". Fishing for Norwegian lobster (aka scampi or langoustine) in the Kattegat had all but ceased, and the long-term build-up of pollution meant it could take decades to recover. And by that time a new peril will have overtaken us.

With sudden urgency, marine scientists are now talking about "the other CO2 problem". Its victim is not the polar bear spectacularly marooned on melting ice, or an eagle driven out of its range, nor even a French pensioner dying of heatstroke. What we have to mourn are tiny marine organisms dissolving in acidified water. In fact we need to do rather more than just mourn them. We need to dive in and save them. Suffering plankton may not have quite the same *cachet* as a 700-kilo seal-eating mammal, but their message is no less apocalyptic. What they tell us is that the chemistry of the oceans is changing, and that, unless we act decisively, the limitless abundance of the sea within a very few decades will degrade into a useless tidal desert.

In every way – economically, environmentally, socially – the effects of ocean acidification are as dangerous as climate change, and even harder to resist. It has been a slow dawning. Until recently, scientists have had little luck in engaging the public or political mind. The species most directly at risk – plankton, corals, sea snails, barnacles and other stuff that most people have never heard of – seemed as remote from our lives as cosmic dust. It took a clownfish – winsome star of the Disney classic, *Finding Nemo* – to put us straight. In the movie, Nemo gets lost. Now it turns out that real clownfish might do the same.

In early February 2009, the American academic journal *Proceedings of the National Academy of Sciences* carried a paper titled "Ocean acidification impairs olfactory discrimination and homing ability of a marine fish". The sombre language concealed a stark and frightening message. What the researchers had found was that clownfish larvae in acidified water were progressively unable to detect the odours from adult fish that led them to their breeding sites. The implications were obvious. If the fish don't breed, the species will not survive, and what is true for one species must be true for others. In time, the world's fishing fleets will become less a food resource than a disposal problem. What's happening is this:

The oceans absorb carbon dioxide (CO_2) from the atmosphere. As most climate scientists and governments now agree, human activity has intensified CO2 in the atmosphere, causing long-term climate change. The good thing is that the seas have absorbed a lot of the gas and so have slowed the pace of atmospheric warming. The bad thing is that CO_2 reacts with seawater to make carbonic acid.

Since 1800, humans have generated 240 billion tonnes of carbon dioxide, half of which has been absorbed by the sea. On average, each person on earth contributes a tonne of carbon to the oceans every year. The result is a rapid rise in acidity – or a reduction in pH, as the scientists prefer to express it – which as it intensifies will mean that marine animals will be unable to grow shells, and that many sea-plants will not survive. With these crucial links removed, and the ecological balance disrupted, death could flow all the way up the food chain, through tuna and cod to marine mammals and *homo sapiens*. As more than half the world's population depends for its survival on food from the sea, this is no exaggeration.

This is why 155 marine scientists from 26 countries recently signed the "Monaco Declaration", identifying the twin threats of global warming and ocean acidification as "the challenge of the century". It is, nevertheless, a challenge they have taken up only recently. The term "ocean acidification" was coined only in 2003 – by odd coincidence the same year *Finding Nemo* was released and 35,000 people died in the European summer heatwave. Verging on panic in 2005, the Royal Society published a 68-page report in which it calculated that acidification had increased by 30% in 200 years. If we went on as we were, it said, this would reach 300% by 2100, making the seas more corrosive than they had been at any time for hundreds of millennia. In every practicable sense, the damage was irreversible. "It will take tens of thousands of years for ocean chemistry to return to a condition similar to that occurring at pre-industrial times," the Royal Society said.

To non-scientists, the giving or taking of a few decimal points can look undramatic. To experts they mark the difference between life and death. The 30% increase in ocean acidity during the industrial age is reflected by a drop in pH of just 0.1. On current trends, it will fall another 0.4 points to hit an unprecedented low of 7.7 by 2100. By 2300 it could be down to 7.3. Few species living in the sea have experienced conditions like these at any time throughout their entire life on earth. With pH as low as this, it is at least questionable that land creatures emerging from the primal swamp could have evolved into the bony specimens that roam the earth today. And it is certain that the pace of environmental change is far too fast for evolution to keep in step. As a recipe for life on earth, it is about as efficacious as nuclear war.

Scientists have studied what happens to marine life in the Bay of Ischia, where acidity is naturally increased by undersea volcanic vents. At pH 7.8 – the level which, on current trends, will be the global norm before the end of the century – shelled creatures are visibly suffering. Sea urchins thin out and disappear as the acidity increases; so do corals, limpets and barnacles. Sea snails straying into the zone have thin, weak shells, and produce no young. There is another important absentee too – the coralline algae (seaweed with a chalk skeleton) that glues coral reefs together. Without it, reefs become weakened and fall apart. In just a few decades, if the output of carbon dioxide does not abate, this will be the condition of all the world's oceans. Many if not all commercially fished species, including shellfish, will suffer. So too will coral reefs, whose disintegration will leave low-lying coasts in the tropics unprotected from the rising seas and fiercer storms that climate change will unleash. By some calculations reefs will have vanished by 2065, and no-one expects them to survive into the 22nd century.

It is a truism that might have been minted for the Darwin bicentenary. A species once lost is gone for ever. You can't re-wind evolution, or re-invent fish. We are not talking about dispossessing our children, or even our grandchildren's grandchildren. We are talking so many generations into the fog of geological time that we might not even be talking about the same species. We are certainly not talking about low-lying countries protected by coral reefs, such as the Maldives. In future they will not be studying the marine environment: they will be part of it.

Various ideas have been put forward to mitigate the damage and downgrade the outcome from fatal catastrophe to expensive nuisance. It will take some doing.

One idea is "ocean fertilisation", which involves adding iron to the water to stimulate a plankton bloom. The plankton then absorb atmospheric CO_2 before sinking into deep water and locking the poison away.

Another scheme from the top shelf of academic fantasy is "ocean sequestration", which involves sinking waste carbon into the deep ocean where, at depths in excess of 3.5km, the gas will solidify into crystals. A possibly more viable option is "geological sequestration", though it is one that will whiten environmentalists' hair. It involves "capturing" gas from industrial plants and injecting it into exhausted aquifers or worked-out oilfields where it can be stored in the rock. Capacity is not a problem – the North Sea alone could hold as much as 800 gigatonnes, which is approximately 1600 times the UK's entire annual output of industrial carbon dioxide. Neither is the idea merely theoretical. The Norwegian oil and gas company Statoil pumps a million tonnes a year into a saline aquifer.

But the risks quite literally are incalculable. What happens if there is a leak? Drilling and extraction in the oilfields may well have caused subsidence and cracking in the rock. The idea makes no sense unless storage is safe, secure and "permanent" – which in the case of CO_2 means somewhere between 5000 and 10,000 years, or about the same as some nuclear waste.

There is, of course, a fourth option, the simplest and yet hardest of the lot – changing the way we live. Carbon reduction targets need to be more than just green baubles on the faraway policy tree. Greed has driven us to a level of overconsumption which threatens our health, melts the economy and progressively poisons the planet. Unless we can get a grip on ourselves, constrain our appetites and halt the mismatch between consumption and resources, the future is an empty ship sailing upon an empty sea.

Britain's appetite for sea rather than freshwater fish seems to have developed during the early 11th century. This may have been due to the poisoning of waterways by urban effluents; or it may have been a matter of taste, for who would have preferred the mud-flavoured denizens of lowland rivers to the salty tang of cod? For whatever reason, it launched a new age of heroic adventure.

By the first decade of the 15th century, ships from England's east coast were a common sight around Iceland. They sailed in March for a round trip of 1800 miles, after which the survivors would return with salt cod in August or September. In favourable conditions a ship might reach Iceland in a week. In bad, it could take a month. In the worst, the best a man could hope for was to perish swiftly. In 1419, a storm off the Icelandic coast sank 25 English boats in a day (this at a time when the entire fleet might have been no more than 30). That ship-owners were prepared to hazard their vessels, and crews to risk their lives, says much about the value of the trade – it benefited richly from meatless days in the religious calendar.

Faith in the infinitude of the sea was like a religion too. We have long known the belief to be false, and yet we continue to behave as if the seas were stocked by magic. The result has been a programme of increasingly spectacular vanishing acts. Typical of many, the Newfoundland cod fishery, once famous for being more fish than water, collapsed in 1992 because we had eaten the breeding stock – an act of wilful self-harm that would have stretched the credulity of a Neanderthal. The North Sea, too, once seethed with shoals. Herring to East Anglians was like gold to the Incas – it raised them up; it brought them down. Lowestoft in the early 20th century could handle 60m fish at a time, but it was not enough. On a single day in 1907, the drifters brought in 90m. During the eight-week season, from mid September to November, more than 1000 boats would steam south from Scotland to join the harvest, shooting their nets at dusk.

Everything moved to the rhythm of the shoals. Just as the marrying season for farmworkers and their girls was in October and November after the corn had been stored, so the fishwives enjoyed their season between November and February, after the salting of the herring. Now it sounds as quaint as the maypole. For all the usual reasons, plus a few extra (disruption by war, loss of export markets through changing tastes), another golden goose honked its last. In 1967 just a single drifter sailed out of Lowestoft, and ten years later the government banned all herring fishing in the North Sea.

I have heard this described as a "salutary lesson", but 30 years on, with cod on the brink and entire marine ecosystems made moribund, fishermen still plead for the right to clear the seas of everything with flesh on its bones. Scientists advising zero quotas tug Europe's fisheries ministers in the direction of sanity. Nationalism, their domestic fishing industries and the appetites of their electorates tug them towards the chip shop. Better empty seas than lost elections.

My paradisiacal evening walk is on the southern shore of the Wash, part of what is known as fishing area IVc, stretching from Grimsby south to Folkestone, and across to northern France, Belgium and the Netherlands. As recently as 1995, IVc netted 2472 tonnes of cod. Eight years later, in 2003, a dwindling UK fleet landed just 678 tonnes. In four years, total landings at East Anglia's principal fishing port, Lowestoft, crashed from 5400 to 1667 tonnes. In 2004 it plummeted again, to 657 tonnes, which included more sprats (272 tonnes) than the combined weight of cod (135 tonnes), sole (38 tonnes), herring (3 tonnes) and haddock (nil). In the following year, even that would provoke tears of nostalgia – the total cod catch by UK boats in fishing area IVc in 2005 was 206 tonnes.

No East Anglian town now figures in Britain's top twenty fishing ports, and IVc is the least productive of the country's eight major fishing zones. In 2007 its total yield of demersal species (that's bottom- and near-bottom dwellers such as cod, haddock and plaice) was a paltry 1,600 tonnes, worth just £4.7m. Pelagic species (near-surface shoalers such as mackerel and herring) contributed another 3,900 tonnes, worth £1.1m, and shellfish outweighed them all at 12,200 tonnes, worth

£12.7m. Altogether, that is just 17,800 tonnes out of a national total of 610,400 – itself a 1% drop from the previous year. In 2007 the UK fleet landed 205,000 tonnes of demersal fish – a decline of 26% in only two years. The Marine and Fisheries Agency's annual UK fishery statistics run to 104 densely-packed pages in which good news is as hard to find as tuna in Blakeney Pit.

From Gore Point the path swings south to follow the harbour creek into Thornham, a pretty tile-and-flint village that comes inconveniently early in the walk but where you will need more willpower than I possess if you are to resist the temptation of lunch. Then Brancaster, Burnham Deepdale, Burnham Overy Staithe, Holkham Bay... The view from here of an offshore windfarm is displeasing, but at least you see it only on the rare days when The Wash is hazeless. Renewable energy is an issue that divides environmentalists like no other. Its apostles, in the inelegant modern phrase, declare it to be a no-brainer. Opponents and sceptics complain of degraded landscapes, interference with birds and fish, and the diversion of our attention from (as they see it) better solutions such as clean coal and nuclear reactors.

Compared with old-fashioned windmills, the wind turbine is a pared-down masterpiece of modern industrial design with a classic form-follows-function aesthetic. You could say it was graceful, and few would argue. But concrete flyovers are graceful too, with their subtle curves and economy of line, and I respond to them in much the same way. I wish I could like them, but I can't. The government is committed to a "major and rapid expansion" of offshore wind turbines, some of which will be of enormous height, and the Crown Estate is in the process of issuing new leases to the generating companies. The shallowness of the North Sea makes it, in engineering terms, ideal for this kind of development so that East Anglia must brace itself for more. Climate change is also making the southern North Sea windier – average annual wind speeds accelerated from 7.5 metres per second in 1990 to 8.5 in 2008 – so there is the promise of a more abundant harvest too. The late unlamented DTI's onlie begetter, the Department for Business Enterprise and Regulatory Reform (BERR), has been conducting what it calls an Offshore Energy Strategic Environmental Assessment (SEA), which has yielded – with dread certainty, you can hear it coming – an Offshore Energy Scoping Compilation, followed by "a series of Stakeholder Dialogue Sessions". When, if ever, it purges its vocabulary of robot-speak and rediscovers the usefulness of English, one hopes it may find room for words such as "sensitivity" and "beauty". After many years of wading through this kind of stuff, however, I find optimism elusive. The decommissioning of oil and gas platforms could provide a number of suitable sites with minimal extra visual impact (195 will have gone by 2020), but clean horizons in future are likely to be a rarity.

What I do have faith in is the power of this coast to enthral and cleanse. Some psychologists and natural scientists now believe that we carry a "god gene" that predisposes us to religiosity. The point was most famously argued by Dean H. Hamer, a geneticist at the US National Cancer Institute, in his 2004 book *The God Gene: how Faith is Hardwired into our Genes*. What he said was this (and I apologise for crushing a complex argument into a matchbox):

A number of brain chemicals are associated with deep meditative states (for example, in prayer) and with feelings of spirituality or "transcendence". It is likely that a large number of genes are involved in controlling the flow of these chemicals to the brain, of which Hamer identified a single example. (One would have loved it to have been called Isaiah, but it is actually known as VMAT2.) These genes convey a propensity for spirituality – in unscientific language, an impulse to which we are bound to respond. Historically, and for many people still, this response has taken the form of religious belief, though the precise nature of that belief – Christian, Buddhist, Jewish, Hindu, Islamic, ancestor-worship or whatever – depends on birth and upbringing. Others find their outlets in different forms of spiritual expression, most obviously through the experience of music, art and poetry, but also through other meditative forms such as yoga. And, I would add, *pace* Richard Dawkins, sheer awe at the beauty of the physical world. Like great art, or (I guess) communion with a deity, a view of Scolt Head, Holkham Bay or Wells Harbour raises both mind and spirit. The jigsawed view of sandbanks, marshes and creeks from the air as you fly into Norwich from Edinburgh is worth the price of the ticket on its own. Google Earth is almost as good.

Stiffkey, Morston, Blakeney, Cley... The marshes here are the Wembley stadium of birdwatching, but they are like mountain slopes beneath a melting glacier, and vulnerable for much the same reason. Climate change is an unstoppable force. Even as we dither in its path, the sea is bulking itself up, literally expanding as the water warms and becomes more turbulent. We know the massive storms and surges are coming; that parts of England and Wales have no more chance than Bangladesh of staying dry. At Cley and Salthouse, the protective arm of shingle is being atrophied by wind and tide, and the most feared local voice belongs to the flood siren. Here and elsewhere, the sea *will* come. It is a dilemma which the shore-line management plans have yet to resolve.

We know we can't save every town and village. But, though we have argued for years, we still can't decide which bits of coastline to set in concrete and which to abandon to the sea; how, or even *if*, we will compensate those for whom a change of policy will mean the loss of their homes.

At Weybourne the walk takes suddenly to crumbling sandstone cliffs, busy with sand martins and skylarks, where you get a real idea of the pace of erosion. From the old coastguard lookout at Sheringham there is a long view back all the way to the Holkham pines. Then, after a breath of old-fashioned seaside at Sheringham, a last leg inland through woods and fields to Cromer, crab capital of East Anglia and, famously, home to England's very last end-of-the-pier show. In its way, it's as eloquent a symbol of this coast's stubborn charm, its dedication to values that transcend and outlast fashion, as a pint of Yetman's or a nesting tern.

Some parts of this chapter appeared previously in The Sunday Times Magazine, *and are reproduced here by permission of the editor.*

Ron Harold

Ron Harold was born at Maidenhead, Berkshire, was educated there and on leaving school served an engineering apprenticeship in the area. He moved to Peterborough in 1974 to work in engineering but two years later decided to leave engineering to work in nature conservation turning what had been a lifelong passion in to a profession.

His first job in his new career was with the Wildfowl Trust at Peakirk (near Peterborough) and in 1977 he became a Summer Warden for the Nature Conservancy Council at Barnack Hills and Holes National nature Reserve (Cambridgeshire), which became a Special Area of Conservation (SAC) in 2002 and is now managed by Natural England. A year later he was appointed Warden of the Woodwalton Fen National Nature Reserve near Huntingdon, one of Britain's oldest reserves that is now classified as an SAC, a Site of Special Scientific Interest (SSSI) and a RAMSAR site. He transferred to the Holkham National Nature Reserve in 1990 and continued in that post until he retired in 2008 completing a total of 32 years in nature conservation.

His main interests are birds and botany and he has travelled extensively on six continents in pursuit of wildlife. His publications on birds include *The Birds of Woodwalton Fen National Nature Reserve* (English Nature 1990).

Natural Selection

Ron Harold

Keep the Adrenalin Flowing

My association with North Norfolk began in the mid 1970s. In those days I was a budding birdwatcher, living at the edge of the Cambridgeshire fens. Inevitably, in the search for new and interesting birds I often found myself drawn to the North Norfolk Coast and such birding Meccas as Cley-next-the-Sea, Wells Woods, Holme-next-the-Sea and Titchwell. Wild open landscapes always held great appeal so visits to the Norfolk coast were always special and the prospect of discovering sought after birds on one of the United Kingdom's top birding coastlines was guaranteed to keep the adrenalin flowing. In time, as my natural history interests widened I came to fully appreciate the wonderful diversity of Norfolk's coastal wildlife habitats and the wealth of species dependent on them. However, the enjoyment of observing wildlife was tempered by an awareness of the enormous pressures exerted on our wildlife by the demands of modern day life and a changing climate.

It's taken for granted that wildlife must adapt to compete in an environment like North Norfolk that is part wilderness and part working landscape. Our wildlife has developed the ability to co-exist within a non-intensive farming landscape but the combined threats of global warming, changes in agricultural practices, pollution, continued loss of habitat and increased human disturbance have driven many species to the brink. Add to these natural pressures like predation and the vagaries of the weather and it's no wonder our wildlife is facing serious adversity.

A summer stroll along the North Norfolk Coast, at say Holkham, might take you through a variety of habitats that could include woodland, grazing marsh and foreshore. The observant visitor will come across many birds, plants and insects and their wildlife experience would generate an impression that all is well with the countryside. If someone suggested otherwise, the least reaction might be a quizzical look. After all some bird populations are still on the increase and include some highly visible species like marsh harrier, buzzard and avocet and, in a positive response to climate change a number of birds, butterflies, dragonflies and other insect species have expanded their range northwards to the Norfolk coast. These include little egret and Cetti's warbler; speckled wood and white admiral butterflies; small red-eyed and large red-eyed damselfly and Rosell's bush cricket. To a certain extent these gains mask the problems faced by our wildlife; scratch the surface and the reality is that wildlife is struggling to cope.

The coastal strip between Holme-next-the Sea and Kelling Quags comprises the North Norfolk Site of Special Scientific Interest (SSSI). This extensive, diverse and dramatic landscape with its outstanding blend of habitats is afforded a significant degree of statutory protection including Special Protection Area (SPA) and Special Area for Conservation (SAC) – both European Union designations. It is for the most part managed by the nature conservation bodies, Natural England, the Norfolk Wildlife Trust, the National Trust and the RSPB. Our National Nature Reserves at Scolt Head Island, Blakeney Point, Holme-next-the-Sea and Holkham are without doubt among the finest examples of their type in the United Kingdom. Yet despite these positives our coastal habitats and wildlife face an uncertain future.

The Challenge of Co-existence

So, what are the problems? Climate change, fuelled by global warming, springs to mind but other serious issues have been around for some time and must be resolved if wildlife is to prosper. On the coastal belt breeding shorebirds are being placed under intolerable stress by an ever increasing number of visitors to our beaches. Public pressure on the Holkham National Nature Reserve has steadily increased during the last two decades and it's now estimated that visitor numbers exceed one million per annum. On the beach between Burnham Overy and Wells-next-the-Sea, understandably a honey-pot for people, vulnerable species like little tern, ringed plover and oystercatcher vie for space to rear their young. The needs of these breeding shorebirds are very basic. Individual nesting pairs require little more than a small patch of sand and shingle beyond the tide line, close to suitable feeding areas and with minimal human disturbance.

The breeding populations of ringed plover and oystercatcher have suffered serious declines since 1990 when there were 45 ringed plover and 22 oystercatcher territories located between Burnham Overy and Wells-next-the-Sea ; by 2008 these figures had fallen to 11 and 14 pairs respectively. The steepest declines, not surprisingly, were in the Holkham Gap to Wells section of beach where visitor pressure is consistently higher than elsewhere and nests are prone to disturbance and trampling. In this zone the number of ringed plovers fell from 10 pairs to one and oystercatchers from nine pairs to three over eighteen years. Little terns favour colonial nesting which improves the potential for protection as colonies tend to be localised on relatively small areas of beach. Simple signed cordons at little tern sites have proved successful in alerting the general public to the presence of nesting birds. Ringed plover and oystercatcher nesting within the cordons have also bene-

fited to the extent that virtually all successful nesting attempts are now within these enclosures.

Uncontrolled dogs are a serious nuisance for nesting shorebirds and in extreme cases cause birds to desert nests and young or create situations where opportunistic species such as gulls nip in and plunder nests. Ideally, dogs should be on leashes during the breeding season or at least under close control. In effect it's all about awareness and consideration for wildlife. The feckless dog owner is a nature reserve warden's nightmare. I've seen dogs entering little tern enclosures to cause massive disturbance to nesting birds. Bad enough you might think but I have also seen dog owners compound the disturbance by panicking and following dogs into enclosures to retrieve them which only increases the risk of trampling nests and young birds. To be fair, most dog owners are horrified if their dogs disturb wildlife and there are few people like the 'gentleman' who deliberately ignored signs, walked his dogs across a tern enclosure and was then heard to say "I don't care about birds".

The alarming reality is that shorebirds are losing out to people in the competition for space on our beaches, to the extent that prime habitat in the form of shingle ridges (e.g. at Holkham Gap and near the Wells Channel) are no longer viable for nesting birds. This poses a dilemma for Natural England which is duty bound under the European Habitats Directive to maintain wildlife habitats in favourable condition. An attempt to restrict access to one of North Norfolk's most popular beaches would be a political headache and would not be tolerated by local commercial interests or the vast majority of tourists. But questions remain: is it acceptable to tolerate habitats in unfavourable condition where there is no sensible remedy; do we accept that locally recreational pressures have won the day; will current legislation allow this to happen; and would such action set a harmful precedent? These questions need to be addressed.

The intensity of visitor pressure has also led to the incremental erosion of saltmarsh and sand dunes. This is most striking close to main access points along the coast where continued trampling has modified the vegetation and the structure of these habitats. The most obvious example is at Holkham Bay, where visitors arriving at Lady Anne's Drive spread out to access the beach to the east and west. Notable sand dune erosion has occurred locally but the impact of foot pressure is most evident on the saltmarsh where pioneer saltmarsh vegetation has been unable to colonise wide belts of beach to the extent that natural function has been restricted. People related issues are of course a source of concern to those involved in protecting our coastal heritage and it will be necessary to be perpetually mindful of the potential harm that can be done by human activity. Yet in the face of natural threats, such as tidal erosion and global warming, the threat of human impact almost pales into insignificance.

The Forces of Nature

The physiographical interest of the North Norfolk Coast is considerable. The sedimentary nature of the landscape renders it susceptible to constant change that within the realms of normal tidal ranges and weather patterns is beneficial to our wildlife. Prograding dune/shingle foreshore systems protects potentially fragile saltmarsh habitats and species, facilitates the accretion of sediments and reduces scour in creeks. Because of the sea's action these formations are changing continually, variously accumulating and eroding on different areas of the coast. Change may be subtle and only noticeable as time elapses, or they can be dramatic following northerly storms, or exceptionally high tides. Waves battering fragile sand dunes may undermine them to the extent many metres may be lost from a dune face overnight. I've seen the awesome power of the sea punch enormous breaches through the fore dunes in Holkham Bay demolishing huge stretches of sand dune. Initially, after observing such destruction the feeling is one of anxiety but soon the realisation dawns that nature is at work. Stretches of sand dune may have disappeared but the underlying shingle ridge is exposed to provide optimum nesting sites for terns and waders. This natural evolutionary process, having taken place through time immemorial, may now be in jeopardy with the prospect of increased storminess, sea level rise and higher wave heights.

The effects of global warming could be disastrous for North Norfolk. On a coast already battered and eroded by winter storms and tidal surges, the prediction that average sea level could rise by as much as 88cm in the next century is truly alarming. Such a calamity would have far reaching consequences for people and wildlife. The physical character of the coastline could change as sea water flooded extensive tracts of low lying land resulting in the loss of existing freshwater habitats like reed beds and grazing marshes. Some of the county's best loved breeding birds like bittern, marsh harrier, avocet and bearded tit would be hard hit; although birds are equipped to move less mobile species like many invertebrates would perish.

Tourism could also suffer if the coastline and its wildlife became less attractive. Research on the Economic Benefits of Tourism to North Norfolk in 2003 by the East of England Tourist Board for the North Norfolk District Council showed annual tourism expenditure amounted to £357 million and a 1999 study for the Norfolk Coast Project on the benefits of eco-tourism in North and North-West Norfolk concluded that as much as £6.2 million was spent annually by birdwatchers and other wildlife enthusiasts. Tourism is recognised as the key sector of the North Norfolk economy, so any downturn would have serious consequences and could bring real hardship for thousands of dependent people many of whom are among the lowest paid workers in the county.

The Powers That Be

The complexity of the issues surrounding coastal management and climate change place a weighty responsibility on local authorities and conservation organisations involved in policy making. Their efforts to resolve issues are often hampered by rigid EC legislation, local politics and vested interests. The completion of a Shoreline Management Plan for North Norfolk, setting out sensible strategies and objectives across a wide socio-economic and environmental spectrum, should prove a useful tool in resolving complex issues. Another less known document, 'The North Norfolk Coastal Habitat Plan' which is based on scientific analysis of coastal change, attempts to identify and predict losses and gains to coastal habitat. The plan recommends measures to minimise future losses and helps plan habitat restoration or recreation in the event of unavoidable losses. It has no statutory power but can influence the Shoreline Management Plan. There appears to be general support for the long term (100 years) objective to create a naturally functioning coastline in North Norfolk but there is also recognition that practical measures are required now to maintain important sites.

Cley, Salthouse, Titchwell and Holme-next-the-Sea are particularly vulnerable to sea incursion. At Holme the Environment Agency has protected a stretch of dunes shielding low lying freshwater grazing marsh and reed beds with a soft defence structure of closely linked timber triangles, approximately one and a half

73

metres high made of 4x4 fence posts. This allows windblown sand to accrete in front of the exposed dune and facilitates the release of sand during high tides thereby reducing the effect of swash. It is unknown how long this barrier can remain effective but as a short to medium term measure to protect the hinterland it is a proven success.

The deteriorating state of the seawall at Titchwell Marsh prompted the RSPB to explore options for protecting one of the country's best loved and most visited nature reserves which ranks as one of the finest places in the UK to observe a wide variety of birds at close quarters, especially wildfowl and waders. It is a key visitor attraction and a valuable educational facility running an extensive programme of events that cater to a range of age groups and for this reason alone Titchwell is worthy of protection.

Funding from the European Union Life+ Fund for 50% of the total cost of £1.2 million (the balance being met by the RSPB) allowed an ambitious project to get underway in autumn 2009. The plan is to realign sea defences on a small part of the reserve and to reinforce the sea wall behind the brackish marsh. It is a major challenge that Rob Coleman, the reserve manager, will relish. On the seaward side reprofiling the intertidal zone will create new salt marshes and mudflats that will absorb the power of the sea. This work, combined with reinforcing the sea bank, will protect freshwater habitats and allow new reed beds to develop. The RSPB hopes these measures will minimise the impact of stormy seas for the foreseeable future, perhaps as long as 50 years. If, over time, Scolt Head Island continues to extend westward the barrier island should provide greater protection for Titchwell and allow intertidal habitat to accrete. The desire to protect freshwater habitats from the sea is the main driver of the project but it also presents an opportunity to call attention to the land management issues inherent in attempts to mitigate the impact of climate change on our coastline. In the hands of an efficient and proactive RSPB publicity department the public will surely understand and grasp this initiative.

Let it Be?

To some people management projects like these amount to tinkering and, if predictions for climate change are accurate, a waste of time. They might argue a better course of action would be to let nature to take its course and support a managed retreat approach where human settlements are not at risk. Furthermore, taking account of the fact that huge tracts of reclaimed land squeezed between the sea walls and the A149 coast road were once intertidal, large-scale managed retreat seems a feasible option. But you can also argue that what we have now has been hard won and is worth protecting as long as possible.

Go back to the start of the 17th century and the vast area west of Wells-next-

74

the-Sea was an extensive salt marsh protected on its seaward edge by a line of sand dunes. In 1639 John Parker purchased Burnham Overy Marshes from King Charles 1 and constructed a sea wall between Overy Staithe and the sand dunes. He drained and reclaimed the marsh to the east of this wall and his example was emulated by the Coke family who constructed further embankments to the east in 1660 and 1720. Reclamation was completed with the construction of the Wells sea wall in 1859. Since then the reclaimed marsh has been used as pasture and arable crops. In more recent times appropriate conservation management has seen large tracts of wet grassland at Holkham NNR take on international importance for birds. Vast assemblages of wintering wildfowl now gather there and populations of rare and interesting birds have increased. Other species like amphibians, invertebrates and water voles have also responded to positive management and this success is mirrored on wet grasslands elsewhere, e.g. at Holme and Blakeney Freshes. This is a persuasive argument against letting the sea in and allowing nature to take its course.

The threat presented by sea level rise is more significant on the relatively narrow coastline of North Norfolk than in some other coastal counties because the potential inland migration of intertidal habitats is restricted by fixed defences and the chalk ridge south of the A149. The 'roll back' response is a normal morphological process but squeezed between the sea and immovable barriers there is little potential for such movement. To a great extent this squeeze effect also applies to our freshwater habitats because apart from very limited potential for habitat replacement along river valleys like the Glaven and Burn, wet grasslands would have little opportunity to develop in the face of managed retreat.

Habitat for Whom?

A serious problem facing planners is the requirement under SPA legislation to replace habitat that is either lost or significantly modified through managed retreat or related works. A daunting task, seeing that, locally, little in the way of the land that is available or suitable lies outside the North Norfolk Coast SPA. This situation is highlighted at Cley where the breeding habitat of bittern is threatened following the decision to terminate annual maintenance of the shingle ridge. If shaped by the sea the ridge will assume a flatter profile and eventually allow sea water into the reed beds to the detriment of bittern. Despite considerable efforts by all interested parties to find a mere 16ha of land to mitigate the loss of part of the Cley reed bed, the situation is still unresolved. What chance then to find in excess of 1500 hectares of land to replace wet grassland habitats in the event that nature was allowed to take its natural course by way of managed retreat on the North Norfolk Coast?

The impact on individuals and communities must also be considered, not least because any hint of a strategy for large scale managed retreat in North Norfolk is likely to be met with a similar response to that it met in East Norfolk where a great furore erupted following the leak of a Natural England draft paper outlining a strategy to surrender large parts of the Norfolk Broads to the sea. Given that many landowners and others are dependent on the land for their livelihoods, the reaction was understandable. Fortunately, for the time being North Norfolk's sea defences appear adequate, so with a degree of 'tinkering' here and there it should be possible to maintain the *status quo* for the foreseeable future. All things considered the current approach of protecting what we have (if possible) is practical and bodes well for us and our freshwater wildlife. But for future generations of planners, scientists and local communities, managed retreat may be the only option. In the meantime we must look to the inevitable challenges and threats rising sea levels will bring.

Climate change poses a serious threat to the welfare of our coastal grazing marshes which depends on a good supply of freshwater. In most years average rainfall combined with river and spring flows ensures there is sufficient water to maintain desired levels. Climate change is expected to be an increasingly important consideration in the management of wetland habitats especially in southern England and changes in both rainfall amounts and timing could have far reaching consequences for our wildlife communities. In North Norfolk a trend towards drier spring weather is already being noted, three of the last five spring periods having produced lower than average rainfall. On the grazing marshes ephemeral pools provide important feeding areas for breeding wildfowl and waders. They are extremely susceptible to drying out and when they do their value as feeding areas for parent birds and chicks is soon lost as the silty clay substrate has a tendency to bake and crack. The drying out process on the marshes is particularly stressful for breeding waders like snipe and oystercatcher that require soft ground to probe for food. There are no obvious solutions and planning for a potentially devastating declining water budget is a daunting challenge for land managers.

The steady decline in livestock numbers in Norfolk and the UK since 2000 is another major concern for grassland managers and the decline appears to have gathered momentum since 2005 with the launch of the Single Farm Payment. This scheme, introduced through the European Common Agricultural Policy Reform Agreement of June 2003, was designed to replace the existing direct main support schemes like the beef special premium and the sheep annual premium schemes, the new payments being based on the amount of eligible land holdings, in other words an area based system. Under this system there is no obligation to undertake any agricultural production to receive payments as long as you comply with EU standards on, among other things, environmental and animal welfare; this is an attractive option for some farmers.

Couple this with falling incomes, a loss of confidence following the foot and mouth outbreak in 2001 and fears over the outbreak of blue tongue disease and it's not surprising many farmers have pulled out of livestock farming. As a result it is now extremely difficult to find graziers to undertake conservation management on some of our nature reserves. Attracting graziers willing to summer cattle on grazing marshes was never easy as these grasslands tend to be viewed as marginal, low intensity grazing pasture that usually receive little or no fertiliser input.

Concerns for animal welfare due to seasonally wet ground conditions and the presence of deep ditches also influence livestock owners' decisions to graze a site or not. Working in partnership with and looking after the interests of graziers have always been important in achieving good grassland management and this is increasingly necessary. Income from grazing lets has fallen dramatically. In the coastal belt only five years ago some pasture was fetching £30 an acre but is now let for a peppercorn rent. This benefits the grazier but as long as the conservation objectives are being met the fall in income is of no great concern to conservation managers. But if livestock owners continue to leave the industry it's quite possible some conservation bodies may be compelled to establish their own herds in much the same way as the Norfolk Wildlife Trust whose 'Flying Flock' has proved a vital element in the management of heaths, fens and grassland.

The value of grazing for wildlife can't be overestimated because it creates a structure and composition of vegetation that isn't matched by cutting. Cattle, sheep and ponies can all produce optimal sward for any given management prescription under careful supervision. It's generally acknowledged that summer grazing when ground conditions are usually drier and the control of coarse grasses is more effective in the growing season and best for a wide range of habitats and species. This is certainly true for our wetland sites where winter grazing is not an option due to wet ground. The fact that grass doesn't seem to stop growing in winter these days may have implications for grassland management and breeding birds if the trend toward milder winters continues. Waders like lapwing and redshank nesting in grassland prefer a short sward, tussocky structure in spring. This mosaic habitat offers good nesting sites and ample feeding opportunities for their chicks. The structure of this and similar habitats could be seriously compromised as climate change bites. At Holkham NNR the presence of many thousands of wildfowl has tended to obscure what may be an emerging problem. These birds consume prodigious amounts of grass during the course of a winter but with wigeon declining locally and a tendency for pink-foot geese to depart the coastal marshes much earlier these days, unseasonably long grass has drawn attention. This also raises questions as to why some of our winter wildfowl are arriving in smaller numbers and why some species are departing earlier. Again, I suspect we do not have to speculate beyond the effects of climate change and the probability that many wildfowl are now inclined to move shorter distances in Europe to find food and escape the worst of the winter weather.

Uncertainty over sugar beet quotas also raises concerns for the future of the pink-footed goose in North Norfolk. A plentiful supply of sugar beet tops has seen a phenomenal increase in the number of this goose to the extent that in some years perhaps as many as a third of the world population is present. Leaving aside the wonder of huge flocks of knot on the Wash, the sight of vast skeins of pink has to be the greatest wildlife spectacle Norfolk can offer. However, in the event of stringent cuts in sugar beet quotas it's quite probable that the distribution of this fine goose could be significantly altered. Despite the short term increase in beet planting in 2007/08 the long term prediction of a decline in the area of sugar beet plantings remains valid.

Predatory Spirits

Predator control is an emotive issue and a subject most people will have an opinion about. It has stimulated a great deal of debate over the years not least among those working in nature conservation and to a great extent opinion is polarised. I know that when I came to work at Holkham NNR I had serious misgivings about undertaking such work but it was made clear to me that predator control would figure in my new role and I resolved to take it on. My attitude changed early on with first-hand experience of the impact of common predators on the breeding success of ground nesting birds, like little tern, lapwing, avocet and redshank. The main culprits identified were fox, carrion crow, stoat and rats. A predator control programme implemented at Holkham NNR in 1991 targeted these four species

with similar action adopted elsewhere by virtually all the conservation bodies on the North Norfolk Coast. This was a bold action in view of the potential backlash from their members and the general public but once in the public domain the issue generated little disquiet.

The fox is one of the most charismatic creatures you are likely to come across and I have enjoyed many memorable encounters with this animal. Some years ago in the still of dawn I remember watching a dog fox returning to its den its jaws crammed with the carcasses of three young rabbits and I was filled with wonderment. I guess I have a slightly jaundiced view of fox these days but even so I maintain great respect for this efficient hunter. I've spent many nights at Holkham huddled with a mate against a bank or in a cold vehicle waiting for the alarm calls of lapwing and avocet to alert us to the presence of a fox. Occasionally there were opportunities to observe behaviour but more often than not the brightness of an eye caught by our lamp was all that was to be seen. I remember Bernard Bishop, the Norfolk Wildlife Trust warden at Cley, telling me one day how the previous evening he had lost eighteen avocet nests to fox. He was particularly annoyed as they were all close to hatching. This and similar incidents where eggs near hatching were predated led to the conclusion that foxes were targeting nests by the sound of chicks cheeping and tapping in the eggs. We often saw fox systematically searching areas of the marsh and wondered if they were snacking on eggs whilst searching for larger prey for their young.

If asked to justify predator control on our reserves I would emphasise the vulnerability of our ground nesting birds, many of which are in serious decline. It's

also sensible to acknowledge the considerable financial investment that has been required to achieve favourable conditions for wildlife within the North Norfolk Coast SSSI. I accept predator control as a necessary element of management in a countryside environment heavily modified by man's activities and condone it as long as control measures are based on clear conservation objectives.

To view the past through rose tinted spectacles is a typical human trait and many of us tend to think of the good old days in these terms. As a child, the summers always seemed longer and warmer. In the 1950's butterflies, grasshoppers, bees and the like appeared abundant and we almost took them for granted. At that time the caterpillars of 'cabbage whites' were a pest on farms and allotments, meadows resonated with the sound of chirping grasshoppers and hedgerows in country lanes were seemingly full of birds. Such halcyon days are long gone and a walk in farmland these days, even on a warm and sunny day can be eerily quiet.

Many years ago I remember reading extracts from Rachel Carson's *Silent Spring* in which she described the effects of pesticides on plants, animals and humans. Until the publication of this book in 1962 it appears people were generally unaware of the toxicity of pesticides. It's a different story these days with greater awareness of the impact of harmful chemicals on our environment. Despite this and other concerns surrounding agro-chemicals their use continues to increase and insect populations continue to decline.

If we also take account of changes in agricultural practices, including increased specialisation and mechanisation, the switch to autumn sowing of cereals, the intensification of grassland management and the loss of field margins and hedgerows it's no wonder many of our farmland birds and insects have declined dramatically. If you add the catastrophic national decline in the distribution of arable flowering plants and the spectre of climate change the future for farmland wildlife looks bleak. At present the odds seem stacked against our farmland wildlife but it's not too late to address some formidable problems and thankfully we are a long way from a 'Silent Spring' scenario in North Norfolk.

The Wildlife Trusts are Britain's largest voluntary conservation organization and an ambitious project to create a living landscape across the UK identifies key areas for wildlife and provides focus, incentives and opportunities to turn things around especially on farmland. The Norfolk Wildlife Trust has six major Living Landscape initiatives that aim to restore, reconnect and enlarge habitats to sustain biodiversity. One of the main objectives is to create wildlife highways that will link fragmented habitats that could ultimately be required to facilitate the movements of whole communities of plants and animals that may need to retreat in the face of climate change. This measure is crucial to the survival of many tiny isolated populations.

Environmental Stewardship is a government scheme administered by Natural England and open to all farmers, land managers and tenants in England. At the start of 2009 nearly two-thirds of England's agricultural land (six million hectares) was covered by environmental agreements. Because this scheme can be financially rewarding there is an incentive for good land stewardship and for managing land to improve the quality of the environment. The take up in North Norfolk has been very good and a number of exemplary schemes are benefiting a wide range of wildlife. It strikes me that at a time when cereal prices are fluctuating, signing up to a 10 year Environmental Stewardship scheme is a prudent measure to secure known and guaranteed income for that period.

A Heritage in Trust

Environmental Stewardship is a complicated scheme but is essentially a three tier system. The Entry Level Scheme (ELS) is a 'whole farm' scheme geared to encourage large numbers of farmers to deliver simple yet effective environmental management. The Organic Entry Level Scheme (OELS) is also a 'whole farm' scheme, open to farmers who manage all or part of their land organically. The Higher Level Scheme (HLS) which is usually combined with ELS or OELS is discretionary and concentrates on situations where land managers may need support to deliver high quality benefits for wildlife. All HLS applications are supported by a Farm Environment Plan (FEP), a structured survey of environmental features that helps determine a suitable level of management and identifies the potential to create environmental features and habitats, improve public access and manage land for flood management and natural resource protection.

There is an extensive range of management options to choose from under ELS/OELS and a farmer will naturally select options that suit his business, are straightforward to implement and are calculated to achieve sufficient points to be eligible for the scheme and to qualify for payment. These options might include hedgerow and ditch management, the creation of buffer strips and field margins, beetle banks, or unfertilised headlands within arable fields.

The HLS offers tremendous potential for habitat restoration and significant biodiversity gains for farmland species such as lapwing, barn owl, and grey partridge. Arable options, such as fallow plots for ground nesting birds, unharvested, fertiliser-free conservation headlands and creation of species rich semi-natural grassland are among many options available to suit the requirements of a particular farm business and its dependent wildlife. An area of concern is the low uptake of in-field options among many farmers, such as fallow plots for ground nesting birds. Some of these options pay well but because they require fiddly management are often rejected, which is regrettable as they are particularly valuable to a wide range of species.

While encouraging wildlife-sensitive farmland management Environmental Stewardship also contributes to biodiversity on other habitats in North Norfolk, including the restoration of chalk grassland and heath land, arable reversion to wet grassland and reedbed maintenance. Working on inspiring projects like these is life's blood to the conservation manager and it never ceases to amaze me just how rapidly wildlife exploits our efforts to enhance the countryside. In our modern high stress life style people generally have less patience and there is a tendency to expect immediate results, especially where large sums of money are invested. However, patience is a necessary virtue where conservation management is concerned and in some habitats like woodland, where high biodiversity comes with maturity, it can take many years to achieve all the objectives.

Wetland projects, such as arable reversion to wet grassland, the creation of new ponds and ditches have tremendous potential to produce swift results for wildlife. There is a fine example at Marsh Farm, Burnham Overy where an HLS arable reversion to wet grassland project on about 68 hectares has achieved significant wildlife gains, especially for birds. This low lying land was formerly in cereals and required regular pumping to maintain a low water table to accommodate arable production. After careful consideration by all parties the option chosen for management of the site was maintenance of wet grassland for breeding waders. Water pumping ceased at the end of 2006 and a number of water control structures were installed to allow the water table to back up over winter. By the spring the land was transformed into a mosaic of brim-full ditches, extensive shallow water bodies, bare mud and sparsely vegetated areas. Wading birds and wildfowl flocked to the area, many in transit to nesting grounds in northern Europe and Iceland but some like lapwing, redshank, avocet, gadwall and shoveler intent on setting up breeding territories.

In that first season breeding birds included 37 pairs of lapwing (51 in 2008), ten pairs of redshank (23 in 2008) and 16 pairs of avocet (eight in 2008). Cattle grazing, introduced in 2008, will gradually improve the structure and species composition of the grassland and over the next few years survey and monitoring results should show significant increases in the populations of many species like water vole, hares, dragonflies, many other invertebrates, amphibians and plant life. Developing good working relationships with land owners and occupiers is critical to the success of such projects. The burden of dealing with complex habitat management may prove testing for some so it is imperative that advice and support continues to be provided by Natural England if we are to achieve the best results for wildlife and get value for money.

Considering the future for North Norfolk's wildlife it's quite easy to feel a sense of doom and gloom. We are increasingly aware of threats from climate change, melting glaciers and rising sea levels. As we read about the relentless destruction of the world's rainforests, the extinction of thousands of wildlife species worldwide and countless other issues one thing is for certain; the world's wildlife will need to be resilient to survive in the face of so many threats.

Thankfully, it's a lot easier to focus on wildlife issues closer to home. Norfolk is rightly recognised as one of the finest wildlife counties in the UK and this is unlikely to change. Initiatives like the Living Landscape Project and the government agri-environment schemes generate a degree of optimism for the future of our species communities and habitat network. It's also important to recognise the dedication and tremendous efforts of people who work with nature including many volunteers and those working in the voluntary and statutory conservation bodies whose contribution is, and will in the future be invaluable in influencing decisions, and protecting and managing our wildlife heritage.

Nicholas Hills

Nicholas Hills is an architect who was born on the south coast at Eastbourne, Sussex and left school at 16 to become apprenticed to a local architect. He completed his architectural training at Brighton College of Art and Crafts, travelled and worked as an assistant architect in Greece, Denmark and Finland and later became Pilkington Research Fellow at the Royal College of Art.

Architecture – embracing theatre, music and poetry – has been his life-long interest. He would have liked to have become what he describes as "a highly successful practitioner" but is content to fulfil his role as a designer of smaller buildings, mostly houses and mostly in Norfolk, where he has lived permanently for 15 years. He has always enjoyed designing houses – ranging from a house on the Cornish cliffs at Lands End to houses in the Sussex Downs and London apartments. Several of his residential designs have received awards. His other work includes designs for textiles, carpets and stage sets.

He has previously published two books 'Setting Up Home', with Barty Phillips, (Design Centre 1978) and 'The English Fireplace' (Quiller Press 1985) and articles in a variety of magazines.

The Built Environment

Nicholas Hills

Man and the Sea

The coast defines the edge of land; but land defines the limit of sea; or does it? The two are in constant battle, like Titans struggling for supremacy, ever changing; sands shifting; cliffs eroding. This chapter considers the works of man in trying to come to terms with the combination of the two. What have humans constructed on the evolving coastal landscape of North Norfolk, and in response to it, and what are the prospects for the future?

Heathcote Williams in his play *Whale Nation* declares that 'from space the planet is blue, the territory not of you, but of the whale. Blue seas cover 7/10ths of the Earth's surface'. Yet the whale is powerless to alter the limit of the sea. Only men have the means to try to keep the whale's natural element at bay.

Our human responses reflect the threat of the sea to 'our' land, expressed in newspaper headlines when a wave dares to crash over a promenade. Happisburgh, round the coast from here, has all but given up the struggle to resist – as did Dunwich. At Holkham Bay, sand and mud are building up and soon new salt-water marshes will be formed like those of Stiffkey, though the sand comes from another part of the coast.

If the country is like a great tapestry cloth (as it appears from the air), the coast is the frayed edge which men seek to define with any means to hand. Maram grass will hold sand firm for a while. Dredgers will seek to move huge quantities of sand where nature may not have wanted to put it – sometimes only to see their work reversed by the might of an overnight tide. Sometimes we try to colonize the sea, with oil rig platforms and wind generators, ships and bridges. With our breakwaters and groynes, seawalls and gabions, we seek to assert land's struggle with the sea, but more often than not the sea will, in the end, have its way.

This special piece of land is defined by its interaction with the sea – and man's engagement with both. How easily do we forget that most of these coastal villages were once an integral part of the fishing and ship building trade, and that some still are. It is our nearness to the sea that gives us our sense of place, our limits, even our security, all far less defined in landlocked countrysides.

Are we adequately conserving, nurturing and protecting it? Are we respecting its specialness with the buildings that we place on it? Are we respecting those with a long and active relationship with the sea, sailors and fishermen and the buildings which have an overriding right to be near their places of work and retirement? Remember Captain Cat from Dylan Thomas's *Under Milk Wood*:

> *The retired blind sea captain asleep in his bunk in Schooner House....dreams of never such seas as any that swamped the decks of his SS Kidwelly, bellying him over the bedclothes and jellyfish slippery, sucking him down salt deep into the Davey dark where the fish coming biting out nibble him down to his wishbone.*

The Land in Question

Before attempting some answers, let us look more closely at this piece of land. I have tried to walk most of the coastline under examination. Beyond its Western end sits Hunstanton – outside our remit in the strict sense, but significant as a geological marker, and also because the towns that border the stretch of coast under examination contain the concentrations of buildings that influence their rural neighbours.

A late autumn afternoon blow along Hunstanton's layercake-cliffs (possibly one of the county's least sung visual treasures) shows up a coast second to none. I am walking in a painting by Boudin, as I kick up live mussels and pocket them for later. I wonder at the ramped line of red chalk and composite stone as it rises from the present ground level at Old Hunstanton, only to suddenly conclude its upward journey before reaching New Hunstanton and peer into the vertical cracks in the red-brown lower layer of carstone.

The town is not as fashionable as it once was, having now settled down as a place of comfortable retirement, but I at least would like to turn back the clock and find the cleanly undulating sward of grass suddenly curtailed by the ice-cream colours of exposed cliff unblemished by hill-top buildings, except perhaps for the now disused lighthouse which will before long form part of the foreshore.

I recall my childhood memory of the Crumbles, a pebbled expanse to the east of Eastbourne which provided a youthful wartime playground; hands scratched and pricked discovering linnets' eggs in gorse bushes and part of the time a mined defensive no-go land which, to the extreme agitation of my mother, I once crossed on a hot summer's day to go for a swim. The area I trudged over among yellow toadflax and viper's bugloss is now almost entirely built on and irrecoverably lost to wildlife.

Further round the coast, North at first by the compass, lie Holme, Thornham and Titchwell, as we make the gradual transition from cliff to marsh and enter the Saltmarsh Coast in earnest, with its tidal creeks and the remains of its former working staithes that serviced the sea transport of grain, timber, stone and coal.

Onwards to the small boat harbours at Brancaster Staithe and Burnham Overy. I like the local pronunciation of Brancaster as Bran Carster, which seems to emphasise the connection with the Roman castle which once stood here. Then the vast beach at Holkham, popular not just with walkers but also with naturists and film-makers, so vast you can stand on parts of it and see not a soul. Holkham Beach and it ever-reforming dunes are skilfully protected by a belt of pine trees. It is said that an Oxford academic, staying at the Temple in Holkham Park, agreed with the then Earl of Leicester that a swathe should be cut through this belt so that he could have a view of the sea. It has taken over 25 years of subsequent re-growth to remedy the resultant breach in the belt and to restore the vital wind and therefore coastline protection.

Another remarkable Holkham vista can be had by climbing to the roof of St. Withburga's Church in Holkham Park. If you look northwards, you see the relatively untouched view of the coast for miles in either direction, looking out across the reclaimed marsh, what was once a Roman camp and the wilderness and grandeur of the North Sea coast. Turn 180 degrees to the southern view and you have the man-made park completely created in the 18th century and expanded in the 19th century to provide a setting for the Palladian home of the Coke family. It is a symbolic and instructive contrast.

Next comes Wells, proudly 'next the sea', in its own way the capital of the Saltmarsh Coast – best experienced over a dish of crisply fried fish and chips, preferably eaten on the harbour wall, but also remarkable for its own buildings, its fine roofscape of terra cotta, sometimes black glazed pantile, its narrow shopping streets framing the view of the harbour, its remarkable collection of fine period houses and its iconic converted granary jutting out over the harbour (in which we were lucky enough to assemble as writers to reflect on the preparation of this book and to enjoy a unique Norfolk panorama).

On to Morston and Stiffkey, Blakeney and Cley, each essentially defined by their relationship with the sea – not just through proximity but by marine activity and trade. And finally further eastwards towards Sheringham and Cromer, Hunstanton's opposite number, with its great tradition of seaside holidays, crabs and pier show and the aspirational Hotel de Paris.

The coast is punctuated by Grade I and Grade II Listed churches, the towers acting as landmarks and often as beacons for individual villages. For the fisherman working far out at sea, their way home determined by currents and tides, nothing could be a more welcome sight than your own church tower, perhaps with a single bell to position it in a sea harr and the knowledge that the tide is right for sailing homeward.

The quality of these coastal churches as architecture is reflected in their protective listings; Blakeney, Cley, Salthouse on the higher land vie with Thornham, Holme and Brancaster for architectural merit. In many cases churches that were

once on the coast have 'moved back' because of the seaboard deposits of sand and clay brought from further round the shore. In this, the architecture of the villages benefits. Sea rounded flint cobbles present a very different look to the flint as dug up from a chalk seam. Their roundedness can give a façade the look of having been knitted on some giant needles. In the past builders took pride in matching similar sizes of flints in rows. Perhaps for reasons of time and effort this is rarely done today in housing developments, with the result that the randomness of the flint takes on the appearance of a wallpaper pattern, a match perhaps for the swirls of artex plaster used for ceilings by less fastidious builders.

The glories of the church interiors, often with the remains of once colourful rood screens and wall paintings, are exemplified by the church of St. Nicholas, Salthouse. Here there is now an established annual art exhibition which uses the church to magnificent effect. The whitened interior somehow typifies the modern art gallery at Salthouse, and the tall slender aisle windows together with the light from the clerestory combine to provide an interior which would be the envy of many gallery owners. The exhibitions give back to the church artworks, the like of which once adorned such interiors before iconoclasts, suspicious of images defaced them and gouged out the eyes of wooden saints.

The Church of England has a vast responsibility for upkeep and, often with monies from English Heritage, works splendidly to fulfil its obligations. In some cases concerts, such as those arranged by Music in Country Churches, assist in funding for upkeep of these architectural treasures. Even though congregations for weekly worship are small, the churches are nevertheless prized and valued as holy relics in a disbelieving age by villagers, churchwardens and others who look after them with a sense of reverence. They are invariably full at Christmas time, for harvest festivals and continue to serve congregations for weddings and funerals.

There is also a tradition in this countryside of tin buildings, the corrugated iron, once galvanized to prevent rusting, painted in fetching colours when the zinc coating breaks down. The old lifeboat station at Blakeney is a case in point, now housing a warden to care for the birds and seals. Its position enfolded by dunes off Morston provides just that cynosure needed in the bland miles of sand. This nostalgic image, recalling countless tin buildings seen on the Greek coastline, is evoked by Desmond MacCarthy in his café at Wiveton, whilst the 'grass-roots' architecture of Cookies restaurant at Salthouse is a breath of fresh air in the more sober, flint-built surroundings.

That then is the land in question, and I suggest that its exceptional quality challenges us to respect it in three particular ways.

Design and Planning

The first pre-requisite for safeguarding this place is to insist on high quality in what we design and build. Planners are often criticised but rarely praised – and are sometimes perceived as insensitive to public opinion and concerns. My view, based on regular interaction with them over many years, is that they deserve much credit in maintaining a balance and in interpreting Government directives in as fair a way as possible.

We need to remember that local authority planners can only approve what they have set before them, so they are very reliant on the quality of designs presented. They have little potential for innovation, apart from some sound advice, not least as their architects' departments have now been disbanded. And they do have to be responsive to public opinion, however that is expressed and channelled. If local people deplore the quality of developers' designs, machinery exists for trying at least to change them through the appeals process, although nowadays, when it is thought that more dwellings are needed, it may be the design of dwellings rather than the development per se which is placed under scrutiny. I feel that as a general rule there should be no new building or housing developments nearer than two miles from the coast line, but even that, in an area of outstanding natural beauty (AONB), should only take place after very serious consideration within existing village envelopes.

Many planners, as well as local inhabitants cling to the comforting idea of 'keeping in keeping'. This rationale is that plans should only be approved if the buildings in question are thought to be 'in keeping' with their surroundings, whatever that is taken to mean. This can be a dead hand on innovation in design practiced by more sensitive architects but at least controls the output from the shoals of builders and technical draughtsmen who operate at a lower conceptual level.

In interpreting and applying their remit, and acting under Government directives to 'maintain local distinctiveness', the planners have to strike a balance between inherent ultra-conservatism and the opportunity to allow and encourage good quality modern design. Yet opportunities can still be missed to create world class architecture, at least of the standard achieved in Michael Hopkins's refectory for Norwich cathedral; buildings well thought out and innovative in their expression.

Public opinion can be both fickle and potent. How sad it was, for example, that Burnham Market was not willing to grasp the opportunity to welcome and adopt a wonderful design for a new village hall by Sir Nicholas Grimshaw. With its boat-like profile it would have created a lasting legacy and symbol for the village and the area – but no, it was too much for reactive tastes to swallow.

Unfortunately, modern architecture is so often associated with lame duck refits exemplified by King's Lynn's shopping centre, where the quality of building nowhere near matches the confident 18th and 19th century buildings yet remaining in the town and people are understandably suspicious of embracing it. But the successful public building can not only enhance a town or village, but also encourage visitors to come to see it.

Experiments in seaside architecture, such as the well-established white clapboard painted town in Florida called Seaside, would sadly be of doubtful success here either; not that clapboard is essentially foreign to this country but the dampness of the climate would soon ensure that the pristine whiteness of Florida would soon become the damp mildewed decay of The Wash. It should be said however that there is a way of 'baking' timber boarding for facings that is currently popular and which renders it less susceptible to decay. In choosing facing materials for a building locally, however, excavated materials are clearly best. They have after all weathered for several millennia and reflect somewhat literally local colour.

Of course planners and designers must respond to the realities of modern life – such as the place of the car in today's society. In the predecessor to this book, *The Turn of the Tide*, my fellow writer Jim Ring bravely suggested that part of this area should be subject to the same restriction on cars that applies in some cantons in Switzerland – that they are only allowed for permanent residents and that visitors must use public transport, which would of course need to be vastly improved in parallel, including the restoration of earlier railway lines. Perhaps that would be a step too far, but it reminds us not only that our roads are totally unsuitable for the volume of cars we now experience, but also that car ownership and usage has become a dominant and none too benign influence on roads, buildings and public places.

One of the issues with which planners have to struggle is the balance between containment of development within established boundaries, applying policies about village 'envelopes', and over-concentration within existing settlements. One extreme is provided by the Irish – who seem ready to allow their beautiful land-scape to be spotted like measles with cottages whose design owes more to a cata-logue than to good taste, usually painted white (how I wish we could have less white paint in the countryside!) and surrounded by balustrades (from another cat-alogue).

The other extreme occurs when containment policies result in too many build-ings being squeezed in between existing properties, often at the expense of their gardens, so that a pleasing distribution of comfortably spaced housing becomes too densely filled with more houses than open space. Perhaps the answer, after all, is to build to three even four stories high in closely controlled groups, with plenty of space, well planted with trees between them.

Geology and Materials

My second need in respecting the specialness of the Saltmarsh Coast is about geol-ogy and materials.

As we travel from west to east through the area, we also witness the conse-quences of a geology changing with our journey, reflected in the materials used for housing. At the western end of the area, we see the predominance of carstone, the distinctive red-brown sandstone often used as slim tile-like bricks. It gives a well-established look to buildings, and offers a hearty, suntanned if not weathered look. It has been used for private and public housing throughout West Norfolk, where the rock is close to hand; for buildings ranging from the Sandringham estate, manor houses, cottages, even railway stations and farm buildings.

As the geology changes so do the building materials. Around Thornham and Titchwell, the carstone slowly diminishes, to be replaced by chalk, flint and brick combinations (the chalk and flint coming from the northward extension of the North Downs and brick clay from deposits left by glacial moraines from succes-sive ice ages) often under Norfolk's familiar orange-red pantiles. Sometimes the two sources are used in combination – so you will sometimes see a mixture of chalk and carstone being used to produce a chequer board façade or for picking out quoins and details.

Occasionally you can see carstone further afield, as in the handsome post office at Wells. At Houghton, William Kent chose to face the important views of his sta-bles for Robert Walpole in dressed and squared carstone which contrasts most effectively with the lighter stone of the house. There is also an agglomerate stone, occasionally seen in Norfolk buildings far harder than carstone and therefore more difficult to dress in earlier eras without diamond tipped saws.

Fidelity to these geological sources is in my view of huge importance in main-

91

taining local coherence and quality in the built environment. A material such as chalk, carstone or flint provides a constancy running through a collection of buildings, akin to the voice of a lead instrument in a concerto. It is not inconsistent with good and innovative design – far from it. Indeed it helps well designed, imaginative buildings to sit comfortably with their traditional neighbours, with the material providing an all-important link which binds the location together into a coherent whole.

Traditionally, architectural innovations were made from the top down. At a time when the study of architecture was the pursuit of gentlemen, landowners vied to build in the latest style and often to impress their neighbours. That is why Holkham differs from Houghton. Some of the stylistic details filtered down to smaller houses, through lesser architects and artisan builders. Samuel Wyatt picked up the distinctively different Holkham style and constructed some fifty or so buildings for his patron in the same idiom. But the Holkham brick clay (as it is correctly known to geologists) was limited in quantity and ultimately in popularity – more's the pity I feel. Men with 'taste' from Sacheverell Sitwell to later writers deplored the ochre-grey Holkham brick and preferences led back to the use of the redder brick of earlier generations. It is now somewhat unusual to find a new building in the Holkham brick colour, but the clay can still be found north of the Wash, where the seam which vanishes beneath the sea rises again in Lincolnshire.

The area boasts wonderful examples of ingenuity and variety in the dressing of flints and chalk. These are brilliantly surveyed in *The Flint Architecture of East Anglia* by Stephen Hart and leave one envious for times when visual effect and the time and trouble taken to achieve them was more important than finishing a building for the lowest cost.

The dedicated work of the Society for the Protection of Ancient Buildings has done much to persuade local builders to use lime mortar again, at least for the finishing of facing materials. In spite of minor infelicities in some artisan work – windows not recessed from the wall's face, crudely formed arches with uncut bricks and other poor quality detailing which will always give a building away – the surface materials will usually weather to match the earlier buildings which have formed the pattern for this recent work.

The emphasis on good matching of material has been strongly encouraged by the planners, helping a place to preserve its traditional character while still moving onwards to reflect modern requirements. The use of such a strict discipline, too often wrongly criticised for excluding innovative modern building, has succeeded in retaining the character which generations of people have come to regard as an integral part of the local scene.

A Bit of Bravery?

There are I fear many ways in which we can spoil this place, some of which I have discussed. Another of these potential failings is not being brave enough in the design of new buildings – and this is my third and last plea. There is a danger, for example, that if we already have a group of mediocre, poorly designed buildings, further buildings will be encouraged in the same style simply for the sake of creating something that is 'in keeping'. Building in keeping with mediocrity should never be allowed. Poor land use is another problem. The elderly naturally prefer to live in single-storied houses or bungalows, occupying valuable sites which could be put to better use through imaginative design, for example creating an apartment on a ground floor with a two-storied house on top, separating access by ingenious ramped earthworks.

The other side of that coin is the vast scope that exists for creative construction. A bridge over the Wash linking Hunstanton with Skegness, perhaps like that across the Oresund linking Denmark and southern Sweden, or that proposed for linking Bahrain with Qatar, but inhabited. It would be like an extended seaside pier replacing those now missing from the two resort towns. Another scheme currently under consideration is to provide a tidal barrage across the Wash combining electricity generation with defence against rising seawater levels which might otherwise flood the whole fen area.

One thing seems certain: extend the small towns and villages of North Norfolk any further and not only their ambiance, but the hard pressed services and access roads will collapse under ever increasing numbers. Many people will think that bold new developments are emphatically what is not needed along the coast. I would argue conversely. No one can stop people coming to enjoy the coast and since the area does not have national park status, there is no legislation which can reasonably prevent greater pressure being put on the existing towns and villages to expand. My view is that many villages have reached their saturation point; if they grow any larger they become agglomerates, no longer places neatly contained within surrounding countryside.

Why not create a new town or village, perhaps on one of the area's many disused airfields, building on the lessons learned from Poundbury near Dorchester? This would allow further building without attenuating existing villages in a ribbon-like development, as has happened in Blakeney and Langham, which increasingly resemble suburbs of Sheringham. Moving a population centre slightly back from the coast would be farsighted in the event of rising sea levels, but they could have a dedicated fast track to the sea via miniature trains cut into the surface of the land, like the one from Walsingham to Wells.

Why should we give in to the North Sea's colonising nature? We need to fight back far more vigorously. Indeed, rather than building on existing land, and since people love to look at the sea so much, should we not think of extending the county out to sea in vast jetties like Dubai's? North Norfolk District Council have made a bold though necessary move at Sea Palling, where offshore reefs have been created which I can see developing in time, providing an extended defence akin to the Curonian Spit off the north coast of Lithuania. Eventually planted with Corsican pines it could perhaps create a whole new holiday playground. Land and sea can work together for sport and recreation as well as the practicality of retaining, if not advancing our coastline.

In Conclusion ...

Achieving the right balance between the various pressures I have reviewed is no easy task. It calls for imagination, restraint, tolerance and a real sense of community.

We have, in all our different ways, a great responsibility to pass on the Saltmarsh Coast looking and being at least as beautiful and welcoming as when we found it. I have argued that our success in doing so will depend on respecting and honouring our traditions and history, and in learning from them; in using our native materials to provide coherence in our built environment; in demanding high quality design and planning, and in a sense of boldness as well as propriety.

The worst of all worlds is mediocrity – when conservatism and 'keeping in keeping' are taken to such lengths that the true character of an area becomes swamped in pursuit of dreary uniformity. The people who designed Holkham or Binham Priory were nothing if not innovators – and it is the constant flow of well-designed but controlled innovation that will both preserve and update the character of a much loved area such as ours.

Being Here

Aspects of Life On the Saltmarsh Coast

Growing Up – *Glynis Anthony*

Somewhere to Live – *Cyril Southerland*

The Rest of the Time – *Sally Festing*

Think Global, Eat Local – *Galton Blakiston*

Glynis Anthony

Glynis Anthony grew up in Wells, attended Fakenham Grammar School and graduated with an honours degree in English from University College London in 1964. She has taught English in Colombia, the Dominican Republic and Japan and was for almost thirty years on the faculty of The Washington International School (USA) where she taught and managed the English programme of the International Baccalaureate.

She published her first book *Colombia Land of Tomorrow* in 1968 and as a mature student gained a Master's Degree in International Education from Oxford Brookes University. Now retired from teaching she remains an examiner for the International Baccalaureate and indulges her passion for travel on long international car rallies.

She enjoys playing tennis, sculling and cross-country skiing and most of all walking on the beach or through the pine-woods between Wells, Holkham and Overy. She still takes piano lessons and is also studying Italian. She lives mostly on the Chesapeake Bay in Maryland, USA but spends long periods of time in Wells at her home in The Granary.

She has been married to Ian Scott for forty-five years.

Growing Up on the Saltmarsh Coast

A Tale of Two Anthonys

Glynis Anthony

My Story

We met for the first time at Brown's in Cambridge. I'd invited her to lunch and asked how I'd know her from hundreds of other pretty, dark-haired students. "I always wear pink shoes," she said.

So, Glynis Anthony, who went to school in Wells and Fakenham in the 1940s and '50s met Rosemary Anthony (surprisingly no relation) who went to school in the same places half a century later. What I wanted to know from her was if growing up in North Norfolk in the 21st century was the same as in the mid 20th or if different, how different? What had changed and what had not?

We had already introduced ourselves and corresponded by e-mail so we felt rather like two friends picking up on a conversation where we'd left off. We seemed to have so much in common in spite of the fact that I was old enough to be her grandmother!

I'd felt a sense of kindred spirit when I read an article Rosemary wrote for the local Wells publication *The Quay* about a summer trip to Mexico as a volunteer in a community development project. There was the same sense of excitement and wonder that I'd experienced going out to Colombia as the young wife of a volunteer (looking for my own opportunities) almost fifty years earlier, an insatiable curiosity, enthusiasm and a willingness to learn.

The Wells I grew up in was very much a post-war society. 'The War' was still the focal point of people's lives. Any reference to time was phrased as "before the War", "during the War" or "since the War". Scores of men like my father came home from the war, already married, but with no homes of their own. Initially we lived with my maternal grandparents, but luckily Wells Urban District Council responded quickly to the situation, building scores of council houses so that by the late 1940s the Northfield Estate was full of young families with lots of children.

We played cricket on traffic–free streets, and after the Saturday matinee at the

97

Regal Cinema we came home to the building sites to replay the cowboys and Indians stories we'd just seen. We rode our bikes round town (I had my first – bright red – at the age of five) and often went down to the whelk houses at East End where smoke rising in preparation for boiling whelks signalled the incoming tide and the return of the fishing boats. We played on rotting hulks at the end of the creek and only went home when we had to. Our homes were small and the one coal fire was often hidden behind a rack of drying clothes; freedom and space were outside. We all walked to the flint-built Primary School on the Polka Road (now a field studies centre) where, in autumn the chestnut trees opposite were loaded with conkers. We kicked through rotting leaves and swung our champions into action.

I loved school. Most of the teachers were kind to me because I was keen to learn and loved to read. The best activity was a weekly BBC radio programme called 'Music and Movement' that we listened to in the 'Hall' a multipurpose room. The narrator encouraged us to react physically to the music, so we danced and swirled, swooped and soared, allowing ourselves to dream and our imaginations to run free. We played hopscotch and skipping rope games in the playground and didn't think beyond the day.

Wells was a great place during the summer holidays, although the beach was a long walk away and the bus that ran between the Quay and the beach cost money, which was in short supply among working class families with children, not to mention that mothers always seemed to be busy. So we didn't go as often as we'd have liked. But on some Sundays we found a fisherman down at the beach who, for a shilling or two, would row us across the channel to the East Hills and collect us when the tide turned. That was our own desert island.

As children we had no idea of comparing where we lived with anywhere else, or of considering whether we were rich or poor. A few children lived in detached houses elsewhere in town that their parents actually owned, but their world was little different from ours. Our knowledge of the outside world was limited to a few books and the fantasy of the cinema. The main entertainment for everyone was the radio. My parents didn't have a gramophone (radiogram!) till I was a teenager and no TV until after I left home.

As we reached the top class of the primary school we became aware that a dramatic event was about to occur. But first came an unexpected one – the great flood. It was January 1953: a dark and stormy night! I was at a birthday party on Church Street, where my grandparents lived, when someone knocked on the door to warn us that the sea had come up over the Quay, had broken through the Beach Bank and come across the marshes, through the railway station and beyond the church. Luckily no-one in Wells was drowned but in the days that followed we watched the carcasses of dead cattle and sheep float up Freeman Street, where people had been rescued from their bedroom windows. And as a junior member of the RSPCA, I joined an attempt to catch the dogs and cats that had survived. It was an exciting, awesome event to many of us children; the only horror was in the newspapers where we saw pictures of devastated towns and villages elsewhere on the coasts on either side of the North Sea.

Then came the event we were anticipating: the Eleven Plus exam which would decide our fate. There were about thirty children in the class and it was expected about a third would pass. The teachers knew pretty well in advance who they would be. In the dinner line one day before the exam I was chattering away as usual when a teacher commented to me "that's not the kind of behavior to take to the grammar school".

I duly passed and life changed. The grammar school was ten miles away in Fakenham. The school buildings stood, secluded by trees, on a rise at the entrance to the town. To me it was a shining palace on a hill, the most exciting place in the world. I could hardly believe my good fortune. There were worries about how the required uniform would be paid for – the maroon blazer with gold trim and the felt hat. Luckily my mother, a skilled dressmaker, made my summer dresses.

We travelled to Fakenham by train – initially a steam one with separate compartments – where we first form girls would swing from the luggage racks showing our suspenders and lisle stockings and attracting the attention of the sixth form prefect in charge – which was our intention as we were all madly in love with him! A crowd of us would swarm down from the Northfield Estate to catch the morning train and then face the harsh north winds on our trek back in the evenings.

School filled my life: not only did I enjoy most of the subjects taught, but I threw myself enthusiastically into almost every activity offered. I played on the sports teams – hockey and tennis according to the season (only as an adult did I realize what a luxury it was to have six lawn tennis courts in front of the main building). On Saturdays we played against other schools travelling to places like Dereham, Norwich and North Walsham. I loved athletics too and for a while held a school long jump record. I sang in the choir and auditioned for every possible part in school plays, Viola, Cleopatra, and Maria in *West Side Story*, revelling in the special privileges for those involved, such as being allowed to come late to school on the day after an evening performance. Luckily the rail services between Fakenham and Wells were frequent so there was (nearly) always a train home!

The school was small and intimate – about 350 students. Yet we came from a huge swathe of North Norfolk. My friend Pippa lived in a hotel in Titchwell, Janet came from Foulsham, Leonie was from Holt, and Cecily from Melton Constable. The headmaster, Stanley Eckersley, a kindly if stern Mancunian, was a widower with no children and I think we were his family. We felt he cared about us. Once I was summoned to his study after winning a local beauty competition. I thought he was going to congratulate me, but on the contrary he expressed his disappointment that I would do something, so, well …. demeaning. He presided over every morning assembly and through the years his message came across strongly: as

much had been given to us in terms of educational opportunities, much was expected of us in return. With privilege came responsibility. We should consider how we could leave the world a better place than we found it. That ethos has remained as his legacy to me.

Because school gave me so much in terms of activities and companionship it wasn't until my later teenage years that I started thinking about what would come next and began consciously to think about where I lived. Yes, Wells was great in the summer, but for the rest of the year it seemed a dead end. There was nothing to do and nowhere to go. I joined whatever there was, a short lived brass band and occasional roles with Wells Dramatic Society (most memorably the lead in 'The Diary of Anne Frank'). But apart from the cinema there was nothing. The Methodist Church tried to run a Youth Club, but ping-pong was a limited attraction. There were no coffee bars or places for young people to meet their friends.

My dissatisfaction with where I lived grew. Neither my instincts, nor my parents or teachers had led me to see its positive aspects. I didn't like swimming, we didn't own a boat, I wasn't the least interested in birds and wild-life. I tried most of the holiday jobs available, working behind a shop counter, waitressing at The Crown and Holkham Victoria hotels, and even seasonal farm work. The summer I was sixteen I was governess to two children at Brancaster Hall. I used the money from that job to visit a pen pal in the Loire valley of France, a trip I made on my own by ferry and train.

As we headed into the sixth form we had to choose our A levels carefully as they would effectively decide our future options. My only careers advice at school came from a casual encounter with my maths teacher, a man with a bristle moustache and tobacco stained teeth. I told him I wanted to travel and see the world. "Well then you should take languages," he suggested. So I did.

More than half my girl friends left school at 16 after taking their 'O' levels. Most went to work in banks. It was a way to earn money for make-up and clothes and have a bit of fun and independence before getting married. It didn't appeal to me and since I loved school I wanted to stay there as long as possible. I had only the vaguest idea of what a university was: like school but with more freedom to choose your subjects and organize your own life? It sounded good to me!

My father, who was an insurance agent travelling around the villages, got lots of questions and advice from his customers. "When's that gal a yours gorner leave school and start helpen you?" Or "What was the point a all that education? She'll only git married!" Luckily my parents, who had left school at fourteen and fifteen, were happy about my staying on at school and proud that I would be the first person in the family to go to university – to University College London, to be precise.

Girls have to get married. I had two objectives in going to college: earn a degree and find a husband. Luckily I managed both.

Rosemary's Story

I told Rosemary my story. How had hers differed?

Like me she walked to the Primary School, which had by then moved up to the old Secondary School at the other end of the Polka Road (it was the 'new' secondary when my mother went there!). She didn't find the work particularly challenging, and was always quick to finish.

Like me she tried dance classes in Wells, like me she became a Brownie, and then a Guide (there were no Guides when I was young). We found we had both played the cello, but I gave it up because carrying it a mile between the grammar school and Fakenham train station became too onerous. Rosemary became an accomplished player and joined the Norfolk Youth Orchestra.

Once in High School – still in Wells, at the Alderman Peel – she found she loved the sciences as well as maths, especially doing experiments. In fact all school subjects were enjoyable – with the exception of PE. Teachers were now encouraging students to think about the future and what kind of life they envisaged for themselves. It seemed as if as soon as you entered high school they were trying to put you on a track. Rosemary hadn't a clue what she wanted to do, but they wanted answers, so she pretended an interest in beauty therapy, hoping that would keep them off her back! In general, teachers were positive and helpful, encouraging students not to mess around and to choose to do something they would enjoy.

One speaker at 'Presentation Day' advised the students at Alderman Peel to "go away" because they could always "come back again". "Go off, see the world and the North Norfolk Coast will still be here when you're ready to return," he said.

I think we agree that this was and is a great place to be young. The 'outstanding natural beauty' of the area, the sea, the beaches, the marshes, creeks and the wide open countryside is a physical delight. There is also the security of growing up in a small community where everyone knows everyone else, where you can walk to school – even High School – and know all the teachers and students. It gives children a very firm anchor in life, a strong sense of identity, a place they are from, that they belong to. Compare it to any city suburb where there is no community, schools are big and supermarkets impersonal. You can say you *grew up* there, but not that you *come from* there – as you do from North Norfolk.

But on the downside you do not have the range of activities you find in larger towns or cities. The daughter of a friend, just going off to university, told me that her parents had to drive her to Norwich on Saturdays to take part in a drama programme, and to King's Lynn for music lessons. A current student at Alderman Peel told me that her parents have to drive her to Cromer to take dance classes. Rosemary would have liked to join a cello ensemble, but that was in Norwich and it was just too much time and hassle.

Then there are the social issues. No places to meet. No cinema (recently one reopened in Fakenham). Drinking vodka on Wells Quay doesn't appeal to many teens other than those who just want to get drunk. One boy who came to Wells at the age of six from a city was shocked to find no shops (or at least what he thought of as shops). Teenagers who come to Alderman Peel High School from the villages complain it's even worse there, not a single shop, often not even a pub, and no transport but parents' cars. Of course they do have TV and computers which my generation did not, but these are very anti-social activities.

On the other hand a Fakenham College student told me there's a good social scene locally, lots of live music, (he plays guitar), kite boarding, wind surfing, sailing and cycle riding. You just have to make a little effort.

Rosemary found that her academic interests tended to isolate her from the rest of her peers who often just wanted to 'mess about' and not take life too seriously. She missed the challenges that would have come from a more competitive class. She wasn't sure how the idea of Cambridge lodged in her brain and made it her first choice for university and says it was almost luck that she chose to take Physics at 'A' level – a vital decision for her future career in Engineering – and perhaps the result of having an inspirational and encouraging teacher. She looked at brochures and leaflets and considered quite trivial factors in her choice. But Cambridge made her an offer of three 'A's at 'A' level (and yet another 'AS'-level) which she achieved, allowing her to study Chemical Engineering at Girton College.

There's some irony here. By the time Rosemary applied to Cambridge all colleges were co-ed and open to her, whereas when I applied there were only two for women. Yet she had to make three 'A's at 'A' level, an achievement far beyond my three fairly mediocre grades that UCL accepted in 1960. Like me she was the first in her family to stay on at school beyond 16 and then continue to university. In her year at Fakenham Sixth Form College she and another student went on to Cambridge; two in one year compares with only two during my seven years at Fakenham.

Of course we came from opposite ends of the academic spectrum: my interests were in the more traditionally female subjects – languages and history; maths and sciences had been considered more masculine choices. In my first year at UCL, I knew a Welsh girl called Mari who was the only girl in first year engineering. She dropped out at the end of the year. Not because she failed her exams but because she couldn't stand the chauvinistic attitude in her department. From a poster at Fakenham College Rosemary learned about a 'Year in Industry' as a gap year training programme which took her up to Aberdeen and although she did mostly administrative and research work she did spend two weeks offshore and benefitted enormously from the whole experience. At Cambridge there was a general generic engineering course to begin with, in which about 25% of the students were women. After a year Rosemary switched to Chemical Engineering where almost 50% were female.

Then and Now

It would seem that educational and career opportunities are vastly greater for children from North Norfolk than in my day as is the amount of information and encouragement. Yet a few months ago a columnist in the EDP claimed that it was harder for a working class child to go to university now than it was in the days of the grammar schools. Of course this is impossible to prove. There is no way to make such comparisons, there are too many differentials and one good reason is that there are virtually no local records from fifty years ago.

No-one denies that the previous system of an Eleven Plus exam leading to a grammar or secondary modern school was elitist (although it still exists in certain parts of the country) and that a comprehensive high school is much more 'democratic' in giving every child a chance to develop at his or her own pace. I had no idea, as a teenager, what a short history the Norfolk grammar school would have; that in little more than a decade after I left Fakenham Grammar School, it would cease to exist. It disappeared almost without a trace. The county archives have no records of it. Its 'log book' was not deposited there. Its scholastic results are lost. Yet this was a school that served the county from Titchwell to Weybourne and as far south as North Elmham and Rougham.

There is a publication called 'Fakenham Grammar School 1923 -73' (though for almost half that time it was a fee-paying secondary school with a few scholarships, not a grammar school) which lists teachers, heads and governors, administrative and domestic staff. It also has photos of some sports teams and school plays and a whole page devoted to speech day guests of honour. But there is no reference at all to academic results – no listing of county scholarship recipients – only a footnote to a scrap of poetry from an old school magazine noting that the writer – Helen Howes – went to Cambridge University sometime around 1930 and gained a first class degree in English.

Sadly, while the Norfolk Education Committee has its files on record they deal with the trivia of approving curtains for a staff room, or tools for groundsmen. They are more concerned with which local dignitaries served as school governors than with how many students went on to university. The only indication of that is in very rough statistics of Norfolk County Council Scholarships that appeared in 'Education in Norfolk, 1950-1960' a pamphlet publication. From a school population that rose from 46,000 to 55,000 over the decade the scholarships awarded jumped from 143 to 469 per year. What a contrast with the present where every school publishes its profile and lists individual school achievement statistics compared to regional and national scores, puts exam results on line and shows exactly how many students have gone on to Higher Education, further training or apprenticeships or entered employment (or not).

When the Education Act of 1946 set up the grammar/secondary modern schools system there was no national directive as to what percentage of children should go to the grammar schools. This was left up to local authorities and it varied dramatically. In Wales and the South West roughly a third passed the 11+ while in Nottinghamshire it was only 22% and in rural Norfolk Dr. Lincoln Ralphs, then director of education, stated in 1951 that the county was "aiming at 15%".

University education was another issue. In the early sixties only 4% of the population attended university; the great majority of them had been to public/independent schools and three-quarters of them were boys. If it was difficult for a working class child to go to university, it was so much harder for a girl. University College London had the best ratio of women to men in the country (9:11), but there were some lecturers, not just in the engineering department, who thought women should not be there at all. One was my first year English tutor, a well known misogynist who thought he could humiliate girls into quitting – and in my case, almost succeeded.

Now students have a vast array of subjects and combinations offered in the sixth form: environmental studies, psychology, sociology, film studies and food technology, things we never dreamed of, and an enormous variety of university courses as well as institutions to attend. It's almost overwhelming and obviously students, especially in remote and rural areas, need help and guidance.

But some factors haven't changed. It's shocking that British teens can still leave school legally at 16. No other developed society considers that an appropriate age to quit education or an appropriate preparation for life in the 21st century, an era when 'life time learning' is a focal point. Local schools have certainly improved dramatically in their ability to help children make the best decisions possible for their own futures. In 2008 only two students leaving the Alderman Peel High School did not go on to further education – and they had jobs to go to.

But how far have local conditions changed? In my day Wells was a working class town full of families. Then the tenants on the Northfield Estate were men who worked on farms, at the Leicester Lime Kilns, were fishermen or did other kinds of manual labour. The boys who left Wells Secondary Modern School were still able to find unskilled – though not well paid – jobs within the community. That is no longer the case. There are few work opportunities in North Norfolk. The biggest employer is the Holkham Estate. The schools, hotels, restaurants, pubs and tourism offer some employment, though some of it is seasonal, yet many of the wait staff at local hotels and pubs are not locals but students from elsewhere – often from outside the UK. It's unfortunate that many children who would like to stay in the area cannot do so because there are no suitable jobs – and even if they find one, they discover that the price of housing is way beyond local income levels.

As long as I can remember local residents have been hoping that 'industry'

would come to Wells and provide employment. 'Attracting industry' was a local council theme. But even having a designated 'industrial site' in the town has not achieved the longed-for job opportunities. Indeed the area, officially, and for a long time, has been one of 'deprivation'. According to recent data more than a third of the adult population of North Norfolk's Priory Ward had no qualifications of any kind – higher than for Norfolk as a whole and considerably higher than for England as a whole. Long term unemployment was also higher. This background makes it extremely hard for schools to achieve good results in terms of national statistics. The current head and the staff of the Alderman Peel High School have made spectacular progress in terms of value added but a large proportion of students at Fakenham Sixth Form College fail to complete a two year course.

There has long been a local attitude of insularity, of people lacking curiosity about other places. It causes local people to accept what they have: "that'll do", "thass good enough" are common phrases. (I know "that'll do" has served me too often.) Many teachers try to encourage their students to aim higher and to look further afield. One Head told me that, through various trips, visits and summer programmes, he tries to encourage his students to look beyond the A148 –even beyond the UK. There is life out there; it is not another planet.

Looking back at the children who have gone on to university, teachers have noted that most of them come from the few professional families in the area, where the parents themselves have degrees or other higher qualifications. Many others still hope to stay around in spite of the lack of employment opportunities and think of Norwich or Kings Lynn as "going away" for further education.

A couple of recent graduates of Alderman Peel, one already at university and another about to go, told me that "if you have ambition or any sense of adventure" you have to go away. It would be nice if at some point they could return, but it's unlikely. One girl, who loves to sail and really appreciates all that the area has to offer thinks she may have found a compromise in training for hotel management. She enjoys travelling and has made many trips to Europe, some on her own, but she always wants to drive past Wells Quay when she returns – just to see the state of the tide!

She also commented that many of her friends from Fakenham College said how lucky she was to live in Wells because she had 'the beach'. She suggests that most local youngsters don't see further than a small stretch of Wells Beach as the most desirable attraction of living in the area and complains that all they do with it is lie on it! How many of them ever go across to the East Hills or walk across the marshes, hike the coastal trails or sail from Wells to Brancaster or Blakeney, she asked? "Very few" she added.

Obviously those students who actively and willingly seek to leave the area are a minority. It is always easier to stay where you are, and wherever you live, picturesque or not, home is home and the tie of family and friends is a very strong one.

Some might call it inertia or as one retired teacher put it "there's a lack of 'oomph' here", no "get up and go", but for others it is a positive decision.

Future Story?

As for the future? Whatever changes future governments may make to the educational system it is unlikely that the make-up of the area's population will feature a higher proportion of school age children. That being so the idea of an all age school – primary through high school – will become more rational as the number of local children continues to fall and the proportion of retirees in the population continues to rise. One obvious drawback – from the point of view of children and parents – is that they will somehow have to cope with longer journeys to school and transport could well be a major issue. Housing for teachers is another problem if the property market in North Norfolk remains as strong as it is now.

This is how the future looked until very recently. Since then the proposals, plans and contracts for off-shore wind farms, their construction and maintenance have created the possibility of different scenarios. The question now is whether the growth of the wind farm industry and activities associated with or spawned by it will mean that more workers with families will move into the area, adding to the school age population. Is this the 'industry' the area has always been seeking? Will it mean more jobs for local school leavers through trainee programmes or apprenticeships? Will it increase the need for other kinds of jobs and services leading to a revitalization of the local economy?

Probably, in the end, it won't make that much difference. The companies involved in the wind farm business have a track record of making little or no investment in local communities, of bringing in skilled temporary workers, not families, and of pulling out of areas as quickly as they moved in. And if they do 'industrialize' the area around the port of Wells, will this put off holidaymakers, tourists, weekenders and retirees, who thought they were looking at an area of "outstanding natural beauty" and find they are looking at and listening to dredgers instead of sail boats and facing mountains of mud instead of miles of golden sands, while that glistening horizon where sky melts into sea has become a forest of whirling turbines. All this could ultimately have a negative impact on opportunities for local children.

Radical changes may well come about as the global village replaces the local village, but the Saltmarsh Coast will remain – altered in some ways no doubt –and local people will remain, "stuck in the mud" or "steadfast", whichever way you look at it, and schools will still be encouraging their students to imagine and aspire. It was a pretty good place to be a child once upon a time....

Cyril Southerland

Cyril Southerland was born in Brancaster Staithe in the house where he lives today. His father and grandfather, who owned the house before him, were both fishermen and Cyril has been fishing for fish, crabs and lobsters from Brancaster Harbour and laying and harvesting mussels and oysters in its creeks for 45 years. He was Chairman of the Brancaster Staithe Fishermen's Society for many years, was instrumental in obtaining funding for and managing the construction of a new fishermen's quay in the harbour and continues to play a very active role in the Society.

He has been Chairman of the Brancaster Staithe Parish Council and, with others, led a very successful drive, in cooperation with the Hastoe Housing Association, to build affordable housing for local people without which many of them would have been unable to live in the coastal villages. He has also been very active in protecting and promoting local interests. He believes the growth of second and holiday home ownership and the area's growing popularity with retirees has created a sustainable new economy and that local people and incomers are mutually dependent. He is optimistic about the future.

Somewhere to Live

Cyril Southerland

I was born at the end of the Second World War and grew up in living conditions that were more or less the same at the end of the 1940s as they had been in the 1930s. Brancaster Staithe relied mostly on fishing and farming. On the farming side the two local farms had a number of houses which housed most of the workers while fishermen tended to be more independent and owned their own properties – bought when fishing was good. Usually these houses had extra ground and sheds to store their fishing equipment.

In the village there were several rows of cottages. Each of these rows tended to be owned by one person who had bought the whole row for probably between £50-£100 per cottage. They were generally let to local people who either worked in agriculture or fishing. This was before the time of the holiday/second home owner so there was no great demand for houses. Nor when they were sold were the prices high. Very often the owners of these rows were just glad that perhaps a newly married couple would come forward to rent a property.

We must also remember that in the late 1950s a lot of the housing in North Norfolk villages was very primitive with no running water or drains. Water was drawn from a deep well in the ground which probably served four properties. There were no fitted kitchens, only sculleries – small rooms where all the washing took place. The toilet would be a small building away from the house which had to be emptied by digging a hole in the garden about once a week.

Although electricity was available from the 1930s the only plugs for lights were downstairs and most people were used to using candles and Tilley lamps so there was no great hurry to put extra lights in. Families had only ever known cooking on coal ranges and even their weekly washes, usually on a Monday, were done in cast iron coppers generally situated in a kitchen or outhouse heated by a coal fire that had been started using wooden sticks. Before the dustmen started calling in the village, the copper fire was also a wonderful way of disposing of household waste, be it an old pair of shoes, clothes, paper or cardboard. The 10 gallon copper had to be filled with water that had to be hand carried to it in buckets from a well anything up to 50 yards from the house. In the early 1950s mains water came through to the villages but the village sewage system was not connected to the main pumping station until the early 1970s.

Back then the villages had no holiday industry such as we know it today. Up to the Second World War most visitors were people who had moved away from the villages either for work or due to marriage who would come once a year to stay with their families. Just after the war one or two caravan sites opened up with approximately eighteen caravans on each site. People would come to them for odd weekends but always for their two-week holidays in July or August, after which the caravans would be closed up for the winter.

Up until the mid 1950s the harbour was mainly occupied by local fishing boats. They fished for whelks, mainly in the summer, but also cultivated mussels and cockles from areas known as lays in the channels and creeks of the harbour. In the early 1930s a sailing club was formed. To begin with this consisted of a few working boats that were sailed by fishermen. Later, people who lived within a few miles radius of the village established a fleet of sailing boats called 12 Square Metre Sharpies and then, with the coming of the caravans, came recreational boating in small sailing boats and on larger boats that were moored in the harbour.

The mid 1950s saw the start of a big change in the life of the village mainly due to the facts that the village school changed from teaching five to fifteen year olds to teaching five to eleven year olds and a new secondary school was built at Hunstanton. All the local village schools fed in to the new secondary school. Before that there had still been the Eleven Plus system which, for years, had given the more gifted village children a grammar school education and at the end of grammar school many young people moved away from the villages to further their careers. However for most of the 11 to 15 year olds the opening of the secondary modern school opened up a whole new world where they met and socialized with children from all the other villages in the catchment area.

With the larger school there were many more opportunities to learn such skills as woodwork, metalwork and gardening for the boys and domestic science and needlework for the girls. This began to steer young people towards job opportunities when they left school. Through leaving the village by bus each day and mixing with other children, their outlooks on life took on new meanings. Finding out how other communities lived and even just talking about their football or cricket teams took children away from their tightly knit communities as they saw other angles on life. It was a time to look at all the further education options that were being made available. By the end of the 1950s village life was changing and would never be the same again.

Changes in the housing situation took a dramatic turn in the early 1960s when a nine acre field in the village was turned over to housing. First, a local farmer who owned the land donated an area on which to build nine dwellings for the elderly people of the parish. A Housing Society was formed which still continues over forty years later and would be a role model for any village. A few plots of land from the field were sold individually. Then a developer started to build several houses at a time and that was when several of the families that had caravans on

110

the three static caravan holiday sites saw the chance to buy bricks and mortar for their long term goals of retiring from town to village at a later date.

That was also when more and more people were discovering the Norfolk Coast and found what seemed to them property bargains. But those property bargains were way out of the reach of local people whose wages did not match those of the towns and their industries. Young people who went on to further education were moving away from the villages and also leaving their parents, who were by then perhaps middle aged, to continue to enjoy village life. What happened in a lot of cases was that the young people moved away, found partners and settled down to bring up families perhaps coming back to the village for holidays or to visit their parents and families. But what happened in some cases was that when the parents of children who had settled away from the village died, the easiest thing for the children to do was to sell their parents' homes. As house prices increased around the coast this may have helped them to pay off their own mortgages. But this trend also reduced the number of houses available for local people.

One of the ways in which local people kept their homes in villages was by acquiring Council houses built by the local Council and rented out at affordable rents. Most villages had a Council estate and certain criteria were laid down by the Council to enable local people to live and work in the community. General opinion supports the view that although the policy of allowing tenants to buy the houses they rented benefitted the new owners it also meant that many Council houses were no longer available for local people to rent.

The 1970s saw a big change in the coastal villages. People who had come in the pioneering days of caravans, progressing perhaps to holiday houses, were now at an age to retire and wanted to switch from the busy world of towns and cities to quiet lives in the country. Over the years there have been many tales of new residents who ask where all the street lights are or moan that a tractor woke them up at 6.00 a.m. coming through the street. Neighbours would often receive complaints because their cockerels had been crowing at dawn. Some people would not accept that a countryman's home was also the place where he ran his business – be it a fisherman with fishing gear in his yard or perhaps a builder's yard surrounding a builder's house.

This often caused friction in the early days because, for generations, the true Norfolk people had lived side by side with a true understanding of each others' way of life. It would be unfair to tar everyone with the same brush because over time, and with tolerance from both sides, things settled down and what we have found in most of the villages is that after settling in and finding new friends a lot of these people have wanted to become part of the community. They become involved with the various organizations such as the church, the Women's Institute, the camera club or one of the numerous other activities that take place over the course of the year.

This was also a changing time in the workplace. Farming was becoming more

motorized with the result that many men left the land. Very often a farm employing 20 men could manage with just four or five. This resulted in a lot of people travelling out of their villages daily to work on industrial estates on the edges of towns.

The 1980s and 90s really brought the beginning of the circumstances we have today. It was a time when work suddenly became more available locally as a number of new job opportunities opened up. Owners of holiday homes needed to keep their gardens tidy because the last thing they wanted to do when they came to the village was to spend all weekend cutting grass or pruning roses. And the enterprising local chap would purchase a van or a trailer and a grass cutter and he was in business, perhaps agreeing to maintain the grounds of a house for a set fee for the year. And people who moved in to the villages often needed work doing such as building repairs or decorating and this work also created job opportunities.

Fishing has changed dramatically over the last 20 years. Whereas before we would send most of our catch wholesale to inland markets, a big percentage now goes to local outlets created by the demand for local produce by people who have either moved here or are visiting the Norfolk coast and want a product that is local to the area. And the hotels and restaurants that serve this produce also need large numbers of staff. The way I see it tourism has been good for us. The way we used to work – selling our fish to wholesalers – was not ideal for us but we now have enough local demand we can sell almost everything we catch in the area. Sometimes we sell to Coles, the wholesaler from Lowestoft, but mostly we sell direct. We all work separately and we don't poach each other's buyers and it works because there's enough local demand to keep us all busy. The other reason it works is that what we used to call the holiday trade is now a year round trade. People come here all year round and a lot of people who had holiday homes have retired here so they're here all the time which means our trade is steady. And this has created jobs for many local people... which brings us back to the housing situation.

By the 1980s with most of the Council houses in the District having been bought by their tenants, it was becoming increasingly difficult for local people or anyone who wanted to live and work in this area to obtain affordable housing. And that situation led to the beginnings of local housing societies. In Brancaster Staithe the Hastoe Housing Association (a national organization that operates throughout Southern England) approached a local farmer for land on which to build new housing subject to Section 1.06 of the planning code that allows land outside village 'envelopes' to be used for housing if it provides affordable homes for local people.

The first development of six houses, which consisted of two or three bedroom homes, was such a success that a few years later in the neighbouring village of Brancaster a larger estate of 12 houses was built and quickly occupied and it has been very rewarding to see so many children from the estate attending the various playgroups and schools in the area. To meet further demand for accommodation Hastoe built four more one-bedroom flats at Brancaster, all of which are occupied, and I understand Hastoe is now looking at another site at Brancaster Staithe because demand for affordable housing remains strong and the new development would balance the supply of housing between Brancaster and Brancaster Staithe. These schemes have provided housing for local people. Most of them are in regular jobs. Some are young people fishing in one of the seven boats that now work out of Brancaster. Some are self employed. Some are working at Brancaster Golf Club on the greens or in the clubhouse. Some are working in pubs (thirty-two of them at The White Horse alone). The people who come here want local fish and vegetables and fruit so local businesses provide them.

And that's just an example of how many jobs have been created by the new opportunities that have come from the growth of the holiday trade and second homes in these villages. When Hastoe first came here they needed support from local people. They told us that in some places they got a lot of resistance from local people who didn't want things to change. And there had been some of that in Brancaster back in the 70s when a new estate called Branodunum was built and outsiders moved in and said they didn't want locals. But Brancaster Staithe is a cohesive community. It hangs together. And local people and outsiders have always mixed well, perhaps because we always made the newcomers welcome. So when Hastoe was interested in building affordable housing here we all – locals and incomers – welcomed it because everybody sees the needs of other people and not just their own.

And you can see how this community is still growing because everyone who wants to can find a place here and can find somewhere to live. Brancaster School is expanding. There used to be twenty pupils there. Now there are sixty! And that's because younger people have come here from other places or young people who were born here and have come back have started new businesses. Locals can only stay here if there is work and there is work, largely because incomers have come here. Some of the new people work on computers. That work can be done here as well as anywhere else and it means their families can have a high quality of life they can make a decent living too. Some of them also found they can live here and work somewhere else, in King's Lynn or Norwich, and commute to work and have all the benefits of living here with their families.

What does all this mean for the future of local people and what has changed compared to years ago? I think the paramount issue must be the employment situation. People are still leaving the village in search of careers which means moving away and severing their ties with their communities. But some people whose families have always lived in these coastal communities and were maybe thinking of leaving have changed their minds. They thought about what a wonderful place this is and as new jobs became available they began to feel it was much more worthwhile to bring up a family in this environment with all that it has to offer than to struggle with the hustle and bustle of city life.

In the last fifty years village life has seen many changes. I am very optimistic that with the support for affordable housing moving forward at such a pace, an increasing range of available work and the high quality of life we have here there is no reason why instead of dying villages they can become even stronger local communities.

Sally Festing

Sally Festing is variously a poet, biographer, radio playwright, reviewer, journalist, art, social and garden historian. She was born in Cambridge and lifelong connections with East Anglia have fostered a deep interest in the links between man, art and landscape. She lives in Manningtree and Burnham Overy Staithe, which she has known since 1947. For many summers her family inhabited a bright green railway carriage with an outside pump and for many more, a wooden, single-storey village School House. In these early years she danced round the Maypole with local children.

Skipping boundaries between art and science, she has written academic Garden History articles, profiles for the *New Scientist*, and a decade's worth of pieces for the two *Times Educational Supplements* (mostly in the Arts pages). In 1977 her first book, *Fishermen,* came out with David & Charles. Five books followed, of which two art biographies went into Penguin Paperback. A third revised, enlarged and much-illustrated edition of *The Story of Lavender* came out for Easter 2009 with a chapter on Norfolk Lavender. The book lists c. 30 UK lavender farms and takes the story of cultivation world-wide.

Sally has contributed widely to poetry magazines, chaired Leicester Poetry Society, read at the Wells Poetry-by-the-Sea, and had three radio plays based on poem sequences on Radio 4. She runs a Poetry Society Stanza in Manningtree, and the second of two slim books of poetry (*Salaams*) is published by Happenstance Press, 2009.

The Rest of the Time

Sally Festing

"I visited gardens even during the notorious wet summer of 08. It was pouring with rain and I thoroughly enjoyed it. There were thistles as tall as me in the herbaceous border. The owner said 'I have to leave them for the goldfinches'."

Sue Everett, Brancaster

"If I get a moment, I paint the Norfolk skies. They're gorgeous and they're free."

Rosemary de Whalley

"Eline chose the site. We love the wild view over the marshes, and she said when we retire, you must play golf. That's why we're here."

Dicky Gilbert Scott, Burnham Norton

"This is the area to show people interesting things."

Ian Burrows, naturalist, Sculthorpe

What do people do when they're not working? I soon began to think there are as many answers as there are people, and rather as E.H. Gombrich affirmed in his classic art history (there's no such thing as art, only artists), I posit that it's the do-ers who substantialize spare time. Only to people, after all, does time have relevance. That said, much of what we do on this somewhat arbitrarily defined coastal stretch is what others do the length and breadth of Britain: tinker with computers, follow FaceBook, watch television, play Bingo, eat out; and outside, there's sport: lots of it. Three young men building our garden wall, all Saltmarsh dwellers, play football and ride motorbikes in their limited leisure: the job has more local flavour than the hobbies.

There are fuzzy boundaries; dog walking, for instance, can be largely perfunctory. Here it's different judging from the endless parade of canines celebrating foot paths and sea walls. A woman was yelling at a seal-like Labrador hotly pursuing dab chicks on the drainage cutting beside Overy Bank. The sun had disappeared; the cold set in. "They'll break the ice if necessary", she said proudly. Duty, relaxation and a resonance with landscape are entwined. It's not so often dog walkers are on their mobile phones.

Falling in love with the area is something I can date to the engagement between my bare young feet and the dried hexagons on Overy's Cockle path, as if I had been in touch with the centre of the earth. A very physical rapport multiplied by the strong arms of the estuary, and its tapestry of samphire, pinks and sea lavender; the muscular sloosh of mud with its scattered congregations of birds. Larks rising to high and light-dispensing summer skies. Sunsets. The chill surprise of bathing. The wind coming at me, swearing across virtually hedgeless furrows, salt marsh and sand dune. Physical discomfort can be a bond that works on us subliminally. There is something brash and cathartic about the wind. Used to it, I wear wooly vests, keep my hair short. Maybe it takes a certain kind of person to respond to its rawness. We get more involved with the landscape and this becomes fundamental to our sense of identity. It happens with people moving in entirely separate spheres of interest. Among those with whom I've spoken, some were born here; others, exposed during childhood, settled when they could. Like Andy Turners' youthful sailing in a lug sail boat at Burnham Overy, Ian Burrow's early lust for North Norfolk birds brewed in him for fifty years before place asserted its claims. While several of the women married into the Saltmarsh, contributing in what they might easily have found a restricting ambience.

Brought up on the marshes, wildfowler Mark Frary said, "You get exercise and fresh air; it's putting your wits against nature." It's as though the place occupies him, so that he's always had a sense of vocation. When he's earning a living he goes crabbing or with the lifeboat out to sea. Edward Allen learned to sail in front of the Blakeney Hotel when he was eight. When his parents built his lovely farmhouse, he was still in a pram. Like the varied obsessions I encountered, Lord Buxton's with birds began at the impressionable age of seven or eight. Brought up mainly near Epping Forest, he took family holidays in North Norfolk. Half a century later, he realized that most of the cattleyard at Stiffkey's Old Hall Farm could be swept away to re-mould a landscape expressly for birds. Ian Burrows had less precedent to follow yet one of his first memories is of reading to the class at a village primary school from a book on the features of Widgeon. A bird-watching club's termly outings took him from Northamptonshire to Cley and, in the end, birds offered scope for a hobby and profession so closely knit it's difficult to say where one starts and the other ends.

My protagonists were not selected at random; to some extent, all have been leaders or initiators. The first need of a community is somewhere to meet. With this in mind, several, teamed with supportive partners, strove to save or adapt buildings for the purpose. Angela Dugdale's decision to run operas for children found its nucleus in an eighteenth century flint grain barn just outside our designated area (Kelling) and Henrietta Faire ran an arts programme in a theatre extension she and Tom designed in their centrally placed village home. Others, filling offices in sport, music, arts clubs and the Church, running tours for prospective country-lovers, or laying out a pioneering bird sanctuary, have affected ways in which many, in turn, spend time.

Carla Phillips's allegiance to the Saltmarsh began so long ago, it's easy to forget that she met Bernard in Paris and, basically, she's a New Yorker. Homing in on Wells by way of Norton and Overy, the couple finally discovered where they wanted to be. "Twenty years behind the times," reckoned the male contingent of a couple tucking into Monday lunch at The Jockey. Is Wells in a time warp? The town won an extended battle against a supermarket. It doesn't have a MacDonalds or rows of Fast Food outlets. Even its Amusement Arcades are fairly traditional. There's an excellent butcher, and an independent newsagent. Like Burnham Market's bookshops, Cley's working pottery and the good pubs in variety throughout the Saltmarsh, this is highly relevant in a country that's lost nearly 30,000 independent food, beverage and tobacco retailers over the past decade; fifty specialist shops closed every week between 1995 and 2004 and the number of second-hand book shops halved in three years this century. An astonishing number of retired academics decide to live in Wells, and the town's resistance to mainstream trends has to be part of the attraction. "Bernard ordered books from Johns Hopkins University, and one from the University of Virginia. The library took it in their stride."

Thanks to the secondary school there's a cross section of ages, and a bigger proportion of indigenous people than the villages despite the high number of retirees. A thriving shopping street, twelve fishing boats that bark in and out on the tide and its business as a port, have kept the town alive. Unlike a string of neighboring harbours, Wells never silted up and prospects of an offshore wind farm bring moves to dredge for access to larger boats. We live in an unequal society and this is reinforced in the villages where lack of jobs and housing work against the resident working class. Wells by comparison is large enough for a healthy diversity; the most obvious reason for the relative inclusiveness on which Carla focuses. "The little port dates right back to when there were several manors, not just one, so there was a certain division of loyalties. The house we live in was probably owned by a wool merchant. There's this underlay of mercantile, fishing and commerce which keeps working its way through. People settled for the benefits of a resident population, not merely boats or farming."

Seventy-odd clubs include one of the many Men's Discussion Groups instituted throughout the country in the 20s by the BBC: Wells is the only one left and this must say something about the town's stability and self-containment. Naturally, there are clubs for every sport, allotments, an RLNI Lifeboat, Maritime Museum, an active Historical Society, Theatre, Cinema and various activities set round the old Maltings and Granary. As the Harbour Room in Blakeney's British Legion Centre has become the social heart of the Glaven Valley's five parishes, Wells' Maltings hosts its poetry festival.

Typical fare include the WI, Probus, and Lions who raise money for local causes. There's an Art Club with members ranging from amateur to professional, a Guy Fawks Day Committee who take turns to monitor the bonfire that's been lit for successively for 100 years and a Carnival Committee who run a popular week-long gallimaufry of events. Faith in the parliamentary representative, Liberal MP Norman Lamb, appears to foster an integrated spirit. "Pressure groups gather to a cause even when they don't agree about all sorts of other things." Burnham Market, too, has its Probus, Round Table, an active Phoenix Women's group and a B.M. Women's Luncheon Group with a waiting list. On the first Monday of the month, participants (70+) turn up smartly dressed. If not perhaps as hooked on the arts as their Wells equivalent; gamely, they take cruises and coach trips that simultaneously bond and widen horizons. But like the Horticultural Society and slightly posher Gardening Club, the women's groups reflect an institutionalized social inequality.

Involvement in the social and religious fabric of a community entails a huge, sometimes selfless effort. "Wells has been a very ecumenical town with its different sects and retired vicars and priests," Carla said. There's an Anglican Church and bell ringers, a popular Methodist Church, an Evangelical Congregational Church that opens for services from time to time, a Catholic Church, and a long established Quaker Meeting that draws from afar. Falling congregations (a universal situation) are to some extent compensated by what ex-teacher, Kate Clodd, described as very proactive branch of Churches Together whose ecumenism is expressed right through the year, liaising between the churches and schools, the Fairtrade Town group, Bereavement, Carnival, and sports bodies. A good crowd join the traditional silent Easter walk down Staithe Street with a wooden cross, and at Christmas, schools are involved in the design and production of a card that goes to every house in town. Plans are afoot to hold Taize evenings "offering time to stand back reflectively and prayerfully".

Everywhere, communities benefit from retired people with skills and the readiness to impart them; those who've been involved with education being prime movers. It can't be altogether chance that my selection included Andy Taylor, an educational administrator; Peter Russell, lecturer at Leicester University and Warden of Hall, Angela Dugdale who was Director of Music at Greshams, and Jim Woodhouse, ex Headmaster of Lancing College and previously of Rugby. Among various bids to welcome children to Church are those started when Jim and Sarah Woodhouse moved into her aunt's old house near her first home at Cley Mill. Sarah was soon writing and arranging the services for Wiveton's St Mary's that now reach a climax twice a year. On Easter morning, with the skilled support of flautist, Wyatt Earp, leading slightly Pied Piper style, a church-full of mixed ages enact the Resurrection in a miniature garden with a leafage of branches held up from pews and nave. The next challenge is to draw in teenagers. "This might work if we held the service in the evening, on a week day, with pizzas to follow, but we haven't quite got the tonnage or the energy yet."

The relevance of Church to its congregation was also a catalyst for Angela Dugdale. As Henrietta Faire has played the organ in Burnham Overy's tiny bell-towered St Clements, so has Angela often played in Salthouse's airy hilltop All Saints. It was during one such service she noticed that no one attended from the village; the building was, as it were, aloof. Four challenging years later, after embarking on a wholly unexpected journey, she was ordained a Priest. Pertinently, Jim Woodhouse enlarges on Angela's contribution, "An enormous amount of fund-raising takes place of a very sociable and often artistic kind, often as it happens, tied in with music. Angela not only runs a Consort Choir with members from the local area but raises an orchestra from a very talented group of young instrumentalists whom she once taught. As she enriches our musical life from the east, so does Gresham's from the south." Angela didn't start with Norfolk connections. Keith Dugdale did, and successive moves in Kelling village brought them the unroofed barn that has become a multipurpose amenity. Opera productions starting in the barn with Benjamin Britten's *The Little Sweep* (in 1983) led to a series of ambitious productions.

Even the quality of its charity relates back to the Saltmarsh as somewhere people choose to live. Tom and Henrietta Faire knew they wanted Overy as a home, but not to be deprived of urban culture. To create it, they converted the old post office with its string of garden outhouses into an imaginative versatile space where

121

the drawing room doubled as a stage, and the dining room as an auditorium seating up to thirty-six. ("The rostrum folds down on hydraulic rams. The drawing room floor comes up with lots of gurgling oil through pipes, and we winch the seats out into the auditorium.") For ten years The Balcony ran to packed houses. People would travel up to fifty miles, mostly to art films, but to jazz and classical concerts, the occasional play and one ballet. To cover costs, each film had to run for two nights, a big commitment on top of full-time jobs and family. One of the perks of enterprise is the support it rallies. Like Angela, Henrietta inspires a strong sense of loyalty, and many artists and directors with Norfolk bases extended their goodwill.

Some sow the seeds; others are drawn into cultivation. Country dancing, or Carpet Bowls are both good integrators. With matches involving 100 villages and competitors from all over Norfolk, a retiree might be talked into chairing the Norfolk Association for Carpet Bowls. Embroidery would be a more sedate, if equally engrossing pastime for, say, a pebble-covered one-time school. Between times, the competent entrepreneur could help introduce computers at local primary schools, become involved in the Norfolk Coastal Project (monitoring mobile phone masts, footpaths etc in an AONB), and Vice Chair the local WEA or commodore the Sailing Club. He or she might become Treasurer of a Harbour Trust, Clerk and Chair the Parish Council, run the Village fete, or edit the Parish Newsletter. This done, the retiree, a trifle worn perhaps, could initiate support for a local Community Hospital. Peter and Chris Russell had enjoyed holidays at The Moorings before they settled in Overy Staithe, since when the village has been the beneficiary.

The regret they most often mentioned is failure to attract the wary indiginous working community. Henrietta's Arts, and Tennis Club haven't either, and few local people living in Overy sail. Some do from Burnham Market but Carol Coutanche at the Boathouse, doesn't see it as a village 'thing'. It's a mistake to generalize and Andy Turner, Secretary of the sailing club, celebrates the great exception. "Peter Beck's been Secretary and Treasurer basically for the last 40 years, while Melba held the social side together. Peter built eight OKs, one each winter, in the late 60s and early 70s. That's why Overy is a centre." The local community spend a lot of their time tending houses and gardens for property-owning summer visitors. Allotments make a refuge, there are their own gardens, and some play sports. Photographs of rugby teams in the Village Hall suggest there used to be a good club in Overy though today's younger generation have to trek to Fakenham to play. Bowls is booming, and this says something about the population because bowls is an older people's game, one moreover that seems almost to dictate the life of Helen and Don Scoles. At Thornham they play indoors in winter, out in summer, mostly during the day.

I'm wary of pigeonholing 'incomers' and 'locals', knowing how we allow definitions to take hold of what constitutes progress and judge everyone and ourselves by them. At the same time, it feels almost a duty to point out that when the size of a group drops below a certain level, members can feel threatened and defensive. This affects their behaviour which polarizes the whole community. With more and more houses on the Saltmarsh bought as second-homes, there's the danger of a small place turning in August into an almost homogeneous Public School holiday camp. Even caravan sites have become gentrified. If we want mixed communities in which everyone feels valued, affordable housing schemes would seem to be half the answer; the other half being to provide jobs.

Like golf and shooting, sailing brings in money; what's important is that it's fed back into the community. And sailing clubs are booming; Overy's OSSC with 300 members, Blakeney's club with 200. Potential secretaries, however, are always scarce, that's why Andy Turner agreed to man the post before he moved to Overy. It was a strain, to which the club has reacted by liaising with the Parent/Teacher Association at Burnham Market Primary School. With luck the effort will recruit future enthusiasts. Andy's mother spent her last fifteen years in two railway carriages in Gong Lane, since when, he's competed in world sailing championships. "That keeps you on your toes. My best was 29 out of 80 which doesn't seem very high but I was pleased." Regatta time is the apogee of the sailing year. Some come on holiday and bring their boat. All sport, in Andy's view, has got more competitive. "That's how we win gold medals." Yet racing at Overy isn't "really serious"; there's not enough water and the tide goes out too quickly. Serious sailors enter the North West Norfolk Week. "It's total concentration; and quite a slog having to move your boat from place to place for 7 am starts each morning on the tide."

Fifty years ago there was a preliminary sort of 'mucking about' in boats; we rowed. We knew the name of every boat in the harbour (some of them are still around), and where the oyster catchers laid their eggs. Knew all the ins and outs of the creeks, our hands and knees intimate with muddy banks and sea purslane. Enviously I and my siblings gazed at sailors until the year we hired an old 12 foot lug sailing boat from Billy Haines. Jill wouldn't go unless wind and tide were with her. Often we pulled her home from The Island and she was no light weight. Sharpies always seemed to us the aristocrats, and Overy, Brancaster and Wells are the only places in the UK where they race. Nearly all were built pre-war of half-inch mahogany planks; unsurprisingly, owners are said to spend twice the time on maintenance they do sailing.

Each harbour has its specialties. Besides an inflatable rescue boat, Blakeney have their dory. Instead of Sharpies, they boast most of the gaff-rigged Cockles. An eponymous club based at Morston race on good tides without any rules. "They just go," said Edward Allen, ex-Commodore of Blakeney's sailing club. Edward puts the club's main attraction down to Blakeney's being such a beautiful place to sail in. Other perks are the tiny pebble clubhouse with a reputation for hot chocolate and bacon sarnies, where he can sometimes be seen with his tool kit. There's free boat-parking in the Carnser and they're said to produce the most comprehensive Year-Book in North Norfolk. Families come from as far as Swaffham and London, while a sturdy founder member goes back to 1939; racers, straight sailors, and supporters who concrete slipways and mark buoys. Besides the Morston- and Blakeney Regattas, activities like wiggling through a very narrow creek to Morston, to make Cley Windmill for a picnic, a 'Little Safari rally', summer suppers and barbecues on the marsh are arranged by sailing clubs – generous support to what Andy thinks is the perfect sport, "You start as early as you like and finish when you're dead."

Much the same might be said about golf; equally buoyant and patently more resilient in Brancaster than in other parts of the UK where clubs are shedding a slightly stuffy image, reducing fees, and even (horror) advertising for new members. No such predicament ails the Royal West Norfolk Golf Club with its total

membership over 900, a five to ten-year queue for hopefuls, and dues which add up to several thousands in the first year. It's an image they wholly endorse. "We're very traditional. We haven't changed in many respects since we were founded in 1892. The club house has retained a Victorian feel, it's part of the atmosphere of the place. Junior members can join when they're twelve and become full members at twenty-five. It's a great family thing."

Dicky Gilbert Scott reinforced the family element. His father played passionately, joining Brancaster's Club before the First World War. He held a club at the age of four and duly became a junior member. Then came W.W.II followed by working life in London. After thirty years he resigned, rejoining before retirement because Eline knew he'd be happy consorting with midges in the surprising light. The old dedication and skill were still there. As a member of the Senior Golfers' Society for the UK, he has played against the equivalent in Canada and America.

"It's an internal game; there's only a ball to hit. If your opponent plays well, you

feel obliged to, but there's a bunker on the right that makes all the difference because it upsets your focus on playing the shot." The traits required, Dicky suggests, are patience, humility, focus and persistence. At my prompting he added discipline, important too, he allowed, for an architect. He comes from an illustrious line of architects whose credits include two knights, St Pancras Station, the Captain of the RWNGC, and the telephone box. "I enjoy competition and it took my mind off architectural problems. Brancaster has the most wonderful golf course, world renowned for its natural hazards. The sea's insurgency has altered the course but there are the views and the wind plays an enormous part."

While wind and views are inherent to the Saltmarsh, Holkham's 25,000 acres offer, more specifically, humanised scenery and the wilder periphery. For shooters, there's the lure of country, a spirit of camaraderie and skill in making a bull's eye of a moving target. As the place where 'driven shooting' started, the estate has a long-earned reputation to maintain. Two of ten keepers are Norfolk men and Head Keeper Nick Parker comes from Yorkshire. This doesn't explain what was to me unfamiliar lingo, codifying an equally unfamiliar life style. For some reason I've never felt the primal call of the man with his instinct and his gun.

For each keeper on his beat, vermin control constitutes a large part of the job. But in the season everything revolves round shooting days, when 'the guns' are Lord Leicester and Lord Coke's guests or groups of public contracted to shoot a pre-arranged number of birds (from seventy to 200) on what are known as Let Days. Whether they're duck coming to flight ponds, pheasants, English partridge, or wigeon, Nick sees his role as enhancing the sport. "We push pheasants into a woodland. Bring the woods in like a big fishing net. Round them up like sheep. We get them to an area where we've got control over them, then we flush them as they start to fly. As they take off they see the line of guns and they honour the guns and go up and up. So you're presenting high pheasants which are flying fast. Trickle them out in five's, ten's, you'll shoot a lot more." At the end of the season, Beaters are invited to join the shoot on what is called the Keeper's Day or Cock Shoot. "They like to keep the females for breeding," Mark Frary said. "If there's too many males about they fight and things go horribly wrong." Without regular beaters, Nick would be obliged to find up to twenty for every shoot. Fortunately, local wildfowlers are happy to serve. Mark goes beating in local syndicates for £25 a day, a pleasure he puts before the money.

Vice-Chairman of Wells and District Wildfowlers Club at twenty-seven, and already a member for fifteen years, he enlarged on a club founded in the 60s, with over 100 members. Every bit as esoteric and selective as Brancaster Golf Club, WDWC has always more applicants than it can accept despite a stipulation that members live within 15 miles of Wells. At first, the rigorous code that protects the responsibility of the arms-carrier sounds burdensome, but to the initiated, the rules are part of what binds. Blakeney has its equivalent, as do Brancaster and Overy combined, of which the latter requires that members are born in the villages with Common Rights. Once a member is approved, he or she (one or two women are enrolled) must be accompanied for a year. During this time they're not permitted to shoot, yet an accompanied youth can borrow a gun provided he has a certificate, which rather refutes the prohibition.

Wildfowling on the foreshore runs five and a half months from 1st September, and restrictions on the 'bag limit' tend to be higher than those self-imposed. Intense observation is the chief appeal, though Mark wouldn't wildfowl if he didn't enjoy eating the catch. Spending anything between two and ten hours a week on the hunt, he plucks a bird in twenty minutes and stocks his deep freeze during the season. Nature, of course, is unpredictable. "I had a friend on a guest permit; I'd been watching the geese for three days before that. They'd been out feeding on the moon the night before and sat on the beach. We got there at first light, that's about a mile and a half across the marshes. We waited and the geese didn't fly. It was getting to the stage we was going to have to start getting back. Not so much from cold; we'd got jackets and gear on, but we was getting hungry. And they finally flew about ten o'clock in the morning. We'd been sitting out there four hours waiting."

Democratic and environmentally aware, bird watching has to top the list for pleasured leisure on a strip of land with arguably the greatest concentration of semi and professional watchers in the country, all feasting on the available panoply of sky and bird and deep horizons. This can hardly be more important at a time when cuckoos are down to the half their number in a few years, and Britain has destroyed half its wetlands since the Second World War. Ian Burrows is on the Council of the Norfolk Ornithologist's Association which has several reserves in Norfolk. Come April Fool's Day, he spotted his first Blackcap of the year. It was a drake, and sat in a willow, token of a vibrant world.

Until 1996, he was lecturing in micro-biology in Papua New Guinea, spending every spare minute watching Birds of Paradise. Then, suddenly, he and Jane were in North Norfolk where he led bird-watching trips, supporting the community by lodging participants in local pubs, hotels and B&Bs. Jane runs her own tours as well as assisting Ian run Sicklebill Safaris. Until the recession made the cost prohibitive, he took parties annually back to the Tropics. Concentrating now on home territory, he has stretched his repertoire to cover the whole gamut of wild life and local history. One side effect of his expanding expertise is the attractive *Food from the Wild* (2005).

There are different ways of being alive to the world we inhabit; seeing it with detachment, first-hand, rather than as a mediated thing. That this brings its own rewards is patently true at Stiffkey's Old Hall Farm. The Stiffkey River drove its way through the chalk ridge leaving quite steep bluffs, and this created what has become an undulating 500 acre estate unlike flattish neighbouring countryside.

Grass meadows at the coastal boundary are very low-lying; here, Highland Cattle, and elsewhere black ewes add an exotic aura. The former suit because they don't get foot rot, the late Lord Buxton observed. Flooding the lively trout stream into vast areas of wetland has all happened over the last 25 years, making a habitat with which he was both delighted and proud. "I never thought I'd see it all as I planned. These are the best views in Norfolk. Where the land was dry as a bone, we've made a whole lot of fens and reed beds." Twin passions, natural history and conservation, occupied much of Buxton's adult life, during which he served on almost every Government body involved. It was after all this, he decided to remodel and replant on an 18th century scale. From the dining room of the farmhouse, the view of lawn, lake and trees retreats like a stage set; everything new except the old trees on the skyline.

The public sees the conservation site from footpaths and rights of way, further access is not anticipated; after all, it isn't for people but for the huge quantity of wildfowl and waders who live in comparative luxury. On the first really fine day of the year, we toured grounds of which he knows every inch. A part-time keeper from the Holkham Estate looking for rats reminded me that for the two wardens, keepers and pest controllers, the job is unending. "We have a certain amount of anxiety with black backed gulls and herons, but foxes we're pretty hot on." Otters and badgers occur; sixty-three avocets were fledged last year without loss. "That's top of the pops for North Norfolk!" Critical of the dredging conducted by River Authorities, Buxton believed there are times when nature is best looking after itself. Having performed its small miracle for the birds, the Stiffkey Stream runs sweet and unmolested.

It is the second day of March, 12.45 pm and 'Hoste Arms (17th Century Coaching Inn)' emblazons a swinging sign at the south end of Burnham Market. Sun blinds the front windows, outside which trestle tables advertise what has become a thriving stop-off for the traveller. Couples, mostly, drink red wine, beer, lager; their accents betray a far-flung clientele. The pity is that we're hemmed in by cars, and still more cars, before the eye reaches pink and yellow painted houses on the far side of the wide thoroughfare.

At the other end of the village, The Jockey compensates in intimacy for a less fashionable corner. Alan Miller moved from Loughton three years ago and renamed one of several Lord Nelsons. To celebrate a Newmarket racehorse he jointly-owned, photographs of the gelding, and comely shirts in racing colours decorate the pub's interiors. What does Alan do when he's not working or sleeping? Reads *The Racing Post*. Customers relax over a pub-lunch. After fifty-six years in Hanover, the couple from Brancaster via Hilgay feel that the Saltmarsh is a big improvement. The female component thinks the environs are pretty; and so is she. Unsurprisingly perhaps, the male ranks his favourite pastime as being 'in bed with

128

the wife'.

    I wouldn't have got that at the Hoste Arms.

Galton Blakiston

In 1979, a 17-year-old high school student set up a stall at Rye market selling home-made cakes, biscuits and preserves. The range became 'Galton's Goodies' and was so successful that Galton Blakiston abandoned plans to be a professional cricketer and decided to become a chef. Within two months he was working at the renowned Miller Howe in the Lake District where he became Head Chef and later worked in New York, Canada, South Africa and London.

In 1991 Galton and his wife Tracey set about finding a location for a friendly and informal country hotel with a relaxed ambience and excellent food. Morston Hall is now one of Britain's leading country hotels. In 1992 it was named Newcomer of the Year by the AA and was joint winner of the award for Country Hotel of the year (with Chewton Glen). Today, with a CATEY award, a Michelin 'star' (since 1998), Three AA Red Stars and Three AA Rosettes, Morston Hall is recognised as a great hotel and restaurant.

Galton was 2001 UK Craft Guild of Chefs 'Chef of the Year', and East Anglian Chef of the Year in 2002 and 2003. An Aladdin's Cave of Blakeney lobsters, Cromer crabs, Morston mussels, Cley Smokehouse kippers, Didlington honey, Norfolk apples and local wild mushrooms allows Galton to work with the best seasonal produce for his renowned no-choice, four-course dinners and hearty breakfasts.

Galton shares his passion for Norfolk produce and the skills of Morston Hall's kitchen in cookery demonstrations and appears on Anglia Television and the BBC promoting seasonal and Norfolk produce. There is, he says "No finer area" than Norfolk, although he admits to bias. He is the author of *Morston Hall Cooking*, *A Return to Real Cooking* and *Summertime*.

Think Global, Eat Local

Galton Blakiston

A Backwater of Brilliance

The salt marshes are a really fragile ecosystem... on the extremities of our islands in far-flung places such as West Wales or Cornwall. Quite often, they are in locations that are not readily accessible by car or even on foot, giving them a feel of wilderness: the last bastion before the sea.

This sense of remoteness, of North Norfolk hanging off the edge of East Anglia – which is in itself out on a limb from much of Britain – has had a huge impact on local food. What's grown and harvested, where it's sold and, most importantly, the lack of proximity to large cities allows North Norfolk to forge its own food identity, relying largely on what's grown within a few miles of our door, and focusing on seasonality and freshness long before they became buzzwords. A backwater of brilliance, you could call it.

What truly makes local food distinctive is that we have no option but to play by the seasons... some things only come in at certain times of the year, so you are limited to what's available. This is a real joy, though, as you anticipate the seasons much more and relish the foods while they are in season, rather than eating insipid versions imported from the other side of the world all year round.

Eating foods in season means you're eating them at their best – they haven't been forced, so freshness and flavour are as good as they can be. Seasonal foods should also be cheaper and won't have clocked up the air miles. You can get so many things locally – even sweetcorn, which needs to be eaten as soon as possible after picking, so we can capitalise on that rather than have it sitting on a supermarket shelf for days with the sugar turning to starch. Anything freshly harvested has to be miles better than something that's been sitting on a shelf for days, wilting. We also used to get peas that had been caught in the machine which meant they were unsuitable for processing – they were real petits pois and full of that just-picked sweetness that is really unbeatable.

Perhaps born of necessity over the centuries to feed the local population, but also due to the very fertile soil and favourable climate, Norfolk is an important farming county. There's an awful lot of seasonal produce grown here for the rest of the country so it's a great garden to pick from...it makes total sense to make full use of it.

From Your Own Backyard

It drives me mad when people put on the menu where the beef is from...surely it should be a given that the meat you're cooking with is from your own backyard? We've made a point of doing it for 17 years and you just do it. I make a precedent of nowadays only serving fish that was caught in the North Sea as there's no need for me to look any further. It's a great seasonal thing to do. Anything you can do to cut down on mileage and transportation has to be good and guarantees that food is as fresh as it possibly can be.

I also think the open landscapes and wild nature of the area mean that you really experience the seasons and notice them, so this then triggers the thoughts of different foods. Although summer is the best time of the year for food, there's also something quite special about early autumn when the shooting season is on and there's lots of game about. Reliance on seasons also makes for more creative cooking – in the winter months when there's less to choose from you have to come up with other ways to cook and present the ingredients so that the menus remain exciting and different.

The relative remoteness of East Anglia and especially North Norfolk is a double-edge sword. There are no motorways infiltrating and criss-crossing this area of the country. As a result, it takes quite a while to get anywhere but the up side is that it's still something of a wilderness with a strong sense of what makes it different from other parts of Britain – the last outpost of the way things used to be done. So we rely on local shops, local producers, local farmers just as we've always done, which means that eating seasonally and buying locally is second nature. The nearest supermarket is in Fakenham, 8 miles away, so while people may do a big shop there once a month, it's more practical and enjoyable to rely on the local shops for fresh food. This keeps the local shops going and means they make a decent living – and makes people more aware of where the food has come from.

Local Producers, Local Shops

If there was a supermarket down the road, it would threaten the livelihoods of these local shops and small artisan producers and dilute the dependence we have on local produce. At the moment local producers can supply local shops which keeps everything fresher and really local. It's all about taste. Madam housewife wants things beautifully presented but why would you want to taste a foreign strawberry jetted in from another continent – a British strawberry is a beautiful thing and has so much more flavour. As I get older I get more and more adamant in my views about home-grown foods. I'm not interested in produce from Chile or Kenya when you compare it with what we have round here.

There is probably nothing you can buy here that you can't get in London, although very local versions of foods such as Morston mussels (which, not surprisingly, I view as the best in the country!) would be hard to find as they're snapped up by locals! But availability is not the issue – the issue is all about freshness. There are times of year when things are quite scarce – it's a fanciful idea to be able to put out a menu of local food 12 months a year and still have the variety.

Local gems are things like honey... I'm concerned about the decline of honey bees and am keen to get my own hive so I've got honey to cook with. Not having enough bees to pollinate the crops is quite alarming. Having a hive is another thing I can do in my own little way – and we've got the perfect garden for them, full of bee-friendly flowers. Sea trout is another local speciality and very seasonal... you probably wouldn't get Norfolk sea trout in London, or grey mullet. Most of the fish that comes in to London is from Cornwall and Devon. We're not big enough so our local boats tend only to service the local area which again keeps that parochial feel.

Locally Unique

Some foods are, of course, unique to this area. In North Norfolk, the salt marshes are a rich source of samphire, rightly championed by chefs and food writers as one of the country's best indigenous ingredients. Yet promoting it could, ironically, threaten the very future of this marsh succulent, which is only available from June to August, by drawing people's attention to it and making it fashionable. Any

decline in stocks of samphire would have an environmental impact on the food chain, as it's an important foodstuff for wintering birds.

Celebrity chef Rick Stein recently found himself in hot water for singing the praises of samphire: the plant is protected by the Wildlife and Countryside Act 1981, which makes it illegal to gather it. Moreover, only those whose homes give on to the marshes are allowed to gather it and then only enough for a 'feed' for their family. Samphire could become a victim of its own success, its very existence jeopardised by finding favour with the foodies. But its saving grace could be the distance from the North Norfolk coast to gastronomic centres such as London as well as the fact that tidal currents put people off from trying to collect it.

Another thing that helps the 'eat local' philosophy is that Norfolk has a very dry microclimate. Farmers have had to diversify massively in the past 20 years since I've been here, to move with the times, but essentially the climate makes for wonderful soft fruit as well as things like blueberries which, in many parts of Britain, have to be imported.

Local strawberries are fantastic. We get ours from Wiveton Hall, where there are extensive pick-your-own fields in a very sunny spot overlooking the salt marshes to the sea. They provide us with strawberries, gooseberries, raspberries, blackcurrants and some vegetables. Their gooseberries are particularly good: almost wine-like purple in colour, they are left on the vine longer for a more intense flavour. It's being able to tap into such local expertise that allows you to find the very best ingredients for cooking. And as these lovely summer berries are seasonal we preserve them as jam for the winter months, another good way of extending availability.

We are a big county for growing potatoes. There is a new variety, Juliette, grown on the other side of Coltishall. It's a lovely, waxy potato perfect for salads. Almost on a monthly basis there's something new that someone brings in. Norfolk – especially this area near the coast – has always been a very good area for growing malting barley for beer, and there are small microbreweries sprouting up all over the county, which produce very good beer. There are plenty of wind farms around too, so the issue of heating polytunnels and generating power for use on farms is also forward-thinking.

Foraging and Experimenting

People are very progressive and the climate allows them to experiment. This could be a throwback to the time when it took three days to get to London, so we had to rely on what was available around us or we would have starved! We don't need to bother too much with bringing ingredients in as we have so much on our doorstep and I think that's a philosophy that's prevalent. You don't necessarily realise what's here unless you get out and about... wild fennel is everywhere as is sea kale.

The foraging thing is quite important and I think that in years to come people will be amazed we didn't do it more. You can of course use wild garlic and Alexanders. Eating local can be taken a step further if we know what's out there. We are moving on apace in our general knowledge of produce. Samphire is very seasonal but can be pickled, which is what people used to do to ensure a supply during the winter. Samphire is wonderful with new potatoes, peas, beans, sauteed...things that grow together locally often partner each other brilliantly, such as gooseberries or strawberries with elderflowers, blackberries and apples, mint and new potatoes, lobster and samphire.

It tends to be the smaller things that interest me, like quinces. In October someone with a quince tree in their garden will bring some in. You don't need that many quinces to make the most fantastic jelly. We also benefit from locals selling directly to us: there's nothing better than a bloke turning up at the kitchen door with a trailerload of fish saying, 'Do you want them or not?' Norfolk's also a great county for growing rapeseed and rapeseed oil is becoming really popular. I love it for cooking as it has a higher burning point than other oils and more omega essential fatty acids. Also, unlike olive oil, it doesn't have to be imported so is better from that point of view too.

As well as samphire, the salt marshes are where you'll find 'Stewkey Blues', a nickname given to the local cockles with dark blue shells found in the salt marshes a couple of miles along the coast at Stiffkey, locally known as Stewkey. The name Stiffkey actually means 'island of stumps' – a reference to the tree stumps that are found in the marsh. The village once boasted a harbour, now silted up, and this provides the perfect breeding ground for these lovely rich, meaty cockles. They're unique to this area but not widely found – you need to know someone who knows where they are. I love putting them on the menu, along with Morston mussels, as it introduces them to people who may not be aware of them already.

Threats and Protections

These foods are all wild but protected. The people who gather the mussels would claim that there's too much red tape and testing but in fact these foods could easily be overfarmed and this would affect future yields. Cod is very protected. My local fishmonger only ever goes for line-caught cod, or long-line cod, rather than net-caught, which is the way forward. In fact, newspaper reports this month have said that the number of cod in the North Sea mature enough to reproduce is now 40% higher on average than in 2000 [according to the International Council for the exploration of the Sea]. At the same time the number killed each year through fishing and other natural causes has decreased by almost 15% since the turn of the century. So it's a bit premature to talk about stock collapses and blame the fishermen for everything.

I don't know how much GM is produced in Norfolk. We're often seen as a backward county but I think it's a joy – time hasn't changed things too much. And the lack of supermarkets means that locals don't expect their carrots to be perfect – local produce should look misshapen! In the future, if there's more pressure on the agricultural system to produce more food, then they may have to switch to GM to ensure higher yields and less crop disease.

Local is Better

North Norfolk is seen as quite affluent and people are prepared to spend a bit more on a chicken, duck or whatever, but the difference in flavour is massive – if you buy a chicken at the farm shop I can guarantee the flavour will be so much better. All the local butchers make their own sausages too from local pork and natural casings, which are quite important. It's important to keep things simple and not mess about with them too much. We are very fortunate. When supermarkets came on the scene a few decades ago, just as the package holiday became popular, people were seduced by being able to buy exotic foreign produce, but I think things are coming full circle and now we're appreciating what we've got a lot more and rediscovering our own rich food heritage.

Norfolk sees a lot of incomers – people who retire here, or those who holiday in the area – who tend to be discerning about food as well as having money to spend on it. One of the things they love about North Norfolk is the wealth of locally produced meats, sausages, fruit, vegetables, fish, seafood and cheese. Binham Blue cheese is an example of this. When the woman who makes it first came to us we weren't that keen but she went away and refined it and now you can't find a deli in Norfolk that doesn't stock her wonderful blue-veined cheese.

As a chef, when I'm on televison or in my books I can wax lyrical about a local product, like Binham Blue, which helps spread the word so then people come to Norfolk looking for it. Some chefs keep their sources and 'finds' very close to their chest, but I can't see the point in doing that...it's great to champion brilliant things and introduce them to a wider audience. For me, the joy of discovering something truly special is in sharing it. Using locally produced foods can even extend to unlikely candidates such as a wonderful English rose wine, sourced from Chilford Hall vineyards in Cambridgeshire – another example of what our temperate local climate can bring forth.

Fish and seafood are major local ingredients. I insist on serving fish at its best, so see no point in buying imported exotic varieties when there are myriad native species on tap throughout the year – and it's crucial to support local fishermen when times are tough. They're finding it harder to make a living as there are quotas and restrictions on what they are catching and stocks have been dwindling – I

Winter Trees, Letheringsett. Michael Barnham

tend to side with the fishermen as they're the ones I see, talk to and sometimes socialise with and the authorities can make it tough for them. To make ends meet, they're diversifying, with sidelines like digging for lugworms.

Seasonal Thinking

When cooking and eating fish you are forced into a seasonal way of thinking as different fish come into their own at different times: skate, for example, is available all year round, but is definitely at its best in January, February and March, as are herring, codling and mussels. As the sea warms up, we go for lobsters, crab, plaice, turbot, halibut and wild sea bass. Cromer crab is brilliant: smaller and sweeter than the larger Cornish crab, it's truly wonderful in the summer months. Sea bass and mackerel are plentiful too.

Since we've been at Morston, Tracy and I have noticed enormous changes in the variety, volume and seasonality of the local catch. In the early 1990s, sea bass was only caught from May to September, then they would leave, presumably for warmer waters. These days, however, we still get decent-sized beach-caught bass – up to 10lb in weight – in January, although there are of course fewer than in the summer months. Cod caught at Weybourne, Salthouse or Cley invariably weighed in over 5lb, but stocks have diminished to the point where we rarely see a cod over 3lb in weight. Willie Weston, the lobster man, will tell you that last year was an extremely poor year for the crab, but no one is sure why. He says it's not through over-fishing but could be due to their habitat changing but this year things have recovered. Even the seals went away this year although a few are back now. No one knows why they went away – maybe their fish stocks disappeared.

There subtle changes are going on. Winters are generally milder and the seas are warming up a bit which has an effect on stock levels and seasonality. Sea trout are still very seasonal. Mackerel were extraordinary last year. I took our two sons down to Cley Beach and Sam, the younger one who's 8, put out his line with brightly coloured feathers. The line was still coming out from the reel and the whitebait were jumping on the beach in shoals to get away from the mackerel. We came back with 30 mackerel that day! I made a light tempura batter and filleted then cooked them...it's important to educate people – especially children – about the link between hunter-gathering and cooking. It reinforces that local connection. We're also extremely fortunate to be able to catch fish right on our doorstep then go home and cook it but that's exactly why people should value the local foods on offer as we're blessed with wonderful ingredients.

Lobster is a good example of a really local speciality. A huge number of lobsters are caught along our coast in the summer months, from Mundesley to Brancaster, with each village claiming theirs as the best, but the sad thing is that most of them are exported as people here think of them as being extremely expensive or don't want to have to prepare them. They aren't cheap but you can get two meals out of them, using the shells for a bisque or stock. Willie Weston catches several container loads a week, yet they're mainly exported to Spain, where you can see Norfolk lobster on sale for £50 each! Madness...so again, it's all about educating people and persuading them to appreciate what's on their doorstep. Also, in times of recession, profit margins could be cut on such foods to boost sales, although the fishermen do need to earn enough to survive, and selling lobster on to large conglomerates is one way of doing this.

It's tempting to think that pollution could play a part in environmental changes, but I don't think it's an issue as there aren't many boats going out. The estuaries have silted up massively in my lifetime and coastal erosion is another huge issue that could have a knock-on effect for the future of the salt marshes. Thinking about the future and the possible threat to certain fish species, people like me do have a duty to educate people and get them to try other fish that may be new to them.

In the past year or so we have been serving less familiar fish in the restaurant such as grey mullet, which is a beautiful fish – the skin is a bit tougher but flesh-wise it's very similar to a sea bass but probably half the price. I don't think their stocks are threatened at all. We also use pollack, dabs, buts and all those little flat fish. They're easy to cook. Herrings are another underrated fish, as are whiting which are plentiful. People tend to go for the familiar names but there are plenty of others in the sea.

We also need to cut down on wasting food, both at home and in the catering industry. This means that people should eat foods like offal. There's nothing like an ox heart cooked really well until tender, but many people are put off by having tried badly cooked versions. It takes skill to do it really well but it's worth it. In the old days, people knew how to cook all parts of an animal so there was very little waste, but these cheaper foods have fallen out of favour, which is a real shame. It's time to look back and rediscover them.

Willie Weston has a little shop in Blakeney and sells pate, quiches, crab tarts which also helps to use up some of the fish that might otherwise get thrown away. The crab man uses fish heads for his pots, so there's not a lot of waste there. I don't think much local food is wasted as it's tailored to supply and demand although it's difficult with fish as it has such a short shelf life. But it is vital that people try not to waste food or throw it away, but again – down to education – that they use food up in other ways as our grandmothers used to do. We can't go on blithely assuming that food supplies are infinite when the world's population is growing so quickly.

People and Food

Another issue for the future of food production locally will be the willingness of young people to work in the industry. I think the lack of money in the fishing industry is putting people off and there's a definite decline. Cromer used to be a big fishing town but now only a couple of boats go out. It's a worry – in 10 years' time when many of the older guys have retired, there needs to be a new generation coming through who are prepared to go out and fish the local seas otherwise our local ingredients will be threatened if we can't get them. The same goes for fruit pickers. At the moment many of the pickers are from Eastern Europe but if it's true that many of them are now returning, there's an issue there too. They are prepared to work hard and fruit has to be picked when it's ready so you do need a labour force on hand.

Having said that, there's a massive interest in food – I get children from the local private school asking if they can come and work in the kitchen. I suppose the exposure of cooking on TV has had a lot to do with this as it's seen as quite glamorous and there is some money to be made in it. When I first started it was almost a swear word to go into the catering industry – it was what you did if you flunked everything! To eat local people have to have the knowledge and skill to grow, harvest, distribute, sell and cook the foods...it's all well and good having lovely local meat and fish but it has to be prepared for sale or for the pot.

There are signs of growth, though: Holt supports three butchers, even though other businesses may be suffering. The local butcher plays a very important part throughout Norfolk. Hopefully, given that Norfolk is an agricultural county, young people will realise that there will always be work in these food-related areas so the issue of available workforce won't be such a problem.

We are so lucky to enjoy the benefits of being able to eat top-quality local ingredients, grown a few miles away. It's a privilege that mustn't be squandered or taken for granted yet, at the same time, the larger global issues need to be addressed to safeguard the future of this localised way of thinking – and eating.

The Way We See Things

How We View the World ... and Ourselves

Godfrey Sayers

In 1965 a contentious planning application to smother a vital piece of open village ground with houses prompted Godfrey Sayers to form the Blakeney Preservation Society. It succeeded in getting that application rejected and under his leadership successfully opposed other unsightly developments including an attempt to build houses on 'The Pastures'. He served on Blakeney Parish Council for 18 years, chaired the committee that carried out the first major dredging operations in Blakeney Channel since the 1800s and was instrumental in acquiring 'The Pastures' for the village by compulsory purchase. He was the Central Parishes Representative to the Norfolk Coast Project (now Partnership) for eight years; Chairman of the National Trust's Advisory Committee for its Blakeney Area properties; and Chairman of the North Norfolk Coast Advisory Committee for the Norfolk Coast Special Area of Conservation. He wrote the 'Longshore Economy' document that helped unlock a stalemate between English Nature (now Natural England) and local representatives.

He moved to Wiveton seventeen years ago and became a member of Wiveton Parish Council which he has chaired for the last ten years and is proud of the fact that Wiveton was the first Norfolk village to complete a Village Design Statement. He is currently a Wells Harbour Commissioner, chairs the Coastal Harbours Forum and is a member of the Client Steering Group for the Shoreline Management Plan for the North Norfolk Coast. He is also Chairman of the Blakeney Watch House Trust. In his spare time he paints in watercolour.

From the Inside Out

Godfrey Sayers

Comings and Goings

Activity along the jagged fault line that divides incomers and the indigenous people of North Norfolk varies considerably. There are stretches where friction between the two sides results in tremors of resentment and bad feeling. But there are other places where the fault line has all but disappeared, time and common sense have blurred differences, incomers have gradually absorbed the culture and acquired an understanding of local ways, and locals have become less parochial and possessive. Some of the most effective protectors of the local environment were once incomers and many locals now embrace the changes and benefits incomers can bring.

The way people living on the interface respond to it has a lot to do with their personal circumstances and values. Many locals have become rich on the backs of incomers, others have benefitted in a variety of ways from their being here. But many more – having seen their villages and way of life destroyed while feeling helpless to prevent it – feel disenfranchised.

If you asked the first group if they thought North Norfolk was now a better place to live I'm sure they would say yes. Ask the same question of the second group and they would say no. The odd thing is each group would be right because both statements are true. In a material sense this *is* a better place to live than it was. But much that was valuable has been lost in the exchange. The important (and difficult) question is: was it a fair bargain?

On the face of things it is hard to argue there is anything wrong with the new North Norfolk. Who can complain there are now so many fine shops in Holt; there are so many wonderful places to eat all along the coast; or that many a tumbledown cottage has been rebuilt to stand in character with its neighbours?

Those who cannot afford to shop, eat and live in them can. But the fishermen, builders, craftsmen and other suppliers of local products certainly cannot. There are winners and losers. But any analysis of the tectonics that created the fault line must accept that these aspects of well being, while vitally important, are only part of the story, because it is not just about material wealth; heritage and culture, social and physical are also damaged. And while some people have become winners with the new prosperity, all of us – because so much has been lost – have become losers.

From Where I Sit

From where I sit the threats and damage to local identity and character come from several sources. All have urban origins and all have past, present and future dimensions:

- The first set of changes – which largely concern damage done – are demographic, notably the influx of holiday home owners and the sustained shift that has seen local youngsters replaced by elderly incomers who (as a force rather than as individuals) are responsible for much of the erosion of local culture.

- The second set of changes has come from the smothering hand of central government concealed in the glove of unelected Quangos[26] known by acronyms such as NALC[27], SLCC[28], and NCAPTC[29] – that seem intent on putting what remains of local government in a straitjacket of regulations designed to neuter Parish and District Councillors and separate them from their intelligence, initiative and elected responsibilities.

- The third set of potential changes comprise totally invented and spurious housing targets defined by government and promoted by EEDA, that could create the equivalent of several small towns in Norfolk over the next couple of decades and will, if realised, metamorphose this county into Essex. A more immediate and – in terms of landscape destruction – greater threat is the potential impact of offshore windfarms.

- The fourth but not least threat comes from statutory protection to wildlife sites. In the last two decades Natural England, a mega Quango, has gained almost total control over landscape and land use on the Saltmarsh Coast. In the main, the land is managed by voluntary organisations like the National Trust, RPB and Norfolk Wildlife but Natural England lays down the management rules and implements the statutory designations that protect these sites. Its impact on the 'New Shoreline Management Plan' (SMP) is a current case in point. Reclaimed marshes that had been designated for realignment over predetermined timescales linked to anticipated sea level rise will, if Natural England has its way, not be considered for realignment until 'coastal processes make it unavoidable', by which time it will be too late. Natural England should be an equal partner in the SMP process but assumes the power

---

[26] Quango: Quasi Non-Governmental Organization or 'Quasi NGO'
[27] National Association of Local Councils
[28] Society of Local Council Clerks
[29] Norfolk Association of Local Councils

to move the goal posts whenever general interests conflict with their own. I would not normally have a problem with powerful authority doing its best to protect wildlife and wildlife habitats, but I do if an equal authority doing its best for people does not balance that power.

Enough is Enough

North Norfolk was granted Area of Outstanding Natural Beauty (AONB) status in time to save it from the tourist makeovers suffered by Cornwall, Cumbria and other once unspoiled parts of Britain. Much of our built and natural landscape was initially saved but a steady and subtle attrition of the physical environment has continued. That is bad enough but our social heritage has fared far worse. Although lost now, the tightly knit self-sustaining culture once common to many small coastal communities hung on longer here than in most other places, so more people remember it, and much resentment stems from the belief that incomers are personally responsible for its demise. This is understandable but not entirely fair; the loss of heritage isn't attributable to individuals or to deliberate plans, plots or designs; it is a consequence of evolutionary demographics and changes in national priorities.

The last fifty years have seen huge changes in the local population, one of the most striking being that large numbers of local children that have benefitted from improved educational opportunities have gone on to universities and significant careers elsewhere. As a result only a handful of the children of people I know live in Norfolk (few even live in Britain!) and I estimate that perhaps two-thirds of all indigenous children leave for better prospects.

Under normal circumstances that exodus would have dramatically reduced the population. But that has not happened because – in all but perfect step with the departure of the young – there has been an even larger influx of the old. The arrival of retirees in such large numbers has significantly altered local demography as they and second homers have created demand for housing that has driven prices almost completely out of local reach and shifted the allocation of resources from the young to the old.

Over the same fifty-year period the popularity of this coast as a holiday destination has increased to the point at which, in the summer months, the population doubles. Holiday lets (which absorb almost all rentable accommodation) and high house prices have created a very unattractive scenario for local youngsters with limited resources. It isn't anyone's fault. Retirees and weekenders have a perfect right to come here and did not do so with the intention of displacing anyone; this dramatic transition has more to do with evolution than deliberation.

That being the case (we can describe it is an influx rather than an invasion) why is there so much acrimony? Well, the driver has to be the loss of a time-honoured way of life and a very real feeling of dispossession. Finding yourself in a minority in your own place and having strangers celebrate and manipulate your environment and heritage without acknowledgement and at your expense is galling.

The major misunderstanding of many incomers is based on an urban/rural myth of an idealised countryside, a world entirely of the mind, a bespoke creation born of city daydreams, pieced together from imported ideas and images that bears little resemblance to true rural life or the real countryside. Country people are familiar with this idealized alternative from images of the countryside and rural life seen through the eyes of urban-based television programme makers. It's a tidy place, silent except for bird song, bathed in sea and wildflower scented air, a slaughterhouse-free place where verges are trimmed and the realities of what makes the countryside function do not exist.

All of us have the right to realise our dreams, but problems arise when fantasy collides with reality. The timeless stewardship of landscape and wildlife which has always been the responsibility of country people throws up all kinds of unpleasant realities that offend the dreamer's construct. Foxhunting we know about, but any kind of vermin control or attempt to balance the natural order is viewed as problematical – even for wildlife managers.

A Beatrix Potter, fluffy bunny kind of anthropomorphism is a big part of the urban rural myth. There is no understanding within it of how the natural countryside works. From this perspective it is a wild and natural environment, which of course it isn't. It is an entirely man-made creation that has to be managed at all times to remain in balance. Until that fact is grasped there can be no proper understanding of how it works.

So much rural heritage has been lost because it did not chime with the incomer's template. But rural heritage has also been lost because incomers thoughtlessly erased anything too subtle to register through a lens smeared with romantic urban Vaseline. In the last few decades many urban dreamers have found the wherewithal to realise their dreams in the bricks and mortar of a country retreat. And in places like Burnham Market the sheer numbers who have gravitated to the same place has compounded their impact. In such places they have begun to make the dream real by creating idealized but artificial environments and through glossy magazines have inflicted these fantasies on the rest of us.

Had those people arrived with the intention of integrating with the people they found here they would have been made very welcome. They have preferred instead to live out an irritating fantasy that infuriates locals and blinds them to seeing how wonderful this place is. By demoting local people to the status of 'walk-on extras' they also deny themselves any opportunity of learning from them. To see the place and not the people is not to see it at all because any community is the sum of those who live in it, maintain it, and whose forebears created it.

With the cream of local youngsters leaving for higher education and better prospects elsewhere, incomers tend to base their assessments on those who remain and often conclude that low local incomes are a result of low aspirations and deficient imagination, intelligence and motivation. Although they have decided to come here because of the quality of life, they fail to see that some youngsters have decided to stay for the same reason – or having done well elsewhere, come back well before retirement, precisely because they are willing to trade-off lower compensation for other satisfactions. Instead, they are apt to say things like *"These people should pull their fingers out and do as I did. Get up off their backsides and work, then they would be able to afford a house."*

Such outspoken incomers – usually those who deny their presence has created a problem – are mostly self-made, highly motivated people for whom it is understandably difficult to grasp such a simple concept as being content, indeed harmoniously happy, with a life bound by relatively unchanging circumstances. Maximizers all, most of them simply don't grasp the difference between maximizing and satisfying.

People making a perfectly reasonable living based on what the land or a particular patch of sea will support do not seem ambitious. Local fishermen catch more or less the same amount of fish and shellfish each year and cover rising costs by charging a little more for what they catch – aided in recent years by the many new restaurants that have sprung up in the area – rather than by trying to catch more. And the ambitious incomer might well say – told that in recent years incomer fishermen with bigger, faster boats have been going ever further out to sea to deploy unsustainable numbers of pots thereby damaging crab stocks – *"Tough luck: they should have been more aggressive!"*

A few moments ago I heard a restaurateur on the radio say: *"Our first restaurant went very well and in quite a short time we bought another, then with the profits from those we bought two more and in our enthusiasm we borrowed enough to acquire two more but then when the credit crunch began to bite things got difficult and now we have unfortunately gone bust."* Most locals would wonder why, when you have a very successful restaurant, you would rush out and buy another one and then four more? Why is it always more, more, more....? Over-reaching greed has caused much of the recent economic turmoil in the world. The irony is that it has taken near calamity to make world leaders grasp a reality that the people of this coast have always understood: that life is only sustainable if we live within our means.

Many incomers are also apt to say: *"This place is like everywhere else, it belongs to everyone who lives here"*. The idea seems irrefutable; how could anyone believe a place belongs to some people more than others? But inarguable as it may seem, I do believe that, and as a local am bound to explain why.

This is my home. Generations of my family have lived here. I am related to many of the remaining indigenous population. We are the living representatives of those who created the place and who, like ghosts in the machine, remain in its charm and character. I know this place as I know my own being, my association is visceral; this place is as much a part of me as I am of it, but this almost symbiotic attachment has an emotional cost, because almost as if I had built it I am powerfully motivated to protect it and for me personally there is a terrible sense of failure in having been unable to prevent so much of it from disappearing.

The following is an extract from a submission related to a small and unnecessarily contentious planning application recently sent to the North Norfolk District Council (NNDC), which illustrates the lack of incomers' understanding of rural life and the value of local knowledge:

Dear Sir,

I am a local person who has lived in the Cley area all my life and from that position of local knowledge I would like to support this application on two counts.

First, the principal purpose of the proposed annex is to serve as a retreat for the applicant (or any subsequent owners of the property) in the event of a tidal surge flooding the main house, thereby making it uninhabitable for a prolonged period.

I have witnessed three tidal surges in my life, those of 1953 and 1978 being the most severe. My home was flooded in 1953 and having lived through the aftermath I can assure the members of the Planning Sub-Committee this need is genuine. In fact I would go further and state that unless they have witnessed events of this kind for themselves they are probably not qualified to pass judgment on the validity of the applicant's claim. Salt water flooding brings far more serious and longer-term problems that fluvial flooding.

On November 9, 2007 a tidal surge raised the water in Cley Channel to the very top of the sea bank that protects the marshes that front this property. As good fortune would have it the surge peaked before high water thus avoiding the bank being over-topped. However, it was a close run thing; if the surge had peaked 30 minutes or an hour later the applicant's property would have been seriously flooded. If the widely accepted predictions for increased storminess and sea level rise associated with climate change are accepted by NNDC they have no option than to grant this application. Set against all the advice from the Environment Agency the applicant is demonstrating considerable wisdom in wanting to create a safe haven for herself.

My second point concerns good neighborliness. Even as a child I was made to understand its importance and it is an absolute prerequisite for harmony in small communities. Sadly I have seen very little of that during the contentious course of this application. The reason, I suspect, is that many of today's incomers have little experience or understanding of its value. So instead of overtures of friendship, patience, and goodwill, which can usually resolve these minor kinds of difficulty, we have had months of acrimony, hot air and hot tempers, creating wounds that will probably never heal, just because people have forgotten – if they ever knew – how to live together in harmony.

If pressed I believe most of the objectors to this application would admit that, on planning grounds alone, the justification for this unpleasant situation is pretty thin. This is a minor application that has been given undeserved prominence by the relentless pressure of a few vociferous neighbours and their many recruits. People who will never see this building and have no real interest in it other than as friends of the objectors, and who would otherwise behave very differently, have seen nothing wrong in gathering together to bring as much force as possible to bear on an elderly lady. This situation is disgraceful and should be ended forthwith. The NNDC has the opportunity and power to do that by granting this application.

Between the lines of this letter there is a glimpse of the way a lack of knowledge and understanding on the part of incomers can cause problems. But it also shows that through changes in the make-up of local authorities and the way they function, local people and their way of life can slip off the agenda. Most officers employed by the District, Borough and County Councils come from towns and cities; the majority of elected members, mostly retired incomers, also have urban backgrounds. Urban-minded governance of rural areas is responsible for many irritants (to those who have always lived here), ranging from the allocation of affordable housing to the urbanisation of neighbourhoods by pavements and streetlights.

The Hand in The Glove

The dead hand of divorced governance does not end there. As if urban-minded administrators and legislators were not enough we must also contend with the influence of central government on Parish Councils. A newly invented Quango the 'Standards Board' now dictates how we shall conduct ourselves as councillors, and insists on poorly thought out policing procedures that show an almost childishly naïve view of life in small communities (based I suspect on the belief that all parish councils are like the one featured in the 'Vicar of Dibley').

Government promises devolved power on specific conditions. Parish Councils as they stand are not considered fit for purpose and if they want this illusory power boost must jump through government-devised hoops, the ultimate hoop being 'Quality Parish Council Status'. That status, once achieved, will enable them to deploy speed guns, fine their neighbours £1000 if their dogs shit in the road and generally toe a tightly scripted line of local governance. And – this is the crux – they will only be considered fit to handle these powers if they can show they have eliminated every possible temptation to use their own intelligence or initiative. In other words, we can have new powers in exchange for our electoral mandate to act freely on behalf of our parishioners.

I have been a Parish Councillor at Blakeney and Wiveton for 30 years. I've enjoyed the role for the most part because the councils were assemblies where like-minded people combined their talents and abilities to a collective purpose in a relaxed atmosphere steered by common sense. And there have been many happy outcomes, from relatively large projects like dredging Blakeney New-Cut and acquiring the 'Pastures'[30], to preparing a Village Design Statement for Wiveton and work that led to a 2005 Environment Award for Wiveton Parish Council.

In recent years however the hand of government – through Parish Clerks guided by Quangos like NALC, SLCC and NCAPTC – has intervened. Parish Clerks have been persuaded their councils are unable to operate fairly and honestly by themselves and that they must become the principal managers of parish affairs. They return from conferences armed with ever more complex, bureaucratic and prescriptive guidelines that are not presented as guidelines but as legally binding rules resembling the tablets brought down from the mountain by Moses. It was hardly surprising that one local clerk felt able to call meetings without consulting the chairman and when challenged said, "I do not have to have anyone's permission to call meetings."

---

[30] A large open area in the centre of Blakeney

The new guidelines and instructions seem to assume Parish Councillors are dishonest, self-serving or just plain stupid and reflect a blurred and remote perception of how Parish Councils actually operate. They are an affront to intelligent, public-spirited people who care deeply for their communities and want to make them better. Insult aside, the ever tighter and more prescriptive guidelines that govern council procedures and councillors' behaviour are counter-productive because they restrict rather than enable councillors to achieve good results.

One local Parish Council in a genuine quest to be better adheres to the new guidelines as if its liberty were at stake. As a result it has been neutered. Its 'Standing Orders' have become so restrictive very little real discussion is possible and very little gets done. In contrast, Wiveton Parish Council's meetings are relaxed and informal, allowing us to cover the ground easily and if that ground is rough, the bumps that might otherwise throw us off course are softened by humour and goodwill. As a result we feel we execute the wishes of the parishioners who elected us to act on their behalf. And that is the crux of the matter: Parish Councillors are *elected*.

Our democracy functions by enabling those who are elected to serve with an effective degree of autonomy. If they fail to do that or abuse their positions they are not re-elected. That's how it works and that's how the electorate gets the councillors or Members of Parliament it deserves. We are not elected to dance to a tune composed by unelected third parties hiding behind acronyms and bureaucracy to negate autonomy and abuse the dedication of elected councillors and divert local government toward objectives favoured by themselves and central government. They are free to offer guidance but we are also free to heed or ignore that advice based on our local knowledge, common sense and the brains God gave us.

Meanwhile at Westminster

It is hard to estimate the likely effect of government-driven development on the Saltmarsh Coast. The most obvious is that if the government achieves its current housing targets for the east of England by expanding Norfolk towns and creating new eco-towns there will be a knock on impact which will put much more pressure on the coast and its facilities.

There is also a significant possibility that in their desperation to find acceptable sites for so many new houses, central government and local authorities may heave sighs of relief as the construction programme for windfarms off our coast gets underway. Why? Because the projected numbers of wind turbines off the Saltmarsh Coast is growing almost daily and the sand banks off this coast offer such a perfect location for them they could stretch rows deep from the Lincolnshire coast to Sheringham Shoal. As the pace of windfarm development accelerates demand for industrial facilities and housing for windfarm service workers in Wells could greatly increase. And local authorities could – as they have at Cambridge – find this a perfect hook on which to hang a few extra hundreds of houses and in so doing transform the character of the town.

Initially this expansion could be very good news for Wells and the surrounding area and Wells Harbour Commissioners are working hard toward this end. But it is a Pandora's Box and contrary to the old maxim, you *can* have too much of a good thing. At present, there three things that might help mitigate such development. First Wells Harbour is tidal and shallow, and although dredging will help in allowing vessels of modest draft to use the harbour – unless catamarans or hovercraft are used this is a serious limitation. But if hovercraft and catamarans were used, what then?

The new LDF (Local Development Framework) should protect against unsightly industrial development, although only in places where there was none previously. AONB status is supposed to offer protection but it has been watered down by so much socio-economic stuff over the years it no longer fulfils its original role. Reliance on any of these things could be a mistake; recently I have witnessed just how far the tentacles of central government have reached to overturn such obstacles to its overall aims. With the subtle mechanisms I have already described in

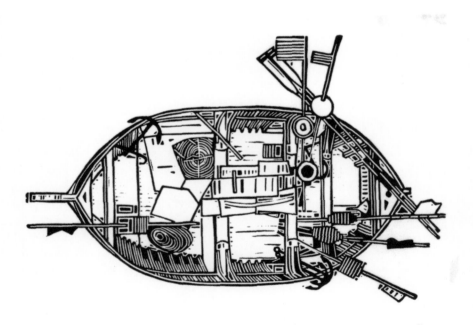

place to influence the democratic process locally, a little government tweaking is probably all that would be necessary to get the goal posts moved. At the time of writing my recommendation would be for Wells Town Council to shoulder some of the Harbour Commissioners' burden and become directly involved because the impending scale of change requires it.

The potential and opportunity for off-shore wind farm development along this coast is enormous, and it takes little imagination to visualise the extent to which it would be changed. It is probably the magnitude of such an obscene level of intrusion that has created a false sense of security. Many people I have met recently do not believe such a thing could happen here; but it can and it will. Off-shore wind-farms could prove very difficult to resist. They are outside planning boundaries which takes away the usual route for objection and in any case I believe this government quite capable of slapping an 'In the National Interest' order on them if opposition looked like slowing things down. The application for Sheringham Shoal has been given the go ahead, the fishermen have quite literally been brushed aside with wind farm craft steaming back and forth through their fishing grounds with no concern for what might be there. Sheringham Shoal is ten miles off and will only really be a visible feature on clear days and then although the turbines are immense it may not be that much of an intrusion, but it is only the first step.

Applications are in train for Docking Shoal and the Race Bank, Outer Dowsing and Triton Knoll all of which will be very visible from West Norfolk's beaches and quiet places. I walk out to Scolt Head as often as I can during the year. It's quite a walk to get there and a fair old jaunt to walk the length of the island, but it is worth the effort. As far removed from civilisation as anywhere in England, its vast emptiness and beauty make it special beyond anything I can describe; it never disappoints. The beach is almost always empty, as is the horizon, but soon, unless enough people oppose them, there will be gigantic turbines just a few miles offshore. Many more are planned between Brancaster and Wells and more to follow further out. The vast triangle of shallow ground off this part of the North Norfolk coast can accommodate many hundreds of them. They are huge in scale and their eye catching and irritating rotation is probably as effective a destroyer of visual tranquillity as it is possible to devise.

Every time I sail out of Blakeney Harbour I feel a pull, a desire to sail out over the northern horizon. I know if I think about it that I would eventually come to the Humber estuary and Goole or Immingham, but that empty horizon offers the opportunity to go somewhere wonderful. That is what horizons do, but it will disappear. This stretch of coast represents probably the last real lowland wilderness in England – maybe even mainland Britain – and if it falls to windfarms nowhere in northern Europe will be safe.

You will by now be in no doubt how much I love and treasure this place. I have lived here all my life and know it with an intimacy few can match. I have also been lucky enough to travel. Nowhere have I encountered anything to compare. But if these windfarms are built I will want to leave because my most precious reason for being here will have been destroyed.

Green vs. Green

I am an environmentalist. I have worked to protect wildlife all my adult life. I have served as Chair of a number of Advisory Committees and Steering Groups for the North Norfolk Coast and in those roles and others have always tried to maintain a balance between the interests of wildlife and people – which in most cases ought, but seldom seems to, mean the same thing.

Many conservationists appear to suffer from tunnel vision, not least the passerine incomers who descend on us in large numbers, block roads and paths and as quickly as they came, leave. During my years of conservation work it became increasingly clear that 'birders' ('twitchers' are not interested) had systematically penetrated English Nature (now Natural England) to protect and promote a narrow interest and had brought with them aggressive anti-fisherman, anti-bait digger, anti-people attitudes. There is no mistaking the unreasonable bias in Natural England's decisions where birds are concerned, sometimes even at the expense of other wildlife.

Natural England and other conservation Quangos have ensured that over the last few decades the North Norfolk coast has been smothered with wildlife designations, SACs[31], SPAs[32], SSSIs[33], Ramsar Sites[34] plus the all-powerful European Habitats Directive. These designations have seriously restricted what people may do in or near these areas. They have made once routine activities more complicated or in some cases impossible. They have become impediments to wider sustainability and have encouraged a stultifying mindset.

In recent years things have improved somewhat. The 'Guiding Principles' for setting up the SAC stressed that: "It is essential that owners and occupiers, right holders, user groups and other local interests should be encouraged to participate in the process at the earliest opportunity." In other words a participatory decision-making process involving a range of stakeholders. Local people contributed to Regulation 33 (the SAC Bible) forcing English Nature to grudgingly accept that local people not only created, but also largely maintain these habitats; however, the pressure that had to be applied to convince them convinced me that within Natural England there was a narrow interest faction whose attitudes contrasted with those of truly good naturalists who know the extent to which traditional 'longshore' activities contribute to the welfare of the natural environment.

---

[31] Special Areas of Conservation
[32] Special Protection Areas
[33] Site of Special Scientific Interest
[34] Convention on Wetlands of International Importance (named after Iranian city of Ramsar)

Outer reefs and islands front most barrier coasts. The North Norfolk coast is a young barrier coast in the early stages of evolution. If allowed to evolve naturally this coast will one day be like that. Barrier coasts and islands are dynamic systems formed by the interaction of wind, wave and tidal energies that erode, transport, and deposit sediments. By absorbing the impact of high-energy marine processes barrier islands reduce erosion on the mainland coast and provide shelter for sensitive coastal habitats.

The south-east of England is sinking due to postglacial rebound and the slow melting of ice during the present interglacial period is raising sea levels. On top of this the world has been diagnosed as having a high temperature, which, if you believe it, is set to rise for many years to come. This has significant implications for our low-lying coast, increased storminess and sea level rise being the most serious. Society's panicked over-reaction to this has produced a rash of predictions as to how much sea level rise there will be, ranging from nothing above the *status quo* to leaving only the tops of the Cairngorms sticking out of the water. However, uncertain as these predictions may be, the precautionary principle alone requires that shoreline management, if it is to achieve its objective of a naturally evolving and sustainable coastline, must take account of it. This puts reclaimed areas of fresh marsh in the front line.

Blakeney Freshes comprises 85 hectares of grazing marshes between Blakeney, Cley and Wiveton. It is made up of reed beds, grazing marsh and low grassy hills called 'Eyes' that were sand dunes a thousand years ago. Over the four hundred or so years since this area was embanked much has changed and the surrounding salt marsh has continued to accrete. Growing imperceptibly with every spring tide it is now several feet higher than the Freshes which have subsided leaving them up to a metre and a half lower than they would have been had they not been reclaimed. The Freshes proximity to the Cley Reserve, the Glaven Valley and the salt marshes make it the jewel in the crown of North Norfolk's coastal reserves. The thought of allowing the sea back in seems perverse but this is an unsustainable situation and the sooner it is addressed the easier the solution will be. Doing nothing means leaving a difficult and dangerous legacy for our grandchildren or a natural catastrophe in our own time. Neither is acceptable.

Such decisions are never easy but the obstructive use of the wildlife designations that protect them could make the decision harder, perhaps impossible, allowing authorities to procrastinate until nature loses patience and produces a solution of her own. So why would losing a valuable asset to the sea be the best option? Well the reality is it would not be lost and to see why it is the best option it is essential to take a broader view that takes account of local people and considers a much bigger slice of time.

If Blakeney Freshes are abandoned the European Habitats Directive would require Natural England to replace it nearby, or if this is not possible, elsewhere.

Some of it (the most important part) could undoubtedly be accommodated within the Glaven Valley, and the remainder elsewhere. Those who claim the Freshes would be 'lost' ignore the fact the area would become extremely valuable salt marsh and mud flats, a wetland habitat that, added to the replacement habitat, would double the area we have now.

If predictions of increased storminess and sea level rise are anywhere near correct, all the reclaimed marshes on this coast would eventually become vulnerable and potentially dangerous. Villages and towns that sit behind sea banks are threatened in a far more sinister way than those that do not. During storm surges sea banks can breach, sometimes catastrophically, and what in other places would be a steady and predictable tidal rise becomes a tidal wave; streets would go from rain-wet to four meters under water in as many minutes. The threat to those who live behind sea banks is deadly.

Blakeney and villages like it that are fronted by dune systems and saltmarshes are much less exposed to these dangers. The dunes reduce windage and the much higher marsh levels eliminate most of the wave energy. Allowing Blakeney Freshes and other suitable parcels of reclaimed marsh along the Saltmarsh Coast to return to the sea would allow these features to re-establish giving natural flood protection that would accrete in step with sea level rise. Using wildlife designations to hang on to wildlife sites as long as possible presents major threats to human life. This reality and the possibility that sea level rise will accelerate accretion (exacerbating the differential between fresh and salt marsh) make the issue urgent.

This of course is a pragmatic and clinical view, but there is another – more romantic perhaps – but no less important view. We each have our own relationships with the world around us and our happiness can have much to do with the extent to which we are in harmony with it, how beautiful we find it, how much we enjoy it through our activities, be they work or play, and perhaps most important through our association with it over time.

Landscape beauty would be enhanced by realignment but people's attachment to the landscape could be a great obstacle. Many local people, particularly the older generation who have lived here all their lives, may not want it to change. Letting the sea back in would wash away memories and long associations and would be felt as loss. The young are excited by the prospect of managed realignment but others may need more persuasion.

From my art gallery on the Carnser at Blakeney I regularly see families pull onto the car park, get out of their cars and with their children run up the sea bank expecting to see the sea. They are always surprised and disappointed. Although dry land finishes where spring tides leave their tangle along the quayside there is a lot of land between Blakeney and the sea.

What if they could run up the bank and be greeted by a breathtaking view of salt water lakes dotted with islands and surrounded by mud flats and salt marshes; sailing dinghies making their way through the old channel which would be navigable even when the tide was out; a small marina for dinghies between Cley and Wiveton where youngsters could learn to sail in safety; a new coast path, a road even, between Blakeney and Cley; a new land and seascape added to the beauty of our coast? The potential benefits for the people of Cley, Blakeney, Morston and Wiveton are incalculable. Wildlife would benefit too; waders on the mud flats, geese on the saltings and ground nesting birds on the islands. Birds live harmoniously with man in the harbour and would do so here.

As things stand an official assessment of what should be done with this area would exclude this option. In fact it would not even be included in the debate. In the 16th century power, money and authority carelessly threw up sea banks ignoring the interests of local people whose livelihoods were destroyed through the loss of the ports and fisheries. It would be nice to think morality and social justice have moved on. But I have no doubt that Natural England and the wildlife organisations would not hesitate to perpetuate the injustice today.

Raymond Monbiot

Born on the Isle of Thanet in 1937 Raymond Monbiot was educated at Westminster School. After a short while as a prep school teacher of Latin, History and English he started a career in the food industry with J Lyons & Co, became a foreman at 19 and trained as a pastry chef making cakes for Buckingham Palace Garden Parties and fruit scones for the Queen Mother (by hand). He later became Managing Director of three of J. Lyons subsidiaries, Managing Director of Associated Biscuits and Chairman of Campbells Soups UK. In 1988 he set up his own food consultancy business.

In parallel he has been a Conservative Party volunteer and has held every volunteer position in the party except that of Chairman of the Women's Organisation. He was Chairman of the National Convention, Deputy Party Chairman and is now one of the Party's Treasurers and Chairman of its Property Company. He was made MBE in 1981 and CBE in 1994.

He and his wife moved to Burnham Market in 2000 where he is Chairman of the Burnham Market Society. His publications include *How to Manage Your Boss, The Burnhams Book of Characters, Characters of North Norfolk* and *More Characters of North Norfolk* and he is a regular contributor to *North Norfolk Living*. He has won numerous prizes for rose growing and he is establishing an orchard of endangered apple varieties and encouraging barn owls in Burnham Market.

From the Outside In

Raymond Monbiot

We moved from the village of Peppard Common near Henley-on-Thames in Oxfordshire to Burnham Market in 2000. We had lived there for 35 years and seen the encroachment of Reading and its commuter belt widening all the time and contributing to the threat that the south-east of England would be concreted over from Swindon to Dover. There had been talk for years about another bridge over the Thames to make the urbanisation of South Oxfordshire more intensive and the prospect would have put paid to the last vestiges of village life we had sought and found when we moved to the area over three decades earlier. In 1999 we made the decision to move and were attracted to North Norfolk which we knew and loved.

We had strong connections with North Norfolk. Rosalie my wife's family has had a holiday home in Blakeney since 1911 and were keen sailors and bird watchers. We continued to spend holidays there after we married in 1961. I was Chairman of Campbell Soups in King's Lynn from 1982 to 1988 and her brother The Rev Hereward Cooke was a canon of Norwich Cathedral.

Knowledge of North Norfolk before we moved was not only an advantage but one of the main reasons for choosing this unique part of England. It was a closed book to many of our friends in the South who knew little about the area except that it was remote. There were a number of inaccurate myths about it. For example that the wind usually blew from the east or north-east, that the road system suffered from the absence of motorways – thank the Lord for that – and that they are clogged at different times of year by transport from the docks, tractors crawling along under their loads of sugar beet and caravans to complete back to back traffic sclerosis. After living in the Thames Valley for so many years these were hardships, in as much as they were factual, with which we felt fully competent to cope.

North Norfolk was 160 miles and 30 years away, offering much of the quality of life we had found and were losing in South Oxfordshire. There is still wilderness to enjoy. The solitude of the mud flats and the marshes orchestrated by the mournful cry of seabirds and the thousands of wild geese in the winter are unique features to be treasured. The sunsets and sunrises are spectacular. It is dark enough to see the stars at night and to rediscover that there is such a thing as silence. I looked forward to resuming my bait digging and setting a beach line at low tide to catch flat fish. I had come to know some of the bait diggers from Blakeney and Morston over the years and to respect the fact that they were counting worms as they dug because they were paid by the score. I knew better than to disturb their concentration with chat. Nonetheless we sometimes greeted each other at 4.30 a.m when a stiff breeze was blowing across the wide open spaces. On occasion – particularly when it was raining horizontally – I might comment on the weather, to be told that it was the best part of the day. These were men in waders with a waterproof sheet tied to their waists to give some protection from the wind and who later in the day took seal trips to Blakeney Point.

For all our familiarity with Blakeney we had never been to Burnham Market until it was recommended in the late 1990s by the hairdresser who worked in the back of a dress shop in Blakeney. Over the years of holidays, conditioned by the days when petrol was short and places to visit few in number, found us usually venturing eastwards. There was not much to visit in those days. Philip Wayre had established an otter sanctuary at Great Witchingham and we used to take the kids there when we had had enough of crafting motor cars and boats in the sand or crabbing on Blakeney quay. We seldom went towards the west unless occasionally to Holkham or Wells.

Burnham Market was a revelation and on first acquaintance was magic. A proper fish shop, butcher, baker, fruit and veg, no supermarkets and a good pub or two……everything except a vet. It reminded us of how villages used to be and we felt we could recapture our preference for village life without impractical isolation. There were trains 22 miles away at King's Lynn if we needed them to get to London. We made interesting and unexpected discoveries. For example there were home-made jams and chutneys on sale in the church in North Creake in aid of the fabric fund. Samphire was available at a cottage gate nearby, as were home grown vegetables fresh as the morning dew and free range eggs. A succession of healthy vegetables was supposedly a contributor to long life in that they contained unusual natural amounts of selenium. A look at the obituary columns was always encouraging in that the average age was nearer 90 than 80.

On the Sunday after our arrival we moved in we were invited to an 80th birthday party and were introduced to at least half the village. Everyone was welcoming and friendly and we were told how nice it was to see younger people. We were both in our middle 60s at the time. It was clear if we were prepared to participate in village life we would have no difficulty in becoming part of it. By the end of the party we had joined the Friends of St Mary's church, the Burnham Market Society and the Gardening Club. We love the fundraising events – sausage and mash suppers, the Christmas parties and the summer fetes and the company of fellow members with common interests. There is always plenty to do and there is no reason to be bored and unoccupied in North Norfolk.

Norfolk like Cumbria and Cornwall leads nowhere geographically and had a traditional suspicion of strangers. In centuries past these were assumed to be up to no good – revenue men, fugitives, ne'er-do-wells and worse. In Norfolk the semi-feudal system is still very much alive although the nature of the community is changing. In its traditionally agricultural community the majority worked for and were tied to the few. Land is still the fabric holding the county together and many big estates are still more or less intact. The status of the landowners' tenants is an important feature in the social order giving one hope that the final crop – bricks and mortar – which has so changed the countryside in Britain will at least be delayed in Norfolk. Dutiful obeisance to the landowner or his tenant has tradition-ally been expected of the 'lower orders' of society – and given.

This is probably the starkest and least comprehensible feature of living in Norfolk which 'blow- ins' observe with wonder. Those who had made a career in the big wide world and either owned or ran multi-national companies struggle to come to terms with this residual archaic social system. Stratification, discrimina-tion of any kind whether it is race, creed, colour or any other categorisation is the fastest and surest way of getting fired in a multi-national company. Citizens of the world find the transition to being citizens of North Norfolk intriguing. Of course it is what has preserved the landscape and the magic but landowners who have been in place for generations are no different to other family businesses be it motor cars, food or engineering where the dynasty produces heirs of varying competence and contribution to the wider community. In international family owned business-es it is reckoned that by the third or fourth generation the founder's earthy zeal and application may have been blunted by more sophisticated education, softer lifestyle and levels of wealth or debt but do little to diminish expectations of entitlement whether earned or not. Class is the most boring of subjects – it is the person with-in that counts.

While worldly-wise retired businessmen and professionals tend to look on tra-ditionalist attitudes with bewilderment and some amusement they are not easily awed by its practitioners.

Of course to be accepted into the feudal society those who are interested must play the game and maintain the distance and espouse the mores set out in its feu-dal strata. They need to be seen in cultural circles – whether artistically interested or not – on the dinner party circuit which is a key source of gossip about the social activities in the county and support the smart charities which tend to lead to con-tinued participation in the social round. This congenial and harmless use of time has its downside. If it means cocooning oneself into a comfort zone of effortless superiority it can also mean turning one's back on or ignoring the majority of Norfolk folk, many of whom struggled to bring up families in hard working and poorly paid conditions. Yet they contain some of the most interesting characters in the county including skilled agricultural workers, service providers and tradesmen. I have written three books about some of these characters.

161

As lifestyle changes in Norfolk, happily the dialect and vocabulary are still very much alive and spread to the younger generation. Because of the price of housing many younger people still live with their parents and retain their roots in the location of their birth. The strong family bond reinforces North Norfolk traditions and brings a reluctance to venture too far away from the family nest. Among other virtues they adopt Norfolk humour which is not confined to pantomimes and variety in village halls. The spontaneous entertainment in greengrocers or butchers shops finds customers joining in and hanging around to enjoy the entertainment after they have been served. It is added value compared to the average supermarket checkout. Keith Loads is a celebrated Norfolk entertainer and does his act on stage in a shepherd's smock complete with crook. "Can I take my car through this ford?" "It's not very deep – it only comes half way up a duck." "Does this bus go to Norwich?" Driver replies "It's got Norwich on the front." "Yes but its got Kelloggs on the side....." There is a mardle society – all are welcome – where one can learn 'Norfolk'.

The county has traditionally been self sufficient. As an example in the big freeze of 1947 Norfolk sought and received little relief from outside. However in the ensuing years Norfolk was discovered as a holiday destination and ripe for the development of second homes. By 1979 when the county was again cut off by snow there was a desperate cry for relief from outside.

The East Anglian character was neatly summed up by Field Marshal Montgomery who would use the Scots and the Welsh to take a position but would rely on Norfolkmen and women to hold it. They are the bulldogs who resist all attempts to dislodge them. Their cussed reliability is a characteristic to be sought and treasured. It takes time to get through the natural reserve/suspicion of Norfolk folk but once you have made your number they are staunch and friendly.

Having bought Eastgate House in Burnham Market we set about a programme of refurbishment and determined to make use of local craftsmen wherever possible. There are more than a dozen builders in Burnham Market and we chose Trevor Manning whose team did an excellent job. We agreed a price for the work at the beginning, vowed we would not add to or change it capriciously and if we wanted more to be done would negotiate the price before it started. Given that we would pay the agreed amount promptly but would not accept bills in addition to the agreed price. No surprises.

If you pay the craftsmen's bills as you go and do not keep them waiting for their money they will recommend you to other craftsmen and you will never be short of a plumber when you need one. Our great local team included a couple of painters who had just started up in business and we were their first big client. They went the extra mile. For example we asked them if there was a dry cleaners in Fakenham and they offered to take our curtains home and ask their wives to take them to the shop and collect them. Trevor Manning recommended them and has made wide

use of them since. He always insisted that his team should be the sort of people who would respect one's house and not let him down.

We had one disaster in the initial construction of the conservatory by a firm of specialists based miles away. We had the good services of David Brown, a retired architect, to supervise the work in the house and I can remember his meeting with the conservatory gang where he said "my clients find this totally unacceptable". They dismantled what they had built and started again.

We have worked hard on the garden from very scruffy beginnings. We constructed a pergola which gives colour all the year round and was a tribute to the skills of the Fakenham Garden Centre. We have planted an orchard of heritage apple trees – mostly ancient varieties dating back at least to 1820 and others a century or so before that. There are hundreds of apple varieties still available yet supermarkets stock only a dozen or so. They have to conform to cosmetic uniformity on the shelf and resistance to damage in transit indicating that they have been picked unripe. Many of these come from the other side of the world. Real Norfolk grown varieties have flavour too and if they don't come in regimented shape and sizes so what. It takes 32 applications of pesticide to grow perfect looking apples and none to grow perfect tasting apples. We also have a grapevine in our greenhouse as all houses built by the Holkham estate had originally. Our best year was 158 bunches of black hamburgh grapes.

We tried to establish a wild flower meadow but our alluvial soil is too rich and grass eventually takes over. We have now mowed it in swathes to encourage barn owls to hunt for voles and have been successful in breeding barn owls in our owl

163

box fixed to a tree in one of our fields. The wild life of North Norfolk is one of its most compelling attractions. We have a nature reserve bordering two sides on one of our fields.

The education record in the past in Norfolk has been poor – particularly for those who failed their 11+ and were regarded as potential field workers in whom the educational system had little further interest. If they were destined to spend their lives on the land they might as well weed the school garden as take lessons. Little wonder that educational deprivation was handed down through generations – no doubt reinforcing reliance on the social system which carried with it the fear of dispossession of house and home. Rosalie Monbiot OBE is a Norfolk County Councillor and cabinet member for young peoples' services. She has been making huge strides with her team to reinforce the efforts of the county's 450 schools to raise standards, and to good effect. She also chairs housing associations and is a governor of Gresham's school. She has achieved the provision of 14 affordable dwellings in Burnham Market – no mean feat given the opposition which emerged in the process. However this was more than equalled by the enthusiasm of local families and is a real service to North Norfolk. These dwellings are the only way Burnham born and bred young people can afford a home of their own in the village, thus preserving a cross section of skills and services that would otherwise have been priced out and lost.

I was presented with a shocking example of social snobbery and segregation soon after we moved to Burnham Market. It was proving difficult to find someone to organise a village event to mark the Queen's Jubilee in 2002. Arrangements had to be set in motion as time was running short. I was asked to find a marquee and get it moving. The celebrations were held on a beautiful day with a church service on the Green and refreshments following, during which it was observed that there were not many 'village people' present but *I suppose they are having their own celebration on the council estate.'*

 Agriculture ceased to employ the bulk of the population – before the war each farm had its cricket team. Mechanisation took over after the war. Successive recessions in the agricultural industry have made an alternative source of wealth creation essential. The EEC regime has disrupted the relationship between supply and demand with set aside, quotas and intervention.

The upheaval resultant from the arrival of ever-growing numbers of second homers and holiday makers from the late 1970s has been seen as a mixed blessing. On the one hand it has brought change – never a welcome condition in a traditionally strong community – and on the other it has brought a new prosperity. The 'blow ins' have come with different and higher expectations of good eating places, the best of Norfolk foods, a wider range of high quality shops, a range of goods and amenities and have brought a lot of money into the county in the process. They have refurbished derelict or run down barns and cottages and provided work for skilled craftsmen.

Burnham Market's transformation started in the 1970s. It had been through a hard time. The cattle market closed and the railway followed suit in the 1950s. The village was generally a bit sad and run down. This was until it was discovered by second homers and holidaymakers. A leading contributor to this new era was Budge Fitzgerald's high-class grocery shop – Bowers. This was one of only two patronised by the Marchioness of Cholmondley – the other was Fortnum and Mason in London!

Today 63% of dwellings in Burnham Market are second homes. The pressure on the next generation to afford to live in the communities of their families has driven many afield and villages are much altered as the tide of visitors ebbs and flows throughout the year.

Burnham Market now has more than 50 shops and many of them rely on visitors buying goods they do not have time to shop for at home and for which they pay London prices. The locals who do not buy scented candles and three different varieties of caviar tend to shop elsewhere.

Each year at Christmas the traders invest in decorative lights for the season and their switch on attracts crowds from miles around. It is a big event and visitors plan their holidays around it. There is a carnival atmosphere with Father Christmas arriving in his sleigh and handing out sweets to the children. The band plays, there are mince pies and hot mulled wine and a hog roast and we all take part in the count down to the switch on. It is a very Norfolk occasion.

The Goosebec flows traditionally throughout the winter and spring, the water rising allegedly from the Chilterns. It flows across the main road 2ft wide and two inches deep and dives underground again on its way to the river Burn. In recent years it has not flowed at all reflecting higher levels of water extraction along its route or maybe as another example of climate change. Visitors are free with their advice about getting the pipe mended somewhere to stop this leak.

In the summer there is the horticultural show and carnival with the fair, fancy dress and decorated floats. These assemble on the Green and process to the sports field led by a band and perhaps the Newfoundland rescue dogs. There are side shows, the flower and crafts tent and home-made cakes on sale for tea. Every year there is the craft fair with a very high standard and large variety of stalls. This is all locally run and inspired and attracts craft exhibits of a high order from miles around. The summer season of concerts attracts a wide audience and the annual art exhibition in St Mary's church has its rota of art sitters to sell pictures by local artists.

The big issue now is the overwhelming number of motor cars in the village. There have been calls for a car park for 25 years and the crowded nature of the village is said to be a disincentive to shoppers. A large number of the cars parked in the village belong to the tradesmen themselves and suggestions that they might

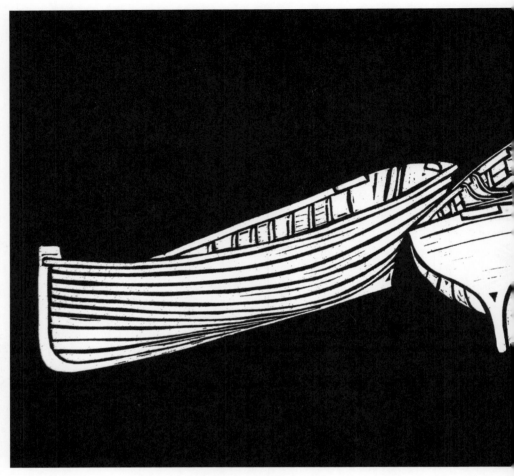

have a car park to make room for customers has all the allure to them of a rattle snake in a lucky dip. Shop workers are on their feet all day and do not want to add to their burden by parking in a remote corner of the sports field or wherever space can be negotiated. There is a focus on a visitors' car park on a field within the village envelope but its owners want planning permission to build some houses as part of the field's change of use. While the case for relief from the cluttered village centre is strong the problem as always is that any relief given will merely bring more cars to fill the vacuum and the village will change its character making it like any other car infested small town. The controversy driven by increasing urgency to do something will probably result in a car park but it will not solve the traffic problem for very long.

The signal that one is approaching Norfolk from London and the South is one's

arrival at the roundabout at Barton Mills near Mildenhall. Newmarket is left behind and the road changes from a wide and modern trunk road to an altogether narrower highway, dividing sandy breckland with its profusion of rabbits on the right-hand side from Lakenheath air base on the left where the RAF meets the US Air Force and which until recently had a strategic role in housing nuclear weapons. It was from here that the raid on Libya authorised by Ronald Reagan and agreed by Margaret Thatcher set forth. I was running an American company – Campbells Soups UK – at the time and we received a phone call from a supporter of Colonel Ghadaffi who had been given instructions to blow up an American company in Britain as a reprisal. Campbells and doubtless others had been identified as suitable targets. By coincidence shortly afterwards I received a phone call from security in the middle of the night that a suitcase was leaning against the perimeter fence at our Manchester factory. We called the police who evacuated the area and called in the bomb squad. After some delicate probing the suitcase was found to be empty, having been stolen off the carousel at Manchester airport. After its contents had been removed by the thief it had been thrown, presumably from a passing car, and ended up against the fence.

I recall this incident every time I pass Lakenheath. It does help to take one's mind off Brandon which now must be one of the more depressing towns of the region. One is surprised that John Betjeman did not give it the same sort of attention as he did Slough. Once one is through this town the way ahead is full of promise. Forest, free range ducks at Mundford – or at least there used to be – and then a long row of interesting pine trees leaning to the wind and weather. Swaffham with its huge windmill now supported by a backing group of lesser ones has some very attractive buildings tucked away off the beaten track. Swaffham also is distinguished by having the only Waitrose store for miles around. Then (when we were living at Cley) on to Fakenham with our very own racecourse, the smallest in the country – once round the track is one mile – which nonetheless attracts some of the best horses and jockeys for its 9 meetings a year. It is compact and the paddock, winners' enclosure, tote and bookies are all in close proximity to the hog roast and the beer tent.

Take the old road, Sandy Lane, between the Garden Centre and the main road for the last mile or so around Fakenham and you come across over 100 chickens and cockerels running around near the River Wensum. Many of these have been dumped on Sid Hooks the 89-year-old owner.

After Fakenham the arrival at Great Snoring and signs to Walsingham help to set up a sense of arrival that is unique and evocative. Walsingham that ancient destination for the faithful is at hand. I discovered later that there is supposedly a tunnel which connects Walsingham with Binham Priory. This folklore received a new reality in the 1930s when road improvements took off the top surface and revealed the skeleton of a fiddler and his dog dating back to the 14th century. The fiddler had been persuaded to enter and follow the tunnel. By continually playing his fiddle he planned to trace its route and destination for the benefit of listeners following his progress above ground. Suddenly the music stopped and 500 years later skeletons of a man and his dog were discovered when the road surface was removed at Fiddlers Hill.

The first glimpse of the sea was always a joyous event for the family at the end of a long journey and as we passed Langham it was laid out in the distance, usually with sailing dinghies dotted about. The realisation that there was nothing between that view and the North Pole was awesome. Such trees as there are along the coast road are bent to the wind in evidence particularly after Cley as one enters that frontier of North Norfolk's defence against angry seas at Salthouse and Weybourne. In the War it stood as defense of a different kind for this was a potential invasion coast. Home Guard detachments performed their duties. At

Mundesley the unit in charge of the single gun pointing out to sea guarded the cliffs and kept it polished and ready for action, but they never had occasion to fire it. However when the War ended they were allowed to fire one shot and the gun collapsed down the cliff.

On the entry to Blakeney there is a 'for sale' sign on the hill offering woodlands. That sign has been there for at least 40 years and is still there. It endures through all weathers. It is unchanging and timeless and says much about North Norfolk.

Jim Ring

Jim Ring is a writer and film-maker based on the North Norfolk Coast. He was born and brought up in London, read biochemistry at Bath University and subsequently read English at Brasenose College, Oxford. In 1984, following a spell teaching Oxbridge entrance, he joined the advertising industry. Over the next ten years he worked at agencies including The Creative Business, Butler Dennis Garland, Yellowhammer, TBWA and WCRS, and ran accounts ranging from Greenpeace to AIDS, Carling Black Label and Orange.

In 1994 he set out to develop two parallel careers. As a communications consultant he advised principally public sector clients: the Defence Evaluation & Research Agency, British Nuclear Fuels, the Health & Safety Executive, UKTI and – more recently – the Food Standards Agency, the World Nuclear Association and the International Atomic Energy Agency. As a writer he published the *Financial Times'* standard text on advertising (*Advertising on Trial*, 1993) a biography of Erskine Childers (1996, winner of the Marsh Prize), *How the English Made the Alps* (2000), *We Come Unseen* (2001, winner of the Mountbatten Prize) and *Riviera* (2004). He has recently completed a WW2 alternative history thriller set in Occupied England.

In 2001 he collaborated on the network TV documentary *Submarine*, a history of the Royal Navy's submarine flotilla. In 2005 this led to his co-founding an independent TV production company. His six part documentary series on immigration, *Incomers*, was broadcast on ITV over the summer of 2008.

Jim learned to sail in the 60s on the Norfolk Broads and in 1989 bought a house on the North Norfolk coast. He now lives there with his wife, daughter and son.

Images: Still Awaiting a Master

Jim Ring

It is this form of blindness that appears to afflict three-quarters of the nation. They cannot see that the ordinary county towns and villages bequeathed to us by the natural good taste of our forebears, the simple domestic architecture, the roll and slip of pasture and arable, well-placed timber, and the homely huddle of stacks and barns is the beauty of England. Not only a large mountain or a spectacular moor.

Lilias Rider Haggard

Yesterday's gone. Yet Hardy's Wessex, Ransome's Lake District, Breughel's Netherlands, Canaletto's Venice, Waugh's Oxford, Constable's Suffolk, Turner's Alps, Lou Reed's New York, Housman's Shropshire and Elgar's Malvern Hills are here today. Last night I dreamt I went to Mandalay again. Tomorrow, I'll be on my way to Arcadia in the Ashmolean in Oxford. Capturing the spirit of a place in prose, paint or quavers preserves it for eternity or at least as long as the world keeps turning. With the North Norfolk Coast poised on the brink of precipitous change, it deserves precisely such embalming to ensure its own unique story is told, perhaps to act as its epitaph.

Such thoughts were very far from my mind when I first visited North Norfolk almost thirty years ago. I had known Norfolk much earlier as a child and had learned to sail on the Broads. Of those reedy meres I had sunlit memories of varnished wood, wind and canvas. Our own coast, barely ninety minutes away by car, was the same county but another country. On that first brief encounter it seemed to have remarkably little to offer. I stayed in Burnham Overy Staithe and must have been reading *My Family and Other Animals* at the time. The place – or rather the weather – reminded me of the opening sentences of Gerald Durrell's masterpiece:

July had been blown out like a candle by a biting wind that ushered in a leaden August sky. A sharp, stinging drizzle fell, billowing into opaque grey sheets when the wind caught it. Along the Bournemouth sea front the beach huts turned blank wooden faces towards a greeny-grey, froth-chained sea that leapt eagerly at the cement bulwark of the shore...

I got very wet sailing a Twinkle Twelve dinghy with the sea-keeping qualities of a sieve in atrociously squally conditions; wetter still on the sea wall in one of those sharp early summer easterlies. When the weather – briefly – cleared, I wandered round the green lanes at the back of Burnham Thorpe in what seemed an agricultural landscape of no particular merit, charm, feature or distinction. Crows cawed. Burnham Market with its church, village green, butcher, baker, candle-stick-maker and Wednesday afternoon closing seemed a throwback to Miss Marple's St Mary Mead. I cannot remember the terms of endearment in which the Burnhams – the whole coast – had been represented to me but doubtless in ways sufficiently attractive to justify driving four or five hours across the country. The place passed me by. It wasn't Oxford or the Lake District, let alone Venice or the Alps. It was hardly conventionally beautiful. Neither to my (very sparse) knowledge had a writer or a painter or composer taken inspiration from the coast and immortalized it. I couldn't imagine returning.

Which of course was why, within a few years, I had bought a cottage here. It was 1989, the year of the fall of the Berlin Wall. A bright future beckoned and all would be well in the best of all possible worlds. So said Margaret Thatcher. 'Some enchantment lies upon the North Norfolk Coast,' wrote Lilias Rider Haggard. Quite against my better judgement the coast had cast its spell.

As they taught me when I used to work in advertising, attitude influences behaviour but more intriguingly actions affect feelings. Having bought my cottage, I began to cast around for reasons to justify its (even then) ruinous cost. Not, I dare say, particularly consciously, certainly not persistently or unswervingly, I set out to find the coast's Hardy or Housman, Constable or Turner. I wanted to persuade myself that I had bought my own little piece of forever.

'The Isle of Mugg,' wrote Evelyn Waugh in *Officers and Gentlemen*, 'has no fame in song or story. Perhaps because whenever they sought a rhyme for the place, they struck absurdity, it was neglected by those romantic early Victorian English ladies who so prodigally enriched the balladry, folklore and custom of the Scottish Highlands.'

At first, despite the acknowledged artistic heritage of the county as a whole, despite the Pastons, Browne, Walpole, Burney, Cotman, Crome, Marryat, Rider Haggard, Seago, Ketton-Cremer, Hartley, Maine and Munnings, it really did seem that the coast itself was similarly lacking in fame. David Byrne of the art-rock group Talking Heads said that heaven was a place where nothing ever happens – or perhaps ever had happened. This seemed to apply here. Like the county as a whole, it was on the road to nowhere. It was a dead end, an appendix, a *cul de sac*, a footnote in history, an oversight and a backwater. If Coke of Holkham claimed a certain credit for the stripling agricultural revolution, its sturdy industrial counterpart had left the coast – the county – largely untouched. The volcanic social and economic upheaval that inspired Charles Dickens's Coketown and created its factual equivalents like Birmingham, Halifax, Manchester and Leeds never erupted here. The railway, that rip-roaring agent of change, hardly disturbed Norfolk's slumbers and scarcely touched the coast. While the new towns and cities teemed with people, money and ideas, the coast seemed the deserted village writ large: the population decimated, unwashed, interbred, benighted and poor. The coast inspired no comment, boasted no fame, and possessed no chronicler.

It was only gradually as I scratched through the surface that a different pattern began to emerge, like a fossil emerging from the sandy coastal soil.

The first interesting evidence I came across was obvious enough. Often billed as the country's first novelist, Daniel Defoe – the creator of *Robinson Crusoe* – travelled the length and breadth of a kingdom that had yet to be united in the early seventeen-twenties. In his account of the journey, *A Tour through the whole Island of Great Britain*, he created an indelible record of this other Eden on the eve of the industrial revolution.

Setting out north-east from London, Norfolk was one of Defoe's earlier ports of call, and his shore is a margin, a brink, an edge where land and sea are genuinely intermingled. Ignorant of the dangers the shallows and storms of the coast posed to shipping, he is astonished by the sight that meets his eyes as he rides north from Yarmouth:

> *The farmers and country people had scarce a barn, or a shed, or a stable; nay, not the pales of their yards, and gardens, not a hogstye, not a necessary-house, but was built of old planks, beams, wales and timbers, the wrecks of ships and ruins of mariners and merchants' fortunes.*

As he follows the coast round from Weybourne he discovers a 'large salt works at Clye', the fruits of which are 'sold all over the county, Holland and the Baltick'; Morston, Wells, and all the 'Seven Burnhams' he describes as 'towns employed in the trade of carrying corn to Holland'; Wells, Burnham and Cley are indeed seaports 'of very good trade'. Some of this is legitimate, some altogether less so. The moralist in Defoe is shocked by the 'great trade driving here for Holland, back again to England...the clandestine trade, or the art of smuggling.' Most surprisingly, he also says that Norfolk as a whole also 'has the most people in the least tract of land of any county in England, except about London, and Exon and the West Riding of Yorkshire.'

This was an eye-opening three-hundred-year-old snapshot of the coast, utterly unrelated to the tidy middle-class playground I saw all around me. Here was an ill-kempt, populous, rough and ready industrious margin, bent on licit trade with Holland and smuggling whatever it could. It earned or stole its keep from both the land and the sea. It was a place where the writ of Norwich – let alone Westminster – scarcely ran. Here was a glimpse of life, a life that had inspired art.

Defoe gave me a clue. Norwich, in the full bright glorious morning of the Blair years, gave me another. A wet afternoon and a tired child drove me into the city's

Castle museum and to revelation in the form of its collection of Norwich School artists. John Crome, John Sell Cotman and their followers, working a hundred years or so after Defoe's tour, echoed the writer's story of a coast not at play but at work.

Take Cotman's *Storm on Yarmouth Beach*. It's mis-titled. The treatment of the storm hints of Turner, yet the real subject is the fisherman and their cart in the foreground, struggling with their nets to glean a living from the restless wave. The retreating line of windmills provides perspective, but also speaks of the labour of men required to give them that day their daily bread. This is not *Storm on Yarmouth Beach* but *Men at Work*. There was more. A note in the gallery tactfully drew my attention to the point that, 'In the seventeenth century the major revelation in landscape painting had been the discovery of visual beauty in the undramatic, unclassical lands of northern Europe.' Crome and Cotman were – I saw – ardent students of the Dutch masters and recognised in the subtle and understated scenery of North Norfolk a likeness to the Netherlands.

The result is a series of land and seascapes which, if rarely centred on the Saltmarsh coast itself, began to suggest – even occasionally to capture – its elusive beauty. Henry Bright's *Windmill at Sheringham* at first seems sufficiently nondescript. Yet the more you look, the more you see. The crotchety grey post-mill and the higgledy-piggledy abutting pantiled granary, the track in the foreground paving the way to the distant parish church, and beyond the hint of bright water; above all, the wide Norfolk sky and the massing clouds throwing deep shadows on the heath below. Brightman shows us the muted beauty of the coast, shows what Nelson's biographer Tom Pocock called the 'muted greens, browns, greys, yellows and blues of Norfolk dunes and salt marshes'.

There for a time I paused. For those who like to see life through the spectacles of books, through the frame of a picture or accompanied by a soundtrack, I had found at least some means of interpreting the coast. Defoe had given me the historical perspective of the same place at very different time; the Norwich School had made me see what hitherto I had not seen. It was something, if by no means enough.

Then came Cromer, Stark, Buchan and Old Shuck. I had seen somewhere an exquisite rendering of Cromer in 1835 by one the most talented of John Crome's followers, James Stark. I also knew vaguely that the arrival of the railway in 1877 had transformed this once lawless outpost, as late as 1864 lacking both pavements and gas, into the fashionable Victorian resort of 'Poppyland'. I certainly did not know that Arthur Conan Doyle had visited the place celebrated and popularised by the journalist Clement Scott, and that Sherlock Holmes's creator had taken inspiration for *The Hound of the Baskervilles* from a story he heard in Cromer's Royal Links Hotel about a great beast. This was the legend of Old Shuck, the phantom that roamed the salt marshes. It was the coast's great misfortune that

Doyle eventually decided to set his tale on Dartmoor. The moor owes its fame to Shuck, *our* Shuck.

John Buchan's adventures of Richard Hannay celebrated the writer's native Scotland and reflected his pre-war wanderings in Europe and Africa, his experience in the Trenches, and his life in London as a barrister and MP. Re-reading this old favourite on an Alpine meadow I discovered I had entirely overlooked the fact that the last of the Hannay adventures, *The Island of Sheep*, features our own coast in the guise of 'Hanham Flats'. I consulted Janet Adam Smith's Buchan biography. This identifies Hanham as Wells. Indeed, anyone who knows its marshes could not possibly mistake it from Buchan's description. In the chapter portraying Hannay and his son staying at the 'Rose and Crown', wildfowling on the January marshes, Buchan tellingly captures the winter coast: the skeins of brent, barnacle, bean and pinkfoot that so characterises it, the power of the winter storm, the sapping bitter cold, the sense of an embattled and isolated humanity eking out its existence on an inhospitable margin, taking what it could from both land and sea. Walpole famously described the denizens of Norfolk as 'roast beef fashioned in human form'. Buchan was more astute. The Hanham men were, 'a class by themselves, neither quite of the land or the water'.

Buchan, too, writing in 1936, portrays the coast in transition. The combination of the arrival of the railway, the silting of the small tidal harbours, and the advent of larger steam driven cargo vessels had strangled the ports noted by Defoe: Cley, Blakeney, Morston, Wells, Burnham. Some alternative form of employment had to be found. Taking inspiration from Poppyland, the building of the Blakeney Hotel in 1923 marked the beginnings of tourism proper on the northern coast. The Moorings in Burnham Overy Staithe followed a year later, complementing the holiday huts and old railway carriages already encamped on Overy beach and Scolt Head island. In Buchan, the innkeeper's wife has lost her husband to an accident logging in the woods. A couple of barges in the creek are vestiges of the once flourishing coastal trade. Hannay and his son are tokens of the future: they are tourists.

I leafed through Buchan's memoir, *Memory–hold-the-Door,* in search of some mention of Wells. I found only an amusing diatribe about modern artists, who were not much to the taste of the conservative Scot. Yet like writers, successors to Cotman and Crome were being drawn in ever larger numbers as visitors to the coast in the thirties. Some of course I knew, like Peter Scott and Matthew Smith. I went to Wells Library in search of more information. There I discovered Ian Collins's study of East Anglian art. 'For painters,' he points out, 'this is a place of bracing holidays, hideaways and hospital stays.' It seemed that Paul Nash and Mark Gertler were among the major artists to visit the coast as a whole, Gertler as a habitué of a sanatorium in Mundesley where he was periodically treated for tuberculosis. The lover of Bloomsbury's Dora Carrington was attracted by the more melancholic aspects of the landscape, better caught by Nash's prose than the rather disappointing paintings of either. 'We walked in a landscape entirely new to my eyes, flat and chequered, with all the trees slanting one way, their branches welded together in tortuous forms by the relentless winds.' Yet like Buchan's, their art reflects the shift on the coast away from work towards play, from a community making its living both from the land and the sea to one serving the tourist trade. Now I tried a cast closer to our own time, the eve not of the industrial revolution but of the Second World War.

I knew of Henry Williamson only because of the Fascist lightning symbol someone had daubed on a wall in Stiffkey close to where he once lived. I had heard of, but not read, *Tarka the Otter*. I was ignorant of the circumstances that had caused him in 1937 to buy Old Hall Farm in the depths of the agricultural depression. In *The Story of a Norfolk Farm*, Williamson explains that he wanted to write about 'a tract of land which seemed to him to be unique, a relic of "Old England"'.

If so, much that he found there seems best forgotten. For those nostalgic about the railway that peeled off the line between Lynn and Hunstanton and meandered its way across to Wells, Williamson evokes decay: 'The train drew into the platform, with its single line, and oil lamps and rambler roses climbing over the faded station name board...'

Much of the coast seemed to be a similar state. There was the Stiffkey schoolmaster who used to 'cane the boys on their hands and continue to strike them until he broke down their resistance with cries and tears'. Until not long before Williamson's arrival, the local vicar had been the notorious Harold Davidson. Only able to minister to his flock in the time he could spare from his attentions to 'fallen women' in Soho, he ended up in a circus, eaten by the lion he was supposed to be taming. Modern conveniences comprised the Night Cart, which had recently replaced the cesspit under the outhouse (Defoe's 'necessary-house') boasted by the village's cottages. For twenty-five shillings a week, man and horse were employed 'to empty the hundred and fifty pails in use by the cottages'. On the farm itself, the principal motive power remained the horse. Williamson's new Ferguson tractor was regarded with suspicion. The writer settled his family in the old granary, a building proof neither against wind nor rain. Pots and pails were necessary to collect the water. This and the remaining farm buildings were overrun with the vermin. There was no running water. A tenant who had paid no rent for a quarter of a century proved impossible to dislodge. In the face of these general difficulties, an alpine winter, the crash of the barley market and a flood of biblical proportions, Williamson failed to make the farm pay. Just before the outbreak of war he returns to Devon. This is not the picture-postcard village of Stiffkey where a former farm labourer's two bedroom cottage now changes hands for £300,000, rather it looks back to Defoe.

Yet, there again, it is. Williamson's is the coast of 'keen Arctic air, of width and depth in the sky and on the earth of sea... of clear lights and distances...of far

extending marsh and watery dykes'. Wells is presented with the thinnest of disguis-
es as 'Whelk, or Whelk-next-the-sea to give it its full name'. It has 'a narrow main
street leading down to a view of the marshes and the sea. A modern grain elevator
arose above an old quay whereon railway tracks were standing. A fisherman in
blue slop and rubber thigh boots passed, under his arm a wicker skep filled with
shell-fish. Two sailing ships were moored alongside the quay. It had an old-time air
which was pleasing to me'. Remove one of the sailing ships and the railway trucks,
and you are in Wells today. Williamson's two summers are less Gerald Durrell's
than those which we ourselves very occasionally enjoy:

> In a warm current flowing into the harbour from beyond the point of sand-
> hills, where white-winged and distant terns were screaming, we bathed
> ourselves, while the gentle flow bore us along the ribbed sands. Was this the
> dour North Sea, this warm and gracious stream which moved us effortlessly
> in an inverted world wherein the sharp chalk wings of terns soared
> themselves swiftly under the blue sky, and the line of remote sand-hills moved
> away from the corner of the eye.

Above all, though, for Williamson, 'the genius of the place' was the wild geese.
'Hark! What's that? A strange jangling, honking, crinkling noise, hundreds of nois-
es all together, high up in the sky. Listen, children! The wild geese coming in from
the sea! This is the Coast of the Wild Geese!'

Lilias Rider Haggard's portrayal of the coast at an identical time was one interestingly different to Williamson's. The youngest daughter of Henry Rider Haggard (*King Solomon's Mines*), she lived for much of her life in her parents' old house at Ditchingham in the Waveney valley. The family kept a cottage at Blakeney, and numerous entries from her 'Norfolk trilogy' of diaries and notebooks concern themselves with the coast. Rider Haggard had not chosen to try to claw a living from the somewhat unyielding coastal soil and could afford a romantic response to her surroundings. Williamson, who edited some of Haggard's material, might accordingly have cast a slightly jaundiced eye over her account of 'one of those Norfolk farms which still seem quite untouched by the coming of machinery, as farms were in one's childhood. The duck pond and the comfortable huddle of buildings crowded together under the shadow of a big barn. A placid sow outstretched in the sunshine contentedly suckled her numerous progeny, next door to a couple of horses at a midday feed.'

Still, Haggard had a sharp enough ear and a very fine eye for the elusive beauties of the coast. There's a wonderful passage on Blakeney in winter in which she convinces the reader of her assertion that North Norfolk in winter is better than summer. 'It was one of those rare winter days, a still day, cold with that clean coldness which seems to come straight from the polar ice, but with a brilliant sun.' Boating out to Blakeney Point past the Watch House, Haggard spots something silvery glinting on the water. Then a herring gull puts up what proves to be hundreds of Brent geese. 'A moment later they were all in the air, quite three hundred of them, stringing out in great skeins across the pale winter sky, swinging over the Point seawards, then turning back in long wavering lines to feeding grounds nearer Holkham.'

Haggard, too, has a tract for our own times. Attending the opening of an exhibition arranged by the Council for the Preservation of Rural England, she cites a story told by one of the speakers about his 'approach to some manufacturers about the removal of a particularly hideous field advertisement. They replied in shocked tones that they would never dream of disfiguring a 'heavenly spot' but saw no harm in putting them in fields'. Haggard comments:

It is this form of blindness that appears to afflict three-quarters of the nation. They cannot see that the ordinary county towns and villages bequeathed to us by the natural good taste of our forebears, the simple domestic architecture, the roll and slip of pasture and arable, well-placed timber, and the homely huddle of stacks and barns is the beauty of England. Not only a large mountain or a spectacular moor.

It is Haggard, too, who wrote that, 'Some enchantment lies upon the North Norfolk coast.' Now, courtesy of Defoe and Crome and Brightman and Williamson and Haggard herself, I was beginning to see what she meant.

I had discovered Henry Williamson (or rather, a transcription of the broadcasts that became *The Story of a Norfolk Farm*) at the apocalyptic time of 9/11 in the unlikely setting of a friend's house in Notting Hill. Williamson had led me to Rider Haggard, and Haggard in turn to more contemporary renderings of the coast. I devoured Jack Higgins, Angela Huth, Joan Robinson, William Rivière, Richard Mabey, Sally Festing, and Kevin Crossley-Holland. Only two of these really caught my heart, ear and eye.

Like Henry Williamson, Sally Festing is a lover of the coast but not of it. The biographer of Barbara Hepworth comes from the Midlands. Her connection was at first as a holiday visitor. It was in this guise that she came to know the fishing community up and down the coast. In *Fishermen* she bears witness to these people. She quotes the folklorist George Ewart Evans to the effect that 'occasionally a body of factual knowledge does exist only in the memories of men and women, and it would be lost, or greatly attenuated, were it not taken down before they died'. Festing continues, 'When I realised just how fast old customs, beliefs, feelings and language were slipping away, it seemed imperative to record the spirit that remains.'

Her approach in *Fishermen* is to allow the men and their families to tell their own stories in their own language in their own way. The result is a record of what Thomas Hardy called 'ways, occupations and customs' that are now on the point of extinction. It's a testament that breathes of courage, endurance, independence of heart and mind and a happy intolerance of authority:

There used to be a postman from Burnham came round with a pony and cart with letters. He had more pheasants in that old cart than he had letters. Nobody ever knew. We'd be down there rabbiting on the hills and I shot rabbits when I hadn't ever seen them, just the twig of the marram. We lived there, that was our hobby. We shouldn't ha' got a drink if we hadn't a gun or dog.

These are Buchan's men, 'neither quite of the land or the water'.

One of Festing's contemporaries is Kevin Crossley-Holland, another outsider who as a child became enchanted by the coast. He made his name as a poet and scholar of Anglo-Saxon, subsequently achieving best-seller status as a children's writer with his Arthurian trilogy, *The Seeing Stone*. He has written about the coast in his recent memoir *The Hidden Roads*, in his poetry, and in his two very fine stories for children, *Waterslain Angels* and *Storm*.

Crossley-Holland's great attributes as a chronicler of these shores are his gifts as a linguist and his rich sense of history. *Storm* is a deceptively simple story about a child's desperate journey to bring a doctor to her sister's child-bed. Crossley-Holland adroitly conjures up the isolation, beauty and fragility of life on the coast, and leaves it entirely to the reader to identify the nature of little Annie's friend in need: the horseman who takes her in search of the doctor. Is he really the ghost of the highwayman's victim? And how does he know with such certainty that Annie's sister Willa and her child will be safe? This story of light and shade, action and reflection, is a miniature masterpiece that won the Carnegie Medal.

Crossley-Holland's poetry includes *Waterslain*, the poet's name for – and portrait of – Burnham Overy Staithe. This collection and some of his other poems about the village represent a very subtle and delicate evocation of the coast – the coast and its characters, too. In some instances he portrays in his own terms precisely those people who Festing had allowed to speak for themselves. In others he veers into pitch perfect evocation of land and sea-scape, perhaps above all the sense of constant flux embodied in the very word 'Waterslain'. 'There it was, and at times not there.' And in both the memoir and *Waterslain Angels* he powerfully evokes the coast he had known as a child, a world of creeks, water pumps and Kilner jars some streets away from plasma screen televisions in second homes.

It was after all this that, quite recently, I turned to one of my favourite series of books. It was not one about this coast at all, but rather that great tract of land far to the west that Thomas Hardy called Wessex in tribute to the Anglo-Saxon kingdom.

Introducing the uniform edition of the novels, Hardy remarks, 'At the dates represented in the various narrations things were like that in Wessex. The inhabitants lived in certain ways, engaged in certain occupations, kept alive certain customs, just as they are shown doing in those pages.' Artists, as Hardy implies, are among other things social historians. The West Country is so much more to us than a place on the map because Hardy has lodged it in the national consciousness and made it potentially part of the life of anyone who can read. Such was Wessex's good fortune. We know what things were like in Wessex.

Likewise, courtesy of the work of the painters and writers I have mentioned – others too – we also know what things were like on the North Norfolk coast.

Yet, of course, we know a good deal less about our coast than we do about Wessex. Shafts of light penetrate the dark backward and abysm of time, but not as many as we would like. We know the Romans were at Branodunum and the Peddars Way and Burnham Market and Stiffkey, but we have little other than archaeological evidence of how they lived and died and nothing other than our imaginations to help us understand how they thought and felt. We know precious little about the Danish incursions of these shores other than the names that were left behind, like -dale, -holme, -toft, -thorpe and -ulph. Thereafter the record slowly improves, but even since the Restoration we have only a patchy and sporadic imaginative interpretation of how the coast and its community have changed, the sense of life as it is lived, here at the quiet limit of the world. In the artists I have talked about, we have some beautiful fragments, some telling snapshots of the coast at particular times, but we cannot see it steadily and see it whole. We have some sense of its metamorphosis from the populous, industrious, lawless margin of Defoe to the de-populated and deracinated Chelsea-on-Sea of today, but not a very clear one. There's little between Defoe and the Norwich School, Cotman and Crome did not really tackle our coast, we only have a chapter of that master John Buchan, there are virtually no serious twentieth century painters, and it is only the non-fiction of Haggard and Williamson that really passes muster. We have no music: no Elgar, Vaughan Williams, or even an Arnold Bax. Despite all the smuggling we have no *Frenchman's Creek*, and despite Shuck we have no *The Hound of the Baskervilles*. Somehow, some quality of the coast remains elusive, has not quite been captured. As Crossley-Holland wrote of the inability of Matthew Smith to respond to where he sometimes lived:

The lines here too Lutheran:
Flat-chested dunes,
the ruled horizontals of marsh and ocean...
Not for him
light honed on a northern whetstone,
the burning ice of aurora borealis;
nor was he the first to flinch
at this ruthless incandescence,
too cutting even for Crome and Cotman
still awaiting a master.

Or as the poet writes in his memoir, 'Dear God, even Mozart sat at the piano and wept because he could not write down the notes he heard, or almost heard.'

I had looked for the equivalents of Waugh's Oxford, Canaletto's Venice and Elgar's Malvern Hills. I had found something, I had found in many respects a great deal, but I hadn't found quite what I was looking for. I had discovered some profound imaginative responses to the coast but I had found nothing that had quite immortalised the area as – say – Housman did for the coloured counties around Shropshire. The late Tom Pocock, writing a few years ago, said, 'At the end of the twentieth century, Norfolk is currently lacking any great native literary talent.' Not so. But our local masters of paint, rhythm and rhyme have yet quite to nail the coast. As Crossley-Holland himself says, we are still awaiting the attentions of that master.

It was also Hardy who made the point that 'a world-wide repute in some cases, and an absolute famelessness in others, attach to spots of equal beauty and equal accessibility.' No world-wide fame attaches to our own coast yet it undoubtedly deserves it. Hardy wrote of the setting of *The Woodlanders*, that it 'cannot be regarded as inferior to any.... scenery of the sort in the West of England, or perhaps anywhere in the Kingdom.' In its own particular way, much the same could be said of our own scenery – and in some respects has been said. Yet – as I say – the coast has not been quite as effectively captured as Wessex.

The consequence of this is that its qualities are insufficiently respected. It may – like oases in the West Country – be designated an Area of Outstanding Natural Beauty, but it sometimes scarcely seems to be regarded as such. Not by central government, not by the local councils in Lynn and Norwich, certainly not by most of the coast's parish councils, and not even by its own indigenous inhabitants. Captain Marryat's daughter wrote that her father on his estate in Langham 'built model cottages and instituted model pigsties; both cottagers and pigs proved averse to anything like progressive movement.' Not much has changed. Certainly, with the draconian plans afoot for development on land and sea discussed elsewhere in this book, it seems there is little chance that the coast will remain true to its designation as a place of extraordinary beauty unless strenuous efforts are made to smother those proposals.

Now is the time to do so, and to do so by galvanising some of our local masters. For not only is a thing of beauty a joy forever, but in immortalising the coast the work of the philistines in whom our county and coast so regrettably abound is made just a little bit more difficult, unpopular, aggravating, expensive, time consuming and – even in Norfolk – uphill. Now is the time to turn our salt marshes into Egdon Heath, lest the dazzling fragments that have been created become little more than epitaphs.

Kevin Crossley-Holland

Kevin Crossley-Holland was born in 1941 in North Buckinghamshire and grew up in the Chilterns (his grandparents lived in North Norfolk). He developed a passion for Anglo-Saxon literature at Oxford, became Gregory Fellow in Poetry at the University of Leeds and later taught in the USA.

Kevin worked as an editor for Macmillan at the beginning of his writing career, before becoming editorial director at Victor Gollancz. He is well-known for his poetry, novels, story collections, translations from Anglo-Saxon and reinterpretations of medieval legends.

His work includes collaborations with composers Sir Arthur Bliss and William Mathias, Bob Chilcott and Giles Swayne, and the libretti for two operas by Nicola LeFanu, *The Green Children* and *The Wildman*, as well as a chamber opera about Nelson, Haydn and Emma Hamilton. He has worked with the photographer John Hedgecoe and the artists John Lawrence, James Dodds and Charles Keeping, and has written a stage play – *The Wuffings*.

In addition to definitive retellings of *The Norse Myths* and *British Folk Tales*, he is the author of *Storm* (1985), winner of the Carnegie Medal; *The Seeing Stone* (2000 – winner of the Guardian Children's Fiction Prize); *At the Crossing-Places* (2001); *King of the Middle March* (2003); *Gatty's Tale* (2006), and, set in Norfolk, *Waterslain Angels* (2008).

Kevin is the author of seven volumes of poetry. His *Selected Poems* was published in 2001, and *Moored Man: Poems of North Norfolk,* with etchings and watercolours by Norman Ackroyd, in 2006. He published his memoir of childhood, *The Hidden Roads,* in 2008.

Kevin has two sons and two daughters.

What Inspires Us?

Kevin Crossley-Holland

Let There Be Light

And God said, Let there be light: and there was light. But as soon as God saw the astounding quality of the light that He had created in North Norfolk, He must have been tempted, mightily tempted to leave it at that: not only to call it Day but to call it *a* day!

There are hours in this landscape when the light is so quick and keen that it articulates each last leaf and shell; when it burns; when we see, or think we see, what we cannot possibly see…

True, I knew a renowned poet living in Norfolk who never wrote for more than twenty minutes at a time, always had his cat on his lap and always had music on the radio. But he was the exception. The fact is that artists do hanker after the sort of working conditions North Norfolk can offer: its light and the space that light reveals, sustained quietness, involvement with elements and the natural world, the relative lack of light pollution, the sense of possibility.

It is, however, perfectly possible to find a place conducive to work – I think I'll resist that word inspiration – without being deeply interested in that place. Once, I wrote a sustained meditation on British megaliths while living in the middle of a Minnesotan forest, and in the same way writers and artists such as P.G. Wodehouse and Patrick Hamilton, W. H. Auden and Matthew Smith have visited or lived in North Norfolk, without making more than incidental use of it or without using it all. It's interesting and fun to know that Wodehouse's *Money for Nothing* is set at Hunstanton Hall, but knowing it doesn't actually help us to any deeper appreciation or understanding of the novel.

What is much more interesting is the way in which the North Norfolk coast has spoken deeply to many artists, some living here, some visitors, some Norfolk born-and-bred, some furriners, and even been seminal to their achievement.

So let me be specific, just as our light is specific and a foe to waffle and generalisation. Our landscape is seven-eighths sky: a vast inverted arena, a sky-dome in which there are often several simultaneous theatres of action. It's a landscape of horizontals – skyline, ribbed fields, decaying ribs of boats – in which verticals, including human beings, often look arresting. It's a landscape of the most subtle colours: shining pearl, pewter, iron, obsidian, many-coloured, mud, olive, lavender...

Sharp-edged as it is, this landscape is also elusive. Witness to how many artists engage with the coastline as well as how many prospective purchasers there are, the manifold galleries in North Norfolk teem with second-rate images. For all the great work of the nearby Norwich School, North Norfolk has not had its Palmer or Constable, its Elgar or Britten, its Dickens or Dylan Thomas.

Another way of seeing our coastline is to think of its components as being in a continual state of flux: a fascinating complex of ocean, sand dune, spit, shingle ridge, creek, saltwater marsh, freshwater marsh and field that all depend on one another, and are never the same from one day to the next.

At one level, the relationship of these constituents is mysterious, arresting, even thrilling. There is little in Britain more beautiful or subtle than an aerial view of the amoebic or anyhow embryonic shape of Scolt Head island and the saltmarshes penetrated by a Byzantine network of shining creeks, and little more dramatic than late sunlight on the faces of the far dunes, ribs of shadow sweeping in over the saltmarsh. But at another level, this shifting scape, and our own attempts to manage it, raise questions about identity, change and survival.

There is of course a paradox in artists finding anchorage in a place that is, of its nature, in a state of flux. But crossing-places are always potent, and many have responded to it.

Let me tell you what I admire. I admire the way in which E. J. Moeran, in the slow movement of his *Symphony in G Minor*, portrays the simultaneous beauty and danger of sand-dune and saltmarsh, and the way in which P. D. James uses them for her own dark purposes in *Devices and Desires*. I admire the dramatic marine paintings of the fisherman John Craske, who showed so graphically the hardship of living on the edge. I admire the brilliant black-and-silver skyscapes of the photographer John Hansell and the way in which, in his etchings, Norman Ackroyd juxtaposes the specific (each reed in a reed-bed, say) with the immensity of marsh or turbulent sky. Almost as much as anything, I admire William Rivière's first novel, *Watercolour Sky*, in which land, sea, sky somehow become one indivisible breathing lung. Above all, I admire (for all his vile politics) the Henry Williamson of *The Story of a Norfolk Farm*, an individual in wartime Britain heroically struggling with his intractable acres, taking the view that a country that 'neglected its soil, neglected its soul'.

Inland, meanwhile, just a breath or two away from the sea and the astonishing, wide beaches where solitaries walk, looking for all the world as if they're the first humans to have been created, are the quiet green lanes that to Sir John Betjeman suggested 'lost innocence', and the crusted villages with their continuities and secrets. On the face of it, they're peaceable, sometimes pretty places, hazelnut cluster of brick-and-flint cottages; in actuality, they used to be little less grim than the village of Dulditch so memorably described by Mary Mann in her unflinching, yet often witty, Hardyesque fiction.

Whereas the coastline breathes flux, these hamlets and villages breathe tradition. First built as passports to heaven at a time when churchgoing was a matter of course, our medieval churches remain architectural wonders, repositories of great art, and places of peace. Outside thick walls, winds swirl, skies swirl, leaves swirl: inside, the tiles are honey-polished, saucered by the steps of the faithful, and there our longings and fears, our passions (and maybe our God) await us.

Almost irrespective of our religious persuasions or the lack of them, churches have punctuated most of our lives. We celebrate our christenings, marriages and funerals within them. In a medieval church, we are at once alone and in a throng. George Barker knew all about this:

I enter and find I stand
in a great barn, bleak and bare;
like ice the winter ghosts and
the white walls gleam and flare
and flame as the sun drops low.
And I see, then, that slowly
the December day is gone.
I stand in silence, not wholly
believing I am alone.
Somehow I cannot go...
(At Thurgarton Church)

As the Church of England wrestles with itself and church attendance falls, it seems all the more desirable that its buildings should be used as places where not only the religious life but the cultural activity of a community is promoted.

In the summer of 2008, the glorious beached ship of a church at Salthouse entertained the most exciting mixed exhibition that I've seen in North Norfolk in a generation, SEAhouse, LIGHThouse, SPIRIThouse, curated by that defender of the faith of East Anglian art, Ian Collins. In this risk-taking show, several artists pointed to where matter and spirit may meet and, so to say, hallow the North Norfolk coast. Floating between the floor and roof of the nave, a swirl of starfish, 'Azimuth' (Liz McGowan) reminded us how to navigate by the stars. A Richard Long-like installation (Margie Britz) elevated clay to the clerestory and revealed the many colours of North Norfolk beach mud. An arrangement of mirrors had us craning our necks and looking over our shoulders, almost entering into the mind of the church's architect; a photograph of the exterior of Salthouse church (Harry Cory Wright), printed on a piece of stretched gauze the size of a large flag, paradoxically enabled us to see the church's interior *through* it; and a small oil painting (Tessa Newcomb), *Then the Light Came*, so utterly defied its frame that a simple unadorned altar and unstained glass window grew as large as the world.

As was apparent from many of the exhibits in this show, the great buildings of North Norfolk – the churches, the halls and houses that have remained in the hands of the same families for generations – continue to attract artists. Not so, however, urban scapes and communities: fishing ports and resorts like Hunstanton and Wells-next-the-Sea, Sheringham and Cromer that somehow combine faded grandeur with vulgarity. The joys of Cromer (including sea-bathing) were noted by Jane Austen and Elizabeth Gaskell, and extolled by Swinburne. But this and the other towns of North Norfolk still await their contemporary laureate.

You don't have to live here or even to be a regular visitor to discover that the place's lineaments may satisfy some inner need. Childhood is a bottomless quarry, and a number of writers – among them L. P. Hartley, Compton Mackenzie and Katherine Pierpoint – have drawn on joyous childhood holidays here. Others have come for a rest-cure, drawn by the coast's sharp, salty air, among them the poet William Cowper ('God made the country, and man made the town') who lived for a few months in Mundesley and often revisited it, and Arthur Conan Doyle.

Parkinson's Law tells us that nature abhors a vacuum, and so it's no surprise that the empty, often bleak coastline abounds with folk-tales. The saltmarshes are full of boggarts, bogles, will-o'-the-wykes, Dead Hands.

When I face south, I'm immediately aware of the presence of the past in this somehow time-defying landscape: here an archaeological dig (such as those underway at Ringstead and Binham), or an avenue of North Norfolk's 'native' tree, the holm oak; there the prehistoric chalkway that leads to the Icknield Way and the Ridgeway; and still almost everywhere, signs of the last world war, cracked and musty pillboxes in ploughed fields, concrete military roads with green spines and blisters.

When I turn and face north, I'm aware of the neverending conflict of land and ocean, and of mighty human attempts to stop or at least stay the sea in her chains. Here, the dykes raised by Dutchmen, and the stony beach at Cley, shockingly rearranged (if that's the word) by a savage storm; there the controlled giving of ground at Titchwell. I'm aware, as was an Anglo-Saxon poet more than one thousand years ago, of the power of the sea itself:

Wherefore my heart leaps within me,
my mind roams with the waves
over the whale's domain... returns again to me
eager and unsatisfied; the solitary bird screams,
irresistible, urges the heart to the whale's way
over the stretch of the seas.

All this is grist to the artist's turning mill. Tides rise and fall – and no wonder we have many words to describe them: flowing, ebbing, dropping, making, on the drag. Then, one morning, the air begins to palpitate. Soon it quivers with the noisy, wild threshing of thousands and thousands of wings, the yelping and honking and wink-winking of a whole colony of pink-footed geese, coming home.

This is what many artists feel about Norfolk. We feel we have come home. We know that the end of each journey is also a beginning. The mind's mist begins to lift, all around there's a lightness and a brightness, and we can walk clean into the possible.

Lady Fraser

Born in Hampstead, London, Lady Fraser first visited North Norfolk in 1946; her family moved from London to Burnham Market in 1958. She worked as Photographic Archivist in the National Gallery, London until starting a family, when she began to support contemporary composers and musicians with Contemporary Concerts Co-ordination, the Society for the Promotion of New Music, the Macnaghten Concerts and finally the Park Lane Group, where she continues as an active member of the Council. She also worked in the Development Office for Sir Neville Marriner and the Orchestra of the Academy of St. Martin-in-the-Fields.

On becoming a widow in 2003, she moved permanently to the family home in Burnham Market where she is now involved as Co-Artistic Director of the Poetry-Next-The-Sea (Wells) Festival, an Honorary Advisor to the Yorke Trust, an Advisory Councillor of Norfolk Churches Trust, Trustee of the League of Friends for Wells Community Hospital, the sole female member of the Interdenominational Fraternal Committee of the Burnham Parishes and Honorary Patron of the Northern Lights Symphony Orchestra.

Finding a gap in cultural activities locally she began to host talks by authors on subjects ranging from Julian of Norwich to 'Going Global'. She has also hosted talks by internationally renowned specialists on musical subjects for the North Norfolk Music Festival. These talks led to local authors approaching her to launch their books, the majority have been young and aspiring and in need of support and patronage and have subsequently gone on to receive widespread recognition.

What Inspires Us?

Lady Fraser

The great triumvirate of sea, sky and marsh-land, each stretching as far as the eye can see. The encircling horizon, confirming, indisputably, that the earth is round.

The North Norfolk coast has been an inspiration for decades to so many artists. It presents itself with a display that holds the on-looker, not confrontationally, but suggesting that an appraisal is needed, a process at once personal, practical and artistic. A prioritizing of ideals and visions. Is there a narrative? There is certainly a rhythm. The artist endeavours to seek out these ultimate answers.

Where and how does the artist belong in such grandeur, in this uniquely feminine panoramic outline, which unexpectedly faces north? Do they sense that they are intruders? How do they proceed with the sensation it arouses and what do they do with their responses?

No passivity is appropriate as the demands reach the deeper aspects of awareness. Perhaps they are even lead to envisage immortality, or immense feats of power in mind, body and spirit.

The threats to the survival of this unparalled coastline persuade even the most reluctant to fight for its future. A struggle, not displaying the conventional techniques of combat, but by applying persistently the artefacts of artistic output.

North Norfolk has a remarkable abundance of architects, painters, sculptures, ceramicists, photographers, writers, poets, musicians and composers who choose to stay and pursue their skills here. They do so in spite of the relentlessly unfriendly wind, which influences the temperature to lower than average throughout the year.

Claims for the choice of, and motives for location are many. They range from fleeing a broken relationship to suffering a loss in income. Others valued finding a location without industry, and more referred to the lack of the distractions and the absence of the tastelessness of the 'bijou', selecting the remoteness and the clarity of an area not en route to anywhere, nor being a solely a passing place. Others claimed that it was easier to find a patron in North Norfolk than in other counties.

These are the overall attractions for the more solitary minded and mildly reclusively inclined artistic people. An underlying searching and yearning, and the seeking a haven, appears throughout. Solitude is facilitated and they find an ease in being alone.

In North Norfolk, the indigenous population offer no frills, and an authenticity almost unparalleled in rural England currently. There is a suspicion, a caution and a dismissal of the intrusive incomer with their image based criteria. A parallel here could be drawn with the unreciprocal landscape, which doesn't woo but presents itself for the observer to evaluate. So it is with those born and bred for generations in Norfolk, who wait quizzically for the dynamic to transform and unfold.

The dominant certainty in the minds of the artists, however, is the tranquillity found here. They find it possible to elevate the commonplace to convey something remarkable. The sense of space, with the enveloping vast skies. There is unanimous challenge found in the elusive and beguiling light. This demands from them the maximum skills.

How to begin to convey, recapture, reproduce? A definition reaches no conclusion. The individual has to delve within himself to solve the indefinable and work through his take on the sine qua non of the North Norfolk Coast.

The extensive tide-soaked beaches provide solace for the meditative, the composer seeking to further their composition or their vision, for the painter to grapple with the germinating creation waiting fruition. The mantra-like footsteps in solitude bring inspiration. The inevitability of the twice daily tide provides a natural metronome, and eases, by its ever transforming quality, a restlessness.

The sea is a variation of nature's own heartbeat.

Most artists are grateful for the acceptance locally of the idiosyncratic and the eccentric – the person who cannot fit any tick box, or cannot be labelled by any 'ism'. There is an undefined norm which accepts and condones. This promotes the creative to pursue their talent, uninhibited and unfettered and so the fragility of their dreams are nurtured, treasured and valued as a locally accepted currency.

Many artists return to a place which provided a haven in childhood with the idea of recapturing halcyon days. They hope the past will remain an ideal setting to develop skills thriving in the freedom of an ideally unlimited spatial background. A maturing of the insights, first sensed in childhood, flowers into a fulfilment, with the experiences of the intervening years contributing to a maturity.

The response to the elusive light, a reflective interplay between sky, sea, and

land, plays a profound influence. Artists observe that in this neighbourhood, all surfaces – horizontal and vertical – and all textures, seem to reflect each other, thus inspiring all the muses of their respective arts to express a deeper awareness. The almost tangible yet elusive quality prompts a mystical reflective stillness. In this setting, the individual seems to experience a paradox of loss of identity, yet artistically gaining an individuality. For the artist, it is the duality of being almost overawed, yet awakened by this withholding passive panorama, in which perspective demands a connoisseurship of execution with much soul searching.

There is no handle to support, no pointers to direct, but the impetus seems to come from an inner recognition that there is a treasure to be conveyed in a colourful, profound composition. The artist feels an inner confrontation of values and identity. This is more than the visual – the inner eye leads the way.

The preponderance of second home properties in the possession of those with wealth, is in direct contrast to the spiralling number of artists and musicians and those who choose to live outside the confines of office restrictions, who continue to select North Norfolk.

Could there be an unseen balance working cosmically? Creative artistic wealth and monetary wealth strangely walking the tightrope, hand in hand? One necessary to feed the souls, the other providing livelihood on many levels for the community.

The threat is that the unchangingness, the spatial freedom and peace should be destroyed. The apprehension is that innovations such as buildings and roads will create intrusion into their creative lives. Yet some artists enjoy changes. They find them a challenge. So it seems that the ripple of paradox recurs in the lives of those most in need of the unique, natural facilities that are the hallmark of the North Norfolk Coast.

Nicholas Barnham

Nicholas Barnham was born at Walsingham in 1939 and was educated at the Royal Masonic School and Norwich Art School. He taught at Cambridge School of Art and for the last thirty years he has worked as a painter and printmaker.

For fifty years the North Norfolk Coast has inspired his *plein aire* landscapes and lino cuts. He has exhibited widely: in London with numerous one man shows, at the Royal Academy of Arts (having been nominated for associate membership), in Germany and Sweden and in Shetland where he lives when he is not living in North Norfolk. Two of his landscapes are in the Government Art Collection, and his work is represented in many public and private collections. He is listed in the *Dictionary of Artists in Britain since 1945* compiled by David Buckman and in *Who's Who in Art 2008*.

This book is illustrated with his drawings and lino cuts. His hand-made blocks have been hand printed on Victorian Albion presses, one of which has been in continual use in Wells for over a century – a fine example of zero carbon print production! He hopes it will continue to be used for another century.

What Inspires Us?

Nick Barnham

To quote Henry Rider Haggard in 1899: 'At every season of the year, at every hour of the day Norfolk is beautiful, but always with a different beauty.' For over fifty years the North Norfolk Coast has continued to inspire me and although I have lived in other places, for instance, the north isles of Shetland, North Yorkshire, Cambridge and rural Essex, I have always been drawn back to Norfolk. It is a pattern that makes clear that 'getting away' from North Norfolk has been as significant as returning to it.

At this stage in my life I divide my time between North Norfolk and the most northerly island in the British Isles, Unst in Shetland, two areas that have in common: sea, sky, ever changing weather, the harshness of the north winds, boats, strangely independent people engaged in similarly demanding occupations as well as the historically fascinating connections created by the herring fishing in the past and mussel farming and – controversially – wind farming today. These two areas of Britain help me, as an artist, to come back to Norfolk with fresh eyes, renewed energy, the benefit of comparison and of being exercised by different demands. There is the excitement of returning and seeing, as if for the first time, a tree, a stretch of sand, a different shape of boat, a field of barley actually ripening, sea lavender and all the subtleties of the salt marsh. On occasion, I look at the horizon and am aware that due north there is an expanse of North Sea some 750 miles between where I am standing and my croft house in Unst, an island farther away from the 'island' of Norfolk than anywhere else in the British Isles.

I have always enjoyed messing about in boats, drawing boats, rowing boats, sailing boats and fishing from boats. I have had the magical experience of working from the deck of the *Albatros,* moored off Salthouse, gazing across the sea at Salthouse church and the watch house at Blakeney. Boats play a significant part in providing my inspiration, particularly as the tradition of building beautiful wooden work boats and crab boats is, sadly, fast disappearing. For me, the visual attraction of the coast east of Sheringham has been seriously diminished by the demise of the traditional wooden crab boats. The traditional clinker built boat has always been 'more than just a boat' – it is a sculpture of the highest quality, a man-made creation that possesses a strand of the spiritual.

Staying with the spiritual, one cannot fail to be moved by the magnificent churches – St Clements at Burnham Overy Town, St Margaret's at Burnham

Norton, St Nicholas at Salthouse and St Margaret's of Cley to name but a few – that inspired John Sell Cotman and his contemporaries and continue to inspire artists today. Regular visits to see the work of the Norwich School at the Castle museum in Norwich have been an essential part of my pattern of life.

Many artists, be they concerned with paint, words or music, pay homage to the influence of the particular men and women who were important at the beginning of their career. When I think of the North Norfolk landscape, the sea and fishing boats, Jack Cox comes immediately to my mind. A man who combined a life of a working fisherman with that of an artist, Jack has been a hero of mine since my Art School days. He found many ways to encourage me, from giving me studio space to providing my first taste of Norfolk beer in the Shipwright's Arms. I was pleased to see his name mentioned in the *Turn of the Tide*. I could easily devote a chapter to Jack Cox, a chapter to boats, a chapter to trees, and a chapter to landscape.

Are there threats to the elements of creative life? Most certainly there are. Some are small and personal; others are huge. The traditional boats I love are being supplanted by a proliferation of plastic and gin palaces, many of which never leave their moorings. Even the future of the Albatros, a source of inspiration for me and other artists, is threatened. Vast, and with intrusive ramifications for the landscape of North Norfolk, are the planned wind farms and all that goes with them. Interestingly, or should I say 'distressingly', Shetland and North Norfolk, my two major sources of inspiration, face this threat to their landscape and their seascape. Massive wind farm developments on land are in the pipeline in Shetland and on/in the sea off North Norfolk. In Shetland the population, deeply concerned, are very much involved and there is a possibility of the projected scheme (part of the plan is to supply 20% of the domestic requirements for electricity for the whole of Scotland) not going ahead. I, as citizen and artist, am particularly concerned about the changes proposed in Wells, especially those concerned with the 'back up' for servicing the wind farms. Particularly disturbing is the plan to invade part of the beach for building jetties etc., and all the detritus that will go with it. Believing that the beach was sacrosanct, I am horrified at the prospect of this intrusion dangerously close to the East Hills, to me one of the most beautiful parts of this, my very special, coast.

To conclude on a more positive note, I have favourite places for painting along the coast of North Norfolk. It is a pilgrimage that I make, and have made for the last half a century, at all times of the year but particularly in winter. Thornham, Brancaster, Brancaster Staithe, Burnham Overy Staithe, Burnham Overy Town, Wells, Stiffkey, Morston, Blakeney and Salthouse (an area incidentally which has diminished over the years) are places unchanged and magical from a creative point of view, thanks to the involvement of and protection by the communities that live in them. Ironically, the only landscape seriously under threat is the one nearest to

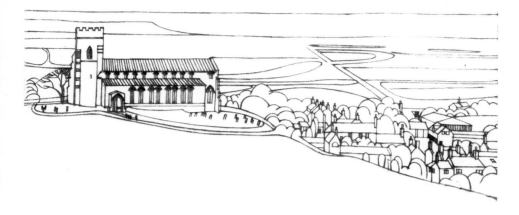

where I live: Wells.

What is it about these areas that so appeals to me? Difficult though it is, I will try to explain. A few miles west of Wells is a spot where I can look north-west and see the horizon, important pictorially because it is where the North Sea meets the north sky. In summer there is usually a soft haze of pale ultramarine and alizarin. In winter there is often a sharp white line. Looking more intently, I see a line of breaking waves against the strip of pale ochre sand; nearer still the salt marsh appears an almost indefinable area of constantly changing subtle colour, mystical, impossible to isolate clearly the horizontal strips of pale light and dark interspersed with glimpses of sea lavender and meandering creeks of sepia mud. Coming closer – the very first sign of man – a group of barns and cottages, very small in the distance, their red brick mellowed by the weather of a century or more combined with flint and chalk looking very fragile and vulnerable from rising sea levels. Nearer still, there is the strong vertical statement of Burnham Overy windmill on higher ground, looking quite magnificent, beautifully restored and belonging indisputably to the landscape, a bold landmark of black, white and vermilion. To complete the picture is a field of oats punctuated by scarlet poppies. What a composition!

From the same spot, if I look west, another delight, one of my favourite churches, St. Margaret's, Burnham Norton, beyond a hedge of dramatic wind blown oaks in their prime, almost hiding from view. I prefer St Margaret's in the winter when the surrounding trees are without leaves, a terrific subject in black and white. Again from the same spot, this time looking south, I see a jewel in the crown of North Norfolk, Burnham Overy Town St Clement's church (St Clement is the patron of seafarers) surrounded by cottages and barns, trees and fields, making a superb united whole of the village. It is an excellent example of organic growth, in both buildings and in landscape, one that could never be deliberately created or planned. It is a matter of miraculous survival across 1000 years of history.

Finally, still at the same spot and having traversed 360 degrees, I look to the north-east and see a Norton creek filling with the incoming tide, Scolt Head Island, sand and marsh in the distance, and beyond that, the North Sea. The masts of small boats are gradually becoming vertical in an essentially horizontal landscape. Wind-blown hawthorns on the edge of salt marsh make up the foreground. From this post I have drawn and painted for years, and hope to continue doing so, this wealth of inspiration that changes constantly with the seasons and tides. I can work here undisturbed for days at a time, even in high summer despite the bumper to bumper traffic on the nearby A149. The only sounds are those of bird song, of wind in the long grass and the distant murmur of the North Sea, combined with the scent – a cocktail of salt, sea, marsh and corn ripening.

My earliest memories are of the magic of living with the North Sea at our doorstep at a spring tide at Burnham Overy Staithe, memories that have coloured my whole life. The essential part that one can only suggest in a painting, in my case with watercolour, is the salt marsh, so ephemeral and ethereal and, with the threat of rising sea levels, so fleeting?

North Norfolk landscape has inspired painters for centuries and continues to do so and I believe will do so in the future with the necessary back up of galleries and, above all, people – usually from outside Norfolk – wanting to acquire original and personal statements about this part of East Anglia. Without this support the 'creative industries' would suffer severely.

North Norfolk is undoubtedly an inspiring place in which to live and work. It is an austere attraction that takes time and weathering to appreciate.

Political Perspectives

A View from the Edge – *Henry Bellingham MP*

A View from Westminster – *Norman Lamb MP*

Henry Bellingham

Henry Bellingham has been the Member of Parliament for North West Norfolk since 2001, having also represented the same constituency from 1983 to 1997. He is currently a Shadow Minister for the Ministry of Justice.

Having grown up and made his home in Norfolk he is passionate about issues that affect his constituency, constantly standing up for local communities both in the towns and countryside, as well as for the environment and small businesses.

Henry was born in March 1955. He studied Law at Magdalene College, Cambridge. Having graduated in 1977 he was called to the Bar (Middle Temple) where he served as a barrister for 8 years.

Henry married Emma Whiteley in 1993 and they now have a young son, Jamie. He is joint secretary of the Lords and Commons Cricket Club, and outside Westminster enjoys country sports and golf.

A specialist in small businesses, countryside and farming issues, defence and Northern Ireland, he was PPS to Malcolm Rifkind (then Defence and Foreign Secretary) from 1991-97.

In July 2002, he was appointed Shadow Minister for Small Businesses, Enterprise and Construction and he held this post up until the May 2005 General Election. After his re-election he was appointed to the Whips Office before becoming Shadow Minister for Constitutional Affairs in November 2006. He then became a Shadow Minister for Justice when the new Ministry of Justice was created in July 2007.

A View from the Edge

An Interview with Henry Bellingham

We spoke to Henry Bellingham on a beautiful spring morning at Burnham Norton, at the Eastern edge of his constituency, which he has served for 22 years.

Not surprisingly, our discussion revealed a deep and thorough knowledge of the constituency – but also a deep affection for it and for the countryside and coast. You only have to hear him talking to confirm that this is an MP combining his local and national roles to good effect, with his roots here and with a well-earned reputation for getting things done.

Having talked to his neighbouring MP, Norman Lamb, about how the governance of North Norfolk is seen from Westminster, we asked him for his views from the other end of the telescope – Westminster and Brussels as seen from here.

Immediately he voiced a theme running right through our conversation: "Both Westminster and Brussels are very remote – not just in where they are but in how they work. They are far too centralised, far too keen on micro-managing from miles way, and on targets set nationally. Small wonder that they can't understand the priorities and needs of a place like this. How can you possibly deal with a complex local issue like sea defences through national decision-making based on a budget owned and operated nationally?"

Quangos

Henry accepts that quangos can play a useful role – for example Natural England and the Commission for Rural Communities (CRC) – but is concerned at the extent to which Westminster and Whitehall set the budget and the culture. "These people need to do the bidding of Ministers, and that comes first." He described Stuart Burgess, the Chairman of the CRC, as a breath of fresh air – someone who understands the countryside and is not afraid to be outspoken – but as the exception rather than the rule. "Too often people feel that these bodies are out of touch. Their top-down system fails to recognise the unique characteristics of each place. Whether it's East Devon, North Yorkshire or North Norfolk, we are all different."

He praises the work of the Government Office for the East of England, "but then we also have the East of England Development Agency and the East of England Regional Assembly. These are hair-shirt times and I fear that they are going to get worse, not better. We simply cannot afford layer upon layer of agencies." He sees the Regional Development Agencies and Regional Assemblies as unnecessary extra levels and confirms that a Conservative government would get rid of them. "We need fewer organisations with a more decentralised brief."

National Politicians and Local Places

Henry fears that national politicians have a poor understanding of places such as the Saltmarsh Coast. "They do come here from time to time, but I am sometimes staggered by the paucity of their understanding, their lack of a real feel for the place. We have real issues here – for example over the inshore fishing fleet and over sea defences."

He is also concerned that their knowledge is often misinformed. "They tend to think of North Norfolk, if they think of us at all, as sparsely populated, wealthy and privileged, full of second homes and without real problems. They don't realise, for instance, that there are two wards in King's Lynn that are among the 20 most deprived in the country, that there are several pockets of high unemployment and serious deprivation here. Every single Norfolk job is vital. That's why the fishing issue is so important."

We asked him about the role of the Minister for the East of England. "Barbara Follett certainly has the interests of the region at heart and does understand its issues, such as flooding dangers. She has been regularly in touch and asked me to contact her for help with problems. But I question the wisdom of having Ministers in these regional roles whose Departmental work has nothing to do with the region in question. We should have a Minister for the region from one of the Departments that have a real impact on what happens here, such as DEFRA. Under the current system, Ministers for the regions have become cheer-leaders for their party."

He spoke of a remorseless drive for commercial and residential development and concern that more and more countryside was being concreted over. "That endangers the character of rural communities – the marshland, the coastland, the breckland. They must be part of living communities, not carried along in the slipstream of this relentless pursuit of growth at any cost."

Priorities

Henry sees three key priorities for the area:

1   We must preserve the countryside and the coast.
2   We must find ways of enabling young people to stay, live and work here – including providing housing at reasonable cost.
3   We must provide more jobs.

He believes that a policy agenda set by Westminster and Whitehall is inimical to those aims.

On housing, he would like to see each village working with Housing Associations to develop their own low cost housing schemes – on the lines that he believes have worked well for example in Brancaster and Burnham Market. "We need a lot more rented accommodation and shared equity housing. This is a case of each community deciding the housing that it needs, especially for young people, working with the experts in the Housing Associations and giving priority to local people."

An Urban View of a Rural World

He believes that urban priorities are far too dominant in current policies. "These people are under huge pressure to deliver an urban, top-down, target based culture. It's not surprising really. If you look at the political map of the UK, with a few exceptions the blue and yellow are the Conservative and Liberal Democrat rural constituencies and the red is in the cities. Labour has been kicked out of the countryside so it's not surprising that it's the cities that they are interested in and will want to look after."

He cited as an example the very important £120 million expansion scheme for the College of West Anglia which was originally given the go-ahead by the Learning and Skills Council (LSC). This would have supported and expanded the creation of the skills needed in rural communities – horticulture, equine manage-

ment, countryside and rural management, farming – alongside other skills needed by sectors such as the residential care homes, the hospitality industry and hair salons. It would have allowed the development of a new site in South Lynn, including a city academy not tied to the national curriculum. He told us that the LSC had announced (and later confirmed) that this expansion, part of a £500 million scheme earmarked for the region as a whole, can't be afforded and had been put on hold. "I very much fear that when final decisions are made the rural areas will lose out and that the go ahead will be given in marginal seats. That would be a real setback for the future skills we need here."

Prospects for Change

Henry anticipates that in the event of a change in Government there would be a definite shift of priorities. "Both the major opposition parties have a much better understanding of rural matters and of what is really happening in a place like this – that we too have problems of drug addiction, of dysfunctional families, that there are young people with drug problems in and out of the region's courts every day, that we need to find ways of stopping them from re-offending, and that mild drug users are coming out of the prisons as hard addicts. These are live, rural issues just as they are urban."

He would like to see the remaining agencies reconfigured with greater powers of local decision-making. "Central government needs to trust local authorities and organisations and then allow them to deliver in ways that suit local circumstances. Yes there should be a tough inspection regime and government should come down hard when mistakes are made – but they should not be breathing down people's necks while they are trying to get on with the job."

Hearing Local Voices

Henry's concern is that local councils aren't trusted by central government and are not given sufficient decision-making power to earn respect from local people. "Places like Wells and Hunstanton should be able to decide how to run their own street lighting, cemeteries, car parking and so forth, so that the services provided by local government would be designed and managed closer to the local people who use them. A Conservative government would strengthen local councils so that they have more, not less influence on decisions."

He asked us whether we knew the name of our MEP. We sadly shook our heads. "You are not untypical – and yet these people have a lot of influence through the European Parliament on matters that greatly affect us – agricultural policy and conservation just to mention two."

"I would like to see someone responsible for representing this county in Europe,

someone who would talk regularly to fishermen, to the local NFU. The UK is going to stay in Europe, but we have to make our representation there more efficient and more accountable."

Keeping in Touch

We asked him about how he kept in touch with constituents and makes sure that he hears their views. He contrasted his role with that of urban MPs. "A rural MP has to operate proactively. In cities it is easier for an MP to be reactive and let the views and opinions come in. But that doesn't work in a constituency like this. You have to go out regularly to meet the local Parish Councils, residents' groups, voluntary groups and pressure groups. And that helps me as well as them; once people get to know you and expect regular visits, you achieve a good flow of knowledge, and a greater awareness of local feelings and concerns, and therefore become far better informed and effective.

"It means that I have direct access to people who can brief me with expert knowledge on matters that are raised in Parliament. And working like that means that the job is far more satisfying and rewarding."

Public Services and Local Government

He sees as the starting point that people value public services but resent paying for them. He paid credit to the Borough Council at King's Lynn for consistently setting a precept below the national average and feels that the services we get are generally seen as reasonable. But he would like to see more roles and services being devolved to town and borough councils and believes that this would produce better value for money.

"I think that the Local Government Review is going to be a big issue at the next Election. If the plan for a unitary authority were to go through as presently planned, we would see a further removal of power and decision-making from local people. That's the wrong way to go."

He sees a direct link between the way in which decisions are made and whether people feel that they are getting a good deal. "If services are run on a uniform model from national level, the odds are that they will be worse. We have had some dreadful examples. The Rural Payments Agency did an appalling job in processing payments when the new Single Farm Payment scheme came in. Farmers were badly hit. Families were seriously affected when tax credits were overpaid and then reclaimed. Student loans were similarly badly handled. All these have been examples of national agencies trying to run a uniform 'we know best' approach from the centre."

"What was once the Department of Social Security used to have an office in King's Lynn where people could go if they had problems over benefits. That was then closed down and they had to go to Norwich. Now the Norwich service has been closed down and they have to go to Burnley. I've nothing against Burnley, but ....!"

He acknowledges that decisions like this have their origin in saving costs and taxpayers' money, but suggested that centralisation actually wastes money. "I see the hand of the big consultancies here, recommending business models based on cost saving rather than effective outcomes. We have seen it in the private sector and especially in banking systems – indeed that mindset may have been one of the causes of the banking collapse; central managers out of touch with the realities of people's lives on the ground. Today if I need to raise a banking problem on behalf of a constituent I can no longer get an answer by talking to a manager in King's Lynn. Often the only way is to write to the Chairman or CEO of the bank and then after a lot of delay get an answer from that level. That one size fits all mentality is neither efficient nor does it save money. They miss out on the opportunity to sort things out quickly and locally."

Henry concluded with a heartfelt message about trust and responsibility: "If you trust people to exercise power, albeit within a strong inspection regime, they will generally deliver, good, probably better results. There is a lot of talent out there, but if you make any of the layers of government into talking shops, the good people will become frustrated and cease to contribute."

Norman Lamb

Norman Lamb is the Liberal Democrat MP for North Norfolk. Before he was elected he was an employment lawyer and leader of the opposition on Norwich City Council. He fought the seat in 1992 and 1997 before winning by 483 votes in 2001 and has since turned a 15,500 Conservative majority into a Lib Dem majority of 10,606.

He was appointed Liberal Democrat Deputy Spokesperson for International Development, became Shadow Treasury Minister, was elected to the Treasury Select Committee in January 2003 and was appointed Parliamentary Private Secretary to Charles Kennedy later that year. Following re-election in 2005, he was promoted to Shadow Secretary of State for Trade and Industry in the Liberal Democrat Shadow Cabinet. He became Chief of Staff to party leader Sir Menzies Campbell in March 2006 and in December 2006 was appointed Shadow Secretary of State for Health.

Until his election, Norman was a partner in the law firm Steele and Co and was recognised as a leader in employment law in *The Legal 500* and *Chambers Directory*. His book on employment law: *Remedies in the Employment Tribunal* (Sweet and Maxwell, 1998) has been described as an invaluable "aide-memoire for experienced practitioners".

He said in his maiden speech in parliament, "We have a duty to make politics much more relevant and to behave in a way that will rebuild people's trust in the political process. It is incumbent on us to modernise the way in which we carry out our business, and to open this place up to young people."

A View from Westminster

An Interview with Norman Lamb

W hen William Ewart Gladstone proposed self government for Ireland in 1868 and the London establishment threw up its collective hands in horror, its reaction had less to do with the implications for English landowners than the threat that London might lose control over a large part of the country. Then as now governance was more centralized in Britain than in any other developed nation. Now as then almost all decisions that directly affect peoples' lives are made in Westminster.

Norman Lamb feels that the East of England, the County of Norfolk and the Saltmarsh Coast of North Norfolk are neither better nor worse off than the rest of England because power is concentrated in London. But he also feels that England as a whole suffers by comparison with Scotland, Northern Ireland and Wales and is troubled by the fact that central control means decisions on local issues and on national issues with distinctively local attributes are largely in the hands of decision makers who may know little and care less about local perspectives and priorities and do not understand local realities.

As Norman Lamb considers the future of North Norfolk he believes the people who live here have far less say than they should have on issues that will directly affect their interests and would be better off if current governance arrangements – in which local autonomy is fragmented across regional, county, district and local authorities and a sub-dermal layer of quasi-governmental organizations – were replaced by a more responsive and less circumscribed system. But he also believes that some of the men and women who work remarkably hard in elected and appointed positions on behalf of their communities – in many cases with little recognition or reward – lack the qualifications and experience that would be needed to discharge greater responsibilities if they had them and that devolution could not succeed unless the most qualified and experienced people came forward to participate in local government.

The One Way Street

On a snowy February morning in his constituency office in North Walsham Norman Lamb points out that Malta is a small, charming and remarkably unspoiled country that in some ways resembles the city-states that once dotted the

Mediterranean Basin. He says that, given its scale (it is smaller than the Isle of Man) it is almost absurd to distinguish between central and local government on this three island archipelago. Nobody, he says, would be surprised to learn that Malta has one of the most centralized systems of governance in the world (and the highest incidence of taxation in the European Union). But he thinks many people would be shocked to know that England is barely less centralized, not least because after centuries of homogenizing central control, this country is more differentiated – geographically, culturally, ecologically, historically and politically – than most. The local issues that worry people in the Northeast are, he says, different from those that worry people in the Southeast and different again from those on the minds of people in the Birmingham Conurbation, Western Cornwall... and the Saltmarsh Coast of North Norfolk.

He recognizes that nationwide policies are the only sensible solutions to nationwide issues; that defence, most infrastructure and many aspects of health, education and welfare are national issues that must be managed nationally; that nationwide standards are the only appropriate standards for product safety, public health and education; and that the bulk of the nation's fiscal resources should be managed from Westminster. But he believes that issues rooted in local realities and priorities should be resolved by the elected representatives of local communities in local authorities, institutions and organizations and that national legislation should allow for the fact that one size rarely fits all and avoid the assumption that everywhere is like everywhere else.

He says the current imbalance of power and responsibility is inefficient because it is – at best – extremely difficult for central decision-makers to grasp local realities. There is an implicit belief, he says, that politicians and officials in central government can make better decisions about local issues than people who live in local communities. He strongly challenges the assumption that 'London knows best' because the evidence shows that is often untrue. The imbalance is also, he says, undemocratic because it imposes unbridgeable distances between local communities and decision makers; because when local views conflict with central policies the centre always seems to prevail; and because local communities have no say in how fiscal resources that flow from them to central government are spent.

But excessive centralization is, he says, only part of the story and another part is buried in tangled, multi-layered networks of regional, county, district and local authorities, non-government organizations (Quangos) and voluntary organizations. While he believes there is a strong case for thoughtful devolution he also believes that devolution in the absence of radical changes in the structures and processes of local governance that affect the Saltmarsh Coast would actually make matters worse. "You could not," he says, "simply shift power within the existing system and expect it would work."

211

Layers of Government

The Regional Layer

Norman Lamb points out that successive national governments have struggled with the challenge of how best to achieve devolution in England and that since the proposed regional assembly for the Northeast (in his words) "came unstuck" in the referendum of November 2004, the present government has made little progress. He also thinks the various regional bodies that exist to serve the East of England are imperfect means of connecting local people with decisions that directly affect them.

The East of England Regional Assembly is independent of central government and exists to promote the economic, social and environmental well-being of the region. But, Norman Lamb believes that very few people know it exists and even fewer know what it does[35]. Much the same is true, he says, of the Government Office for the East of England (GoEast) one of nine regional offices that cover the English counties, each a focal point for delivering national government services.

GoEast is described as the *"Government's eyes and ears in the region"* and is expected to facilitate an *'East of England input'* to the policy-making process by *"working with a range of regional and local bodies including local authorities, businesses, local education authorities, voluntary organizations, the health service and local people to help create sustainable communities and to maximize competitiveness and prosperity in the region"*. The problem with GoEast, says Norman Lamb, is that as with the Regional Assembly, most people in North Norfolk are unaware it exists, a small minority knows what it does, a yet smaller minority can explain the difference it makes in their lives and a fraction of that minority can name the Minister for the East of England or explain the Minister's role.

On the face of things, he says, GoEast looks like a good thing because it promises to make central government better informed and more responsive; to hear, understand and interpret what local people have to say; to adapt national policies to local realities; and to give local communities better access to Westminster. In sum it seems to address many of the issues arising from the imbalance of power between Westminster, regions and localities. But the creation of GoEast and its counterpart offices in other regions was, in Norman Lamb's view, at best a well meaning exercise in window dressing, at worst a cynical attempt to disguise the reality that GoEast is an agency of central government and a top-down institution that leaves the balance of power unchanged. The existence of GoEast, he says, does

---

[35] The Assembly advises government on regional planning, housing and transport issues, including priorities for public spending; scrutinizes the work of the East of England Development Agency (EEDA); provides services to local government such as training, consultancy and advice as the regional employers' organization; hosts the regional improvement and efficiency partnership ('Improvement East') for local and fire authorities; and aims to work with its partners and stakeholders to promote equality of opportunity, eliminate discrimination, promote good relations, well-being and regional cohesion.

not return local issues to local owners and ignores the fact that (with the partial exception of some Quangos) English local authorities have few financial resources and almost no power to raise them and implies that the existing structure of local governance is efficient and democratic when it is neither.

Turning to the East of England Development Agency (EEDA), one of nine regional development agencies whose boundaries coincide with those of the Government Offices, Norman Lamb says that while EEDA exists to promote sustainable development in the region and invests in both the public and private sectors "it has no democratic legitimacy but is nonetheless a player". He recognizes that in recent years the Saltmarsh Coast has benefitted from EEDA grants (Wells has received two grants to support the improvement of harbour facilities and amenities) and that it has a competent staff and a committed Board. But EEDA's mandate, he says, comes from Westminster, its members are appointed by Westminster (although there are representatives from the six County Councils covered by EEDA) and it reports upwards – to central government. The result, he says, is that EEDA lacks local accountability and the situation is not helped by the fact that it has no local offices in Norfolk.

The County and District Layer

Having served on the Norfolk County Council from 1987 to 1991 before being elected to Parliament, Norman Lamb draws favourable contrasts between the elected County Council and the unelected regional bodies but laments the facts that even in fields like education and transport in which the county *seems* to have jurisdiction, its powers are severely limited; that fundamental issues like spending priorities are largely determined by central government on the basis of national criteria; and that the scope of the issues managed at the county level has actually diminished in recent decades. He marvels that in these circumstances so many dedicated people are prepared to spend so much time and effort on County Council business.

Norman Lamb recognizes that the North Norfolk District Council and the King's Lynn and West Norfolk Borough Council which between them cover the Saltmarsh Coast (and quite a lot more) add value by filling the gap between county and town/parish governments and that their roles are particularly important in a large county with relatively poor infrastructure. But he points out that both would disappear under either of two proposals for local government reorganization being considered by the Boundary Commission.

He does not have a lot of time for the Commission, thinks "the whole process of local government reorganization is flawed", doubts if any of the options would change current relationships between national and local governments and believes the choice between a unitary authority and a 'doughnut' solution (in which Norwich would be separated from the rest of the county) is largely irrelevant because neither proposal would devolve power from Westminster. But he is impressed by evidence that larger authorities tend to outperform smaller ones and believes the contrasts are related to the fact that larger authorities find it easier to attract and retain capable staff and persuade strong candidates to run for elected office. In his view the best solution for Norfolk would be a single tier of local government with the power to raise a balanced mix of income and property taxes and to eliminate what he regards as regressive Council Taxes. He thinks England would do well to emulate European countries where local authorities have substantial fiscal autonomy.

The Town and Parish Layer

The oldest town and parish councils in Norfolk measure time in centuries and Norman Lamb says it is sadly ironic that as they have grown older they have become increasingly feeble. He appreciates the fact that some Parish Councils focus their energies on issues and opportunities that do not require significant expenditures and in so doing add tangible value to the lives of people who live there. But he recognizes that other Town and Parish Councils are frustrated by the difficulty of affecting outcomes; that lacking authority to mobilize financial resources they are forced to depend on District/Borough Council 'precepts'; and that they must often address issues on an advisory basis or refer them to higher authority. It is he says, hardly surprising that Parish Council elections are often uncontested although he says it is testimony to the strength of some local communities that so many people are willing to make the best of what could be – if the powers of local authorities were increased and realigned – a more fulfilling job.

Quasi Non-governmental Organizations (Quangos)

Whereas some of the basic structures of regional and local government that affect the Saltmarsh Coast and will shape its future have existed for a very long time, most Quangos are the creations of the last thirty years. Norman Lamb points out that Quangos are by far the fastest growing branch of governance in Norfolk and much of the rest of England although – perhaps because it has so many special, notably environmental and ecological issues – North Norfolk seems to have more than its share. He also points out that compared with other branches of local government many Quangos are relatively well off and that, as Baroness Scott recently pointed out "Quangos are now outspending local government"[36].

Local Quangos cover what he describes as "a swathe of issues", ranging from environmental conservation and protection to business development to the management of the area's largest harbour. Some Quangos – such as the Environment Agency and Natural England – have nationwide remits and work in the Saltmarsh Coast either through regional offices (e.g. the Environment Agency covers North

---

[36] Baroness Scott of Needham Market, House of Lords debate, July 5, 2007

Norfolk from its Ipswich Area Office) or local partnerships (e.g.Natural England's partnership with the Holkham Estate). Other Quangos, such as the Norfolk Coast Partnership, created in 1991 to *'protect and enhance'* the designated Area of Outstanding Natural Beauty[37] are explicitly local, locally funded[38] and mainly advisory.

All Quangos have more or less explicit mandates but few have elected members although some (including the Norfolk Coast Partnership) have elected representatives. Others (such as the Wells Harbour Commissioners[39]) fill vacancies through open advertising, new members being chosen by existing members. Some Quangos are accountable to central government, others to local (County, District, Borough) governments, others, to all intents and purposes only to themselves. Some are directly funded from Westminster, others (such as Wells Harbour Commissioners) operate with their own revenues.

The Wells Area Partnership – one of 376 Local Area Partnerships created to promote sustainable development in England and Wales – covers the eastern and western parts of the Saltmarsh Coast but excludes Holme, Thornham Titchwell, Brancaster, Brancaster Staithe and Burnham Deepdale. Its purpose – like that of other Area Partnerships – is to 'provide the means for their communities to determine actions in their own locality and to influence decisions at the district and county level which affect the services for their area'. Norman Lamb applauds their intentions and the fact that in a short time the Wells Area Partnership has done some useful things (such as promoting the 'Homes for Wells' campaign). But why, he asks "do we need yet another layer of quasi governance by yet another unelected body".

He questions whether the Quango-based business support networks that are supposed to serve area businesses actually *'provide high quality advice to new and growing firms'* and says "the proliferation of Quangos and other agencies across the UK under this (present) Government has only served to confuse small businesses and inhibit their ability to flourish". He has no quarrel with their stated purpose 'to provide small businesses with a support network'. That he says "is a worthy cause". But he believes that "for this network to function effectively, information must be easily attainable and must match the requirements of the business community". Instead, he says, "there is a morass of advice which often appears to be confused and unhelpful to business" and adds that in his view "the Government is not fulfilling its remit, is failing to provide the quality of information demanded by business users and is leaving taxpayers short-changed by manifestly failing to deliv-

---

[37] The Norfolk Coast AONB – which covers a substantially larger area than the Saltmarsh Coast – was created in 1968 under the National Parks and Access to the Countryside Act on 1949.

[38] The Core Funding Partners for the Norfolk Coast Partnership are the Norfolk County Council, the Kings Lynn and West Norfolk Borough Council and the North Norfolk District Council.

[39] A Statutory Public Body first established by Royal Charter I 1667 and subsequently governed by successive Revision Orders.

er value for money".

The Voluntary Layer

Norman Lamb is a passionate believer in the value of voluntary organizations and says they play important roles in the life of the Saltmarsh Coast. Although they are not instruments of governance they play parts that, in other countries are played by government and can exert a strong influence on political outcomes. Two nation-wide voluntary organizations, the National Trust and the Royal Society for the Protection of Birds are particularly important in this area which, in turn, plays prominent roles in the lives of those organizations (the RSPB's reserve at Titchwell is the most visited RSPB reserve in the country). Another national voluntary organization – the RNLI – has a more localized influence but plays a central role in the Wells community which is intensely proud of and works tirelessly to support its lifeboats and their crews.

He also points to purely local voluntary bodies that have been created in response to specific threats and opportunities and have played key roles in shaping outcomes. The 'Save Wells Hospital' campaign, created in 2004 in response to the planned closure of Wells Hospital was, he said, an outstanding example of what can be done through local grassroots action when like-minded people join forces to promote or defend a common cause. He admires the volunteers who have successfully campaigned over several years through many setbacks to ensure the hospital continues to serve the area community. Whereas he thinks the creeping growth of Quangos in the economic, social and political fabric of English life is cause for concern and while he recognizes that nationwide voluntary organizations may sometimes seem insensitive to local thoughts and feelings he believes locally-based grassroots organizations have intense legitimacy and that they will continue to play vital roles in local life.

Power to Which People?

Norman Lamb is full of admiration for the thousands of people in North Norfolk communities who turn out week after week, year after year – on winter nights when they would rather stay home and on summer evenings when they would rather be out and about – to do what sometimes turns out to be frustrating and thankless work in elected and unelected and mostly unpaid positions in local government, Quangos and voluntary organizations. Many of them – local people who bring deep commitment and lifetimes of relevant experience to bear on their responsibilities and people who have recently come to live here having acquired experience elsewhere and now want to add value in their new communities – are, he says, remarkably well qualified for the roles they play.

But, he says, there are three problems, each rooted in the limited powers of local

217

authorities. The first is that although some elected officials, particularly at the parish level, feel they are able to shape local events, others are dissatisfied and frustrated and it is not uncommon for successful candidates to stand down because they feel they are wasting their time. The second is that although the area has rich human resources, many people – long time residents and incomers alike – are unwilling to throw their hats in to electoral rings because they feel they would be wasting their time. The third is that if power *were* to flow from central to local government, some of those whose enthusiasm and commitment is beyond reproach lack the backgrounds, skills and experience that would be needed to make devolution work.

Much the same is true, he said, of local government employees. Although the North Norfolk Coast is a very attractive area in which to live and raise families the limited powers and small size of local government in North Norfolk mean that the most qualified and most ambitious public servants are reluctant to move to what they see as a backwater. As with elected officers, the most capable people will not come forward unless they know they will wield significant authority and autonomy.

Norman Lamb believes that some potential candidates for both elected and appointed offices are also put off by what he sees as a regrettable local trend towards the party-politicization of local government. Party identities are now, he says, "far more prevalent then they were twenty or thirty years ago when there were many more Independents". Then, the further you got from the centre of the English political universe the less party politics mattered: the Norfolk County Council had more than a few Independents; there were a lot of Independents at the District/Borough Council level; and at the Town/Parish Council level everybody (at least as far as the Town/Parish Council was concerned) was Independent. Most people thought that was appropriate because it meant candidates were elected in light of who they were and what they had done rather than what their political party (if they had one) stood for.

Now, he says, local government is increasingly about party politics. The County Council has party machines. And although he is glad that is less true at the North Norfolk District Council he regrets the fact that even local councillors (for example in North Walsham) wear party labels. On most scores he strongly favours devolution as a means of reducing the 'democratic deficit' but he believes the devolution of power from Westminster would inevitably increase the emphasis on party affiliations and that as power and money flowed from Westminster to Norwich, party machines would not be far behind. He is also concerned about the risk that the practise of party 'whipping' (which he accepts as part and parcel of Parliamentary life but thinks would be "ridiculous" at the local level) would tend to grow.

From a Westminster perspective Norman Lamb believes improved governance for North Norfolk partly depends on shifting resources, power and accountability from the central level to a modified system of local governance; partly on creating incentives to attract the most qualified candidates to seek election and employment; and partly (and not least) on persuading local residents that participatory democracy depends on participation. People must realize, he says that no participatory system is perfect and that their imperfections are directly related to the extent people turn out to vote in local elections, the extent to which they remain engaged in local political processes and the extent to which they believe that by voting and remaining engaged in political life they can make a difference.

"Big issues engage people" he says and adds that climate change, whatever its causes, poses major issues for some of his constituents. He recalls how, in 2008, when a leaked report by Natural England persuaded many people in Broadland that the Government had decided not to defend the area against flooding, they quickly mobilized in self-defence. "People are naturally energized when they believe their survival is at stake" he said and adds that people living east of the Saltmarsh Coast (at Sidestrand, Overstrand and elsewhere) now face the threat of losing their homes to cliff erosion and have joined forces to campaign for government compensation.

As Norman Lamb looks ahead at the political future of the Saltmarsh Coast he believes climate change, rising sea levels and coastal erosion will be increasingly important concerns for local people and expects that local communities will be increasingly inclined to mobilize in support of efforts to ensure their concerns are understood by national policymakers. He also anticipates they will become more inventive in finding ways and means to get their voices heard and will use both traditional (press, radio, television) vehicles and innovative (websites, podcasts and video) technologies to get their points of view across. He believes "there is enormous scope to use technology to reach scattered rural populations and to project the views of those populations to the world at large". All of that, he says, is part of the democratic process. But the fundamental need is to change the balance of power, to devolve real authority to a streamlined system of local government and to trust the people to make sound judgments.

Richard Worsley

Richard Worsley is co-Director of the Tomorrow Project, a charity which helps organisations and individuals think about the long-term future of people's lives (www.tomorrowproject.net). He co-founded the Project in 1997, following a series of jobs in large companies. He works with government departments and agencies, companies and voluntary organisations to explore emerging social trends, on which he has co-authored several books. Richard and his wife Stephanie count themselves extraordinarily lucky to have been able to build a new house overlooking the marsh at Burnham Norton. Although the house is only 12 years old, visiting barn owls and the occasional marsh harrier suggest that it has settled well into the landscape. Richard was churchwarden at Holkham for ten years and is a Trustee of various local and national charities and chairman of one. He is rather obsessed by his vegetable garden.

Reflections and Conclusions

Richard Worsley

Durable – If We Look After It

Much of today's debate about where the world is going and what is happening to it is conducted in urban terms. The buildings that are written about are in cities; music is reviewed from metropolitan concert halls, culture at the hands of journalists writing in London office blocks.

There is another life here in the country that is lived in different ways – also struggling to find its own future, and wondering what has happened to its past. Struggling too, as these chapters have confirmed, to come to terms with its relationship with the urban world and its visitors.

But unlike its urban counterpart, country life has natural assets that are more durable – the beauty of its landscape, its wildlife, its light and its silence; and perhaps a greater ability to protect its true nature – as long as we look after it.

This is even more true of this particular piece of the rural jigsaw here in North Norfolk, because the intrusions of man are constrained by our coast. In many ways the sea defines us, in its beauty and permanence, its riches and threats. We don't have motorways in Norfolk, because the sea limits the journey. The sea has given us our priceless marshland habitats. And for many it still provides a living. But we have now planted dozens of windmills out at sea – an outrage to the marine landscape, a vital contribution to renewable energy, or an absurdly miniscule one, depending on your viewpoint.

It is easy to ignore the effect of the landscape. Ronald Blythe's essay *Remedial Scenes* [40] asks 'Does any doctor prescribe landscape these days?'. He talks of

> *'that most exquisite (and taken for granted) of pleasures, of having a rich sequence of near and distant hills, fields, woods, skies, buildings and landscape features of every hue and form fed through one's heart and mind' day after day'*.

And he describes the amazement of Norfolk labourers seeing their wetland landscape miniaturised in a camera lens for the first time by a Victorian photographer 'that this beautiful place was just their poor old marsh'.

---

[40] In *Field Work; Selected Essays*, 2007

Is our striving to keep what we have here a losing battle of conservatism and nostalgia, or can we hold together and pass on to our successors a way of life and a place of which we can still be proud, which promotes the common good of all who live here, which welcomes and is respected by those who visit, and which may even have lessons for others?

We face that challenge at a time when the world around us is changing at an extraordinary pace. Some of that change, for example in medical advances and in standards of living for most of us, has been benign. But there is a less benign side too, not only in the environmental threat by man to the planet, but also in our culture, values and way of life.

Four Perspectives

This book has been about vulnerability – balanced against the staunchness, permanence and continuity of what we have here. These are great strengths, which it will take more than passing fashions and bureaucrats to erode, try as they may.

I am struck by four perspectives – the first from Alexander Solhenitzsyn, deeply concerned that we are sinking into a great maw of consumerism and self-indulgence:

> 'The West has become enmeshed in our slavish worship of all that is pleasant, all that is comfortable, all that is material – we worship things, we worship products. Will we ever succeed in shaking off this burden, in giving free rein to the spirit that was breathed into us at birth, that spirit that distinguishes us from the animal world?' [41]

The three others, more hopeful, are from here in Norfolk:

- Where the late Bernard Phillips revived a moribund magazine, *The Quay*, to create a vibrant, positive and inclusive voice for the town of Wells-next-the-Sea.

- Where the village of Burnham Norton held a street party, attended by 130 of its 90 residents – with beer, bunting and band – simply to celebrate the salvation of its red telephone kiosk and raising questions as to 'Why haven't we done this before and when is the next one?'

- Where on a November Sunday, 200 people gathered in the church at Burnham Thorpe, the birthplace of Lord Nelson. They came to give thanks for the sacrifice of those who died in the two World Wars. Nobody required them to be there and they gained nothing direct for themselves in doing so. But they came in pride and remembrance. This was not a fading gesture from a disappearing generation. The church was bulging with people of all ages, of all

---

[41] *A Warning to the West*. p. 45

roles in life, men, women and children who were simply there to say thank you. As the familiar role of the dead was read out, we recognised the names of families we all knew. We saw their children, grandchildren, and even some great grandchildren standing there with pride, and I reflected that this is indeed true permanence and continuity, unconnected with marketing, the internet, political correctness or the credit crunch.

Watching, Listening and Learning

Perhaps the most appealing quality of country people is their ability to go on learning. I think of perennial wonderment at the yearly changes in the timing and numbers of migratory geese. And of a great authority on tidal flows and estuaries: 'It's different every day. You can't model it on a computer. Just keep watching and learning.'

Yet we are regularly visited and advised by those who claim to know it all, offering instant assertions without evidence and real knowledge about a place and people they only know from afar. I took a perverse pleasure in hearing one such put in his place with pungent irony: 'I wish I was as sure about anything as you seem to be about everything'.

Then I think of Peter Beck, much loved harbour master at Burnham Overy Staithe, known to generations of sailors and visitors for his gentle advice, firm when needed. I recall him listening politely to yet another instant adviser on Overy's silting problems: 'For just £40,000 ('just!') you could bring in a dredger on a high tide and have it sorted once and for all in a couple of days. Why do you people hang about?', and Peter's wise response, 'I think you could just wake up and find the whole £40,000's worth of sand and mud put back exactly where it came from by a single overnight tide'.

Looking Ahead

We asked our writers to look not only at where we are now and where we have come from, but also to look ahead. That is no easy task: by definition we cannot know the future, and if we try to predict it with any certainty we are likely to get it wrong. But there is real value in standing back from the immediacy of the everyday – trying to take a longer-term view and to think about the factors that will bring about change. It's rather like looking at a painting by van Gogh from four inches away – at which distance it is a meaningless set of blobs of paint. But stand three paces back and you have the wonderful, full image.

Our writers have risen splendidly to that task, and helped to answer, or a least to think about the really challenging questions. What will our successors think of the decisions and actions we are taking today and tomorrow? Did we do all that we could to look after the Saltmarsh Coast for future generations?

So how do our writers think we are doing, and what might happen here? Their voices will speak for themselves, especially as they are people who know what they are talking about, and it is no part of my task to seek to summarise them. But reading these chapters has revealed some strong common themes and some deep and abiding impressions.

Who Decides? Who's Listening?

The first of these is a profound sense of unease about the way in which decisions about the Saltmarsh Coast are made by other people.

Many of our writers are concerned about a disturbing gap between local needs and decisions made elsewhere. The chapter by Tim O'Riordan and Sophie Nicholson-Cole gives a sobering assessment of the quality of the consultation by the Environment Agency on their Shoreline Management Plan for the coast to the east of us. They point to the need in future consultations for 'profound and prolonged community engagement' and to learn from their experience.

Shortly before this book went to print I and others were gradually becoming aware of the successor consultation for our own area (unromantically labelled Area 3a by the Agency; the area to the east is Area 3b). From my relatively narrow (Burnham Norton) viewpoint, the alarming proposal that has suddenly revealed itself is startlingly simple: to punch two holes in the long established and highly effective seawall between Norton marsh and Scolt Head, to abandon the seawall and to re-align (code for flood) the marsh by making it tidal after 2025.

No clear rationale is offered for the proposal. No account seems to have been taken of the area's triple protection under the European Habitats Directive as a unique and much loved habitat for rare and migrant bird species - or of the resultant destruction of this part of the Coastal Path. Virtually none of the 36 residents who attended our early October Parish Meeting to consider the proposal had any earlier knowledge of it. And to cap it all the proposal was later described by an EA official as a way of testing out plans for similar floodings elsewhere. Small wonder that the Parish Meeting voted unanimously to oppose the proposal and to ask for it to be withdrawn.

So much for 'profound and prolonged community engagement' – and for learning from experience.

Policies that deeply affect North Norfolk are taken remotely by people in London, with urban priorities being dominant. As Henry Bellingham comments, 'I am sometimes staggered by the paucity of their understanding, their lack of a real feel for the place. They tend to think of North Norfolk, if they think of us at all, as sparsely populated, wealthy and privileged, full of second homes and without real problems. They don't realise that there are real problems here of poverty, unemployment and deprivation'.

His neighbouring MP Norman Lamb makes a similar point, challenging the assumption that London knows best: 'The imbalance (between London and local people) is also undemocratic because it imposes unbridgeable distances between local communities and decision-makers; because when local views conflict with central policies the centre always seems to prevail; and because local communities have no say in how fiscal resources that flow from them to central government are spent. The fundamental need is to change the balance of power, to devolve real authority to a streamlined system of local government and to trust the people to make sound judgements.'

The imbalance between national and local interests is strongly exemplified by a gradually emerging realisation of just what the current plans for offshore wind farms mean for the area. Nearly all of our writers feel strongly about them – though for different reasons and with different views.

The use of wind power is a highly interventionist policy: it has to be because it is incredibly, some would say prohibitively expensive. A new gas fired power station in Pembroke will cost £1 billion. It would cost six times as much to build a wind farm capable of generating similar power. A wind farm producing the same amount of energy as a nuclear plant would cost three times as much.[42] The Government is therefore asking the tax payer to pay for what the market will not. That may be defended on political grounds, though many would dispute it. But if the costs of this policy are to be funded at public expense, the public have as much right to be consulted about whether and how it is implemented as do the shareholders of any corresponding private venture.

In pursuit of what *The Times* has described as the 'fanciful' aspiration of increasing the amount of energy supplied by renewable from the present 2% to 15% by 2020, the Government is placing massive reliance on wind energy, even though its supply is by its nature so volatile. The plan is for an additional 10,000 wind turbines by 2020 – 6,000 onshore (many also in our area [43]) and 4,000 more offshore.

The paucity of consultation about wind energy in Norfolk is no small matter given what is at stake. There is deep concern about the 'modest' (52 turbine) 'Round 1' wind farm already in operation off the Lincolnshire coast and standing in the view from the Norfolk coast. The current plans are for a further 377 turbines much closer to our shore, on the Race Bank and the Docking Shoal, immediately North of Wells, and on the Sheringham Shoal. At the time of writing, the Sheringham plans look likely to go ahead, while the Race and Docking proposals, currently under discussion, are of much greater significance to the Saltmarsh Coast.

---

[42] *The Times*, 13 July 2009
[43] For example on land between Stanhoe, South Creake, North Creake and Syderstone

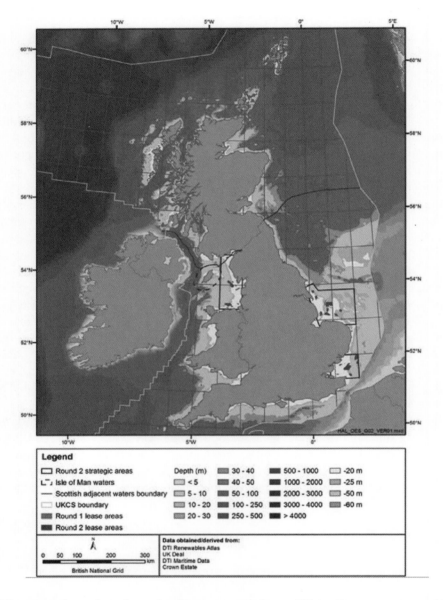

The map above based on the Government's latest White Paper on renewables strategy [44], shows vividly the intensity of wind farm activity for the Norfolk coast as compared with other parts of the UK.

This a large scale industrial undertaking, not just in construction, but in maintenance. As part of the plan for Wells to be the base for constructing and servicing

---

[44] *The UK Renewable Energy Strategy*, July 2009 (CM 7686)

226

the new wind farms, there will need to be constant dredging of the harbour five days a week, using a vessel with a 20 metre boom. (Richard Hardman observes that 'Sisiphus had a greater chance of getting the stone to the top of the hill than the dredgers of keeping this area sand free'.) It is reported too that the turbines will have a 50 year life span, at the end of which they will be cut off at the base, leaving who knows what remains on the sea bed.

These plans have huge implications for Norfolk's tourist and fishing industries. In a small island nation such as this, the placing of turbines on this scale has enormous long-term consequences for both heritage and land/seascape – and yet how much do we read of these in a Government White Paper devoted to renewables strategy? Answer – one small sentence: 'Inappropriately located wind farms could affect landscapes'. No conclusion is drawn or guidance given about what is appropriate – and yet some ground rules about location that is appropriate in terms of landscape and heritage would not only be helpful, but would also make the planning process a great deal less contentious.

But what has Government done to present these plans and implications openly and objectively to those who will be directly affected? There is a feeling amongst those we talked to that the consultation has been superficial and has the appearance of a fait accompli.

Do people realise what is at stake? And even if they do, does the response amount to any more than a wringing of hands and a whimper when set against such a potent, centralised determination to see this policy through to fruition, with all its uncertainties?

Of course there is another side to the coin. Britain cannot go on deriving 90% of its energy from fossil fuels; they are going to run out, they have a damaging effect on our climate and they are far from secure, give the extent to which we depend on other nations for their supply. There is therefore a strong case for us to make the maximum use of renewables. But we need to see the renewable objective in proportion.

Our current (average European) energy consumption is 125 kilowatt hours per day per person (kWh/d per person). If this was to be produced by renewables only, the two biggest contributors would need to be photovoltaic panels and offshore wind farms – BUT the panels would need to cover between 5-10% of the country to produce 50 kWh/d per person; offshore wind farms on the sale necessary to produce another 50 kWh/d per person would fill a sea area twice the size of Wales.[45]

So, let's get real. As David Mackay, on whose work the preceding paragraphs is based, puts it,

'Such an immense panelling of the countryside and filling of British seas with

---

[45] *Sustainable energy – without the hot air* by David J.C. Mackay http://www.withouthotair.com/

227

wind machines (having a capacity five times greater than all the wind turbines in the world today) may be possible, according to the laws of physics, but would the public accept and pay for such extreme arrangements. If we answer no, we are forced to conclude that current consumption will never be met by British renewables.'

It is not therefore an unreasonable policy to seek to make the most of renewables – but with three strong caveats:

- First, we must see their potential in proportion and not give or accept the impression that renewables in general and wind power in particular are the answer to our energy and climate change challenges on their own.

- Secondly, they must be implemented with much greater respect for our heritage, landscape and seascape – and Ian Scott in his introduction makes a powerful case for intensive wind farm development to be excluded from heritage coasts and Areas of Outstanding Natural Beauty (AONBs) such as the North Norfolk coast;

- Third, the planning process must be a genuine one, taking full account of local concerns and interests, rather than being dominated by the heavy hand of Government doing everything within it power, as it seems to many, to overcome objection at any price.

Strong, Distinctive and Special

The second impression left by these chapters is about the extraordinary strength of character of the Saltmarsh Coast – its buildings, its land and seascape, its wildlife, its potential for inspiration, and its people.

In any league table of 'specialness', the Saltmarsh Coat must come near the top. Our specialness comes partly from a prized combination of several different characteristics:

- From buildings and churches, as Nicholas Hills reminds us, unified by the use of local materials of flint and chalk, carstone and pantiles;

- From a unique habitat for indigenous and migratory wildlife described by Ron Harold – with Richard Girling's description of North Norfolk as 'the Wembley Stadium of birdwatching';

- From what it means to be bounded, defined and enriched by the sea;

- From its marshes, and their changing colour throughout the year – with Galton Blakiston's reminder that they 'are a really fragile ecosystem ... in locations that are not readily accessible by car or even on foot, giving them a feel of wilderness, the last bastion before the sea .. a backwater of brilliance you could call it'; Jim Ring quotes the description by Tom Pocock, Nelson's biographer,

of 'the muted greens, browns, greys, yellows and blues of Norfolk dunes and salt marshes.'

- And lastly from its offering of solitude, if you seek it.

We have three sharp insights here into what it is about North Norfolk that inspires the artist, the poet, the painter. Kevin Crossley-Holland talks of how this coast has spoken deeply to so many artists by its 'landscape seven-eighths sky, a vast inverted area, a sky-dome in which there are often several simultaneous theatres of action'; Lady Fraser of people 'seeking the remoteness and clarity of an area not en route to anywhere, not being solely a passing place'; and Nick Barnham (who provided our cover illustration and many of the drawings in these pages) of 'the wealth of inspiration that changes constantly with the seasons and the tides.'

The distinctiveness of the Saltmarsh Coast stems not only from landscape and the physical, but from the human and the personal – the characteristics and values shaped by being here and coming here, and what it means to be here and return here. 'Where else' someone said to me recently, 'can people take such pleasure in coming home?' Sally Festing provides a remarkable snapshot of a sample of North Norfolk people whose energy and initiative through different activities – from cinema clubs to choirs, from PTAs to wildfowling – have done so much to provide the fabric of these communities – 'huge, sometimes selfless effort'.

In their different ways our writers caution us that our distinctiveness may be very vulnerable. Richard Girling warns us against faith in the infinitude of the sea – citing the collapse of the Newfoundland cod fishery because the breeding stock was eaten, and the astonishing decline of cod catches in our North Sea fishing area from 2,472 tonnes in 1995, 678 tonnes in 2003, to 206 tonnes in 2005.

Tributes abound to the character of Norfolk people. Raymond Monbiot quotes Field Marshal Montgomery's reported assessment that 'he would use the Scots and the Welsh to take a position but would rely on Norfolkmen and women to hold it. They are the bulldogs who resist all attempts to dislodge them. Their cussed reliability is a characteristic to be sought and treasured.'

Lord Nelson knew that 'a Norfolk man is worth two of any other'.

I met the purchaser of a Norfolk business who had struggled in his early days here to be a successful boss. 'I learned in due course', he admitted, 'that you don't tell Norfolk people to do things, you ask them how they are done'.

Insiders and Outsiders

The third issue that pervades these chapters is the perennial one of so-called insiders and outsiders. The terms are misleading and unhelpful, not least because we all who live here, or our forebears, were incomers once. But I use them because both our writers and people in the area use them extensively – and because they

undoubtedly reflect an issue that is strongly felt.

The opinions and behaviours that surround the issue are very subjective. Those who are perhaps less sure of their ground go to some lengths to present their 'non-incomer' credentials. In some cases there is anger and frustration – for example over the effect of new arrivals on the housing market; over ill-manners or impatience in shops and on roads from people whose sense of pace, and place, has been conditioned in a more hurly-burly world. I met a man in a lane whose speeding 4x4 had been dented by a barn owl. I wept for the dead barn owl; he wept for his damaged bodywork.

Godfrey Sayers, fisherman and painter, makes a telling assessment, without attributing blame, of how the countryside here has been distorted and disturbed by an externally imposed combination of factors: by demography (local youngsters replaced – in relative terms – by elderly incomers), by regulation and quango activity, and by urban perceptions of what the countryside and rural life should be.

I hope we can play down the insider/outsider issue. We should value the talents and expertise of people who are not here all the time but who come back regularly because they love it, and have much to give, alongside the character, skills and values of people who have been born and bred here – and above recognise the interdependence of both groups.

Cyril Southerland, for 45 years a Brancaster fisherman and former Chairman of Brancaster Parish Council, has no patience with the distinction. He provides a vivid account of the very basic pre-war cottage housing in the village, the arrival of both 'Housing Society' homes and council houses, and the pressures created by the influx of holiday-makers, caravans and second home owners. However he is encouragingly optimistic and pragmatic: 'Over time, and with tolerance from both sides, things settled down, and what we have found in most of the villages is that, after settling in and finding new friends, a lot of these people want to be part of the community. They become involved with the various organizations such as the church, the Women's Institute, the camera club or one of the numerous other activities that take place over the course of the year.'

And So?

The Saltmarsh Coast could be radically different in our lifetimes, and more so in our children's. Nature will herself be responsible for many such changes, especially in the shape of the coastline, constantly shifting, eroding and accreting. And from time to time, we will be forcibly reminded of nature's power in events that may well be more dramatic here than elsewhere. But most of the change will be man-made, ranging from the planting of wind turbines on land and sea to the effect of our leisure habits on flora and fauna described by Ron Harold.

Helping to engage, listen to and then to read the thoughts of our writers has been a huge pleasure and a remarkable insight. Each of them knows and loves this place; each of them has a special expertise. Together, they have provided more than the sum of the parts. Their collective messages come through to me strongly:

- that whether or not the Saltmarsh Coast is destroyed, or is handed on in at least as good a shape as our generation found it, will depend on actions not words by each of us in all our different ways playing our part in collective decisions, and in our willingness to challenge actions and plans that threaten damage;

- that more is likely to be achieved by courtesy and neighbourliness than by anger and division, and

- that this is a place to be proud of, to be safeguarded by our actions and decisions, individual and collective, and never to be taken for granted.

Index of place names